GNOSIS

Boris Mouravieff

Boris Mouravieff

GNOSIS

BOOK ONE
The Exoteric Cycle

STUDY AND COMMENTARIES
ON THE ESOTERIC TRADITION
OF EASTERN ORTHODOXY

Translated by S. A. Wissa,
edited by Robin Amis.

Published for
PRAXIS INSTITUTE PRESS
by
AGORA BOOKS

Published and typeset for Praxis Institute Press by
Agora Books, China Hill, Brightling Road,
Robertsbridge, East Sussex TN32 5EH

Distributed by
Element Books, Longmead, Shaftesbury,
Dorset SP7 8PL

Printed in Great Britain by
BPCC Wheatons Ltd., Exeter

Cover design by Lance Hidy, drawings by Martin Gordon.
We gratefully acknowledge the assistance of L. D., L and S. K.
and J. M. in editing, and G. T. and E. R. in proofreading.

First published in French by
les Éditions du Vieux Colombier,
collection La Colombe, Paris, 1961,
then by les Éditions de La Baconnière,
Neuchâtel, Switzerland, 1969
English edition first pubiished 1989

British Library Cataloguing in Publication Data:
Mouravieff, Boris, *d. 1966*
    Gnosis.
    Bk. 1. The exoteric cycle
    I. Title   II. Amis, Robin
    299.932

    ISBN 1-872292-10-0

'This is wisdom which we preach among the perfect, yet not the wisdom of this age nor of the leaders[1] of this age, which will become nothing. We preach the wisdom of God, mysterious and hidden, which was foreordained by God before all ages for our glory, a wisdom that none of the leaders of this age have ever known.'

(I Corinthians ii: 6–8.)

---

1. In the original: *nor the Archons of this aeon. Novum Testamentum* graece et latine. Textum graecum recensuit, latinum ex Vulgata. Tertio editio critica recognita. Published by Frédéric Brandscheid, Fribourg, 1907, Vol. II, p. 258.

ACKNOWLEDGEMENTS

Our gratitude to Mr Mouravieff for this work is inexpressible but very great. I thank Mrs Larissa Mouravieff for permission to translate and publish the work.

After this my foremost thanks must necessarily go to Doctor Fouad Ramez in Cairo, without whose help this translation would never have been made. He has cleared up many points on which I was not quite clear. No expression of thanks would do justice to the tireless efforts he has put into this translation. My next debt of gratitude goes to Mrs. Jeannot Stevens, since deceased, who assisted with untiring faithfulness in the typing and correction of the manuscript. I only wish she were here to see the final work completed. Last but not least, I extend my thanks to my dear wife Margaret for her patience and devotion during all the time it has taken me to complete the present manuscript.

I thank God for the inspiration bestowed upon me in carrying out some of the very difficult parts of this translation.

S. A. Wissa

CONTENTS

FIRST PART: MAN

The interior life of man. The instability of the *I*. Introspection as a method of work. What we can learn by introspection. The three currents of mental life. Iron filings. Friction, fire and fusion. The Law of Hazard or Accident. The plurality of the *I*. What is man? The body and the soul. The Personality. The three mental centres.

Knowledge and understanding. Consciousness and its functions. Four levels of consciousness: subconsciousness, waking consciousness, consciousness of the real *I*, and Consciousness. The problem of being. Four levels of being. Containing and contents. Knowledge, understanding and savoir-faire.

The Personality is an organism enjoying a certain autonomy. The intimate link with the body. Mastering the latter. Posture of the Sage. Study of the structure of the Personality. The three mental centres: intellectual, emotional and motor. Their structure. The three fundamental types of exterior man: men 1, 2 and 3. Their characteristics.

The three *I*'s of man: the *I* of the body (physical), the *I* of the Personality (mental), the real *I* (spiritual). Their relation in theory and practice. The 987 little *I*'s, resulting from possible combinations of the three centres and their sectors.

SECOND PART: THE UNIVERSE

THIRD PART: THE WAY

THE LANGUAGE OF GNOSIS:
FOREWORD BY THE TRANSLATOR

When translators have translated complex and elaborate literary or philosophical works into other languages, they often make excuses for not giving their readers the original with all its shades of meaning, its subtleties and intonations. The translators of scientific works never do this, as they are certain they have been able to translate the complete content. But although Gnosis is a work of esoteric philosophy — with all the shades of meaning that this implies — its author, Boris Moura-vieff, has insisted on its scientific precision and on the rigorous scientific method which has been followed throughout. He says in the twentieth chapter of the second volume, Gnosis II:[1] *'Just like positive science, this Gnosis is systematic; it is the same as the other knowledge in its systematic arrangement of the Cosmos, in its ensemble as well as in its smallest parts.'*

Gnosis describes the Cosmos and man with equal precision. Wherever both consider the same subject, its method is systematized in exactly the same way as in positive science. Because of this precision, I have sometimes found it necessary to translate the French text word for word, sacrificing elegance in favour of precision.

The three volumes of Gnosis, like the scriptures, are built on the principle that no special terminology is used — just as the gospels were written in Greek and not in Hebrew, which was the ancient sacred language. At the same time, some of the words used have been given very precise meanings which remain the same throughout the book. The only exceptions to this consistency, says the author, are in old translations made by enlightened men.

These special terms are sometimes explained by notes. I have not hesitated to employ words now little used in the English language, but which prove exactly suitable, such as the word 'ensemble' — which means exactly the same in both languages, and 'notion', which once meant the same in French and English but which is now much less used in English, and often in more narrow ways. Here it is used in its original breadth of meaning.

Two other words should also be brought to the notice of the reader. These are 'gamme', translated by 'gamut', and 'échelle', translated by the word 'scale'.

The author has stipulated that the use of simple terms does not exclude a rigorous precision of meaning. (Chapter II, p. 12) This is particularly true concerning certain important French words: *'savoir'* and *'connaître'*, which

---

1. P. 262 of the French text.

are more or less indiscriminately translated by the English term 'to know', but which have very different meanings in French. If the reader refers to the sixth paragraph of the first chapter he would read: '..knowledge leads us towards power.' 'Knowledge' here is the translation of the French word *'connaissance'*, which derives from the verb *'connaître'*. If we turn to the third paragraph of the second chapter we would see that: 'one can know without understanding, while the reverse is not true' and also that: 'to understand is to know with something imponderable added to it'. Here again, 'to know' translates the French verb *'savoir'*.

We deduce from these two facts that since Knowledge (*connaissance*, not savoir,) leads us towards Power, and since knowledge (*savoir*) is nothing but a preliminary step towards understanding, savoir is a kind of inferior knowledge which, though indispensable, neither leads to Power, nor is in itself Understanding. Considerations like this have shaped the translation of this book, sometimes involving a choice between accuracy and elegance. These often difficult choices are summarized in the translation notes that follow.

Translation Notes

As the Translator's introduction says, because of the specialized nature and precise terminology of the French original, we have found considerable difficulty in translating certain French words, particularly where modern English uses one word for meanings clearly differentiated by different terms in the French. The most important examples are summarized below, and sometimes also indicated by footnotes to the text:

Niveau / Niveaux: Levels in the psychological or anthropological sense: 'Abaissement de niveau mental'.
Translated: Level—Levels.
Conflicts with:

Echelle / Echelon —
Echelle: ladder used in a sense of stepladder or sometimes in a different sense as a graduated scale.
Translated: Scale.
Echelon: rung, used in the sense of level (that is static, i.e. it is already there), rung, step—of a stair: one level above another; rank in a hierarchy.
Translated: Step.
This in turn conflicts with and must be differentiated from:

Gamme, in the sense of musical scale of several different but related notes. Translated by gamut — a forgotten English word for a 'musical scale', which is rare but technically correct, if not previously used quite in the way in which gamme was used by the author. The use of this word gamut actually originated in French with Guido d'Arezzo (Klein's Etymological Dict. says '*Gamut,n., range of musical sounds from gamma (the lowest) to ut (the highest) — Coined by Guido d'Arezzo. Fr.*) This word also has more than one meaning in the book, and refers in general to a sequence of events developing according to a musical scale.

Translated: gamut.

Octave: octave as a complete musical scale from Do to Do.

Translated: octave.

Plan: The French word 'plan' is used in what appears in English in two ways, one equivalent to the English term 'plane', the other in the everyday English sense in which an action is preceded by a plan, or as in the Fr. phrase, 'le plan de la creation'. This fortunate double meaning in French does not translate well in English.

Translated: plan OR plane as appropriate.

Words for road, path or track, intentionally differentiated by the author.

Voie: translated way,

Chemin: translated path,

Sentier: translated track.

Words for knowledge and understanding.

Savoir and related words describe knowledge that is 'outside ourselves', information that we may or may not understand.

Translation: knowledge, to know.

Connaissance and related words refer to knowledge which we contain ... the knowing of that which is outside us by that which is within.

Translated: Knowledge, to Know.

These two forms of knowledge are often distinguished in the text by footnote reference to the French.

Comprendre is understanding. This is within us and is limited by our capacity.

Translated: to understand, understanding.

Savoir-faire is knowledge we can successfully put into practice.

Translated: savoir faire.

Older English words brought back into use.

The author distinguishes in French between: *idée* and *notion*, often using 'notion' where normal loose use of English would use 'idea'.

We are doing the same in English.

Translated: idea and notion.

He uses the word *'ensemble'*, (as in *'tout ensemble'*), to describe a loose mixture or combination of different components, often in contexts in which looser use of English would us the word 'whole'. To be precise we have translated this by 'ensemble', correct but now rarely used in English.

Translated: ensemble.

He distinguishes this from various derivatives of the word *'integral'*, which translates loosely into the English words 'whole' or 'complete'. In this text these words are used by the author to achieve greater precision, and his meaning has direct links to the mathematical idea of integration.

Translated: DERIVATIVES OF integrate.

Constatation: French words that exist in English, but are very little used:

A group of words including *'constate'* and *'constatation'*, which are used here with very precise meaning.

Translated: 'constate', 'constated' and 'constatation'.

Psychique: The French word *'psychique'* is translated throughout the book as 'mental', used in the same sense that Descartes distinguished mind from body, so that mind and mental refer to the ensemble of intellectual, emotional and instinctive processes. It is used in this way to avoid the occult connotations now attached to the English word 'psychic' — this usage is marked by footnotes. Where the word 'mental' is used without a footnote it directly translates the French 'mental'.

Translated: mental; *'centres psychique'* translated as 'mental centres'.

Because of their importance, certain of these translations will also be referred to by footnotes.

A number of more general footnotes have been added by the translator and editor. These are marked 'Tr.' and 'Ed.' respectively.

Sadek Alfred Wissa, December 1989

FOREWORD

People interested in esoteric matters will probably have read the book by P.D. Ouspensky, published posthumously by his next of kin, titled *Fragments of an Unknown teaching.*[1] The ideas found in that book were gathered by the author from 'G'.[2] 'G' indicates in that text what is the basis of his teaching: 'for the benefit of those who know already, I will say that, if you like, *this is esoteric Christianity*'.[3]

It is curious in these conditions that the title speaks of an unknown teaching. The Christian Esoteric Tradition has always remained alive within certain monasteries in Greece, Russia, and elsewhere, and if it is true that this knowledge was hermetically hidden, yet its existence was known and access to it was never forbidden to those seriously interested in these questions.

If some passages of the book give the impression, in certain respects, of a syncretic gathering from different traditional teachings,[4] I have no doubt that — in their essentials — the system disclosed by the fragments that form Ouspensky's work originates from revelations issued by that *Great esoteric Brotherhood* to which the Apostle St Paul alluded in his Epistle to the Romans.[5] These fragments are therefore drawn from a genuine source. Yet — as correctly indicated by the title — Ouspensky's book contains only fragments of a tradition which, until recently, was only transmitted orally. And only a study of the complete[6] tradition can give access to the Revelation.

My own relations with Ouspensky, who I knew well, were described in an article of the review *Synthèses.*[7] I must reaffirm here that although Ouspensky had a spirited desire to publish his book during his lifetime, he always hesitated to do so. I myself had stressed strongly the danger of fragmentary disclosure, and uncertainties in the exposition of certain essential points. The fact that *Fragments* was only published after the death of the author, more than twenty years after it was written, supports these assertions.

---

1. *Fragments d'un enseignment inconnu*, Paris, Stock, 1950. (*In Search of the Miraculous: fragments of an unknown teaching*, Routledge & Kegan Paul, London, 1950.)

2. *Fragments*, p. 6. Footnotes have been amended to refer to the English version of *Fragments*. The original references to the French text have been retained thus: [p. 22].

3. *Ibid.*, p. 102 [p. 154] Italicized in the original text.

4. *Ibid.*, particularly p. 15 [p. 35].

5. Romans viii: 28–30.

6. Fr. 'ensemble'.

7. Woluwe-Saint-Lambert, Brussels, Editions Synthèses, issue 144 — November 1957.

The study presented here is directly drawn from the Eastern Christian Tradition: the sacred texts, the commentaries written around these texts, and especially from the *Philokalia* which is, above all, the same teaching and discipline, transmitted by fully authorized individuals. We will find certain similarities between the contents of this study and Ouspensky's book, since the sources are in part the same, but attentive examination and comparison will, above all, show the incomplete character of that book — its deviations from the doctrine. We all know the importance of diagrams in the Esoteric Tradition. They have been introduced to allow the transmission of this knowledge through the centuries in spite of the death of civilizations. Errors on the background of a particularly important diagram[8] were exposed in the previously mentioned article in *Synthèses*. What else should we say of the place given to man in the diagram called 'Diagram of Everything living'?[9] After several considerations aiming to show the 'nullity' of the man who has not esoterically evolved — the very small place which is his in the Universe — in that artificially complicated diagram he has been placed at the level of the Angels and Archangels. This means he has been shown in the Kingdom of God — represented by the superior inverted 'L' — even though Christ categorically affirmed that entry into the Kingdom of God is closed to those who have not been *born anew*.[10] This second Birth is the object and goal of esoteric work. According to the New Testament,[11] the place of *exterior* man, man who has not, so far, produced fruit; whose latent faculties are yet to be developed, is in fact found in that diagram between the two inverted 'L's', where he forms the link between visible and invisible worlds.

There is something else graver still: the concept of the *mechanical-man* has as a consequence his irresponsibility.[12] This is in direct contradiction to the doctrine of sin, repentance and salvation which form the basis of the teaching of Christ.

The greatest genuine faith, human intelligence, and goodwill, are not sufficient to prevent errors and deviations in everything that touches the domain of Revelation but is not totally inspired by it. The errors and deviations of *Fragments* attest to the fact that the book was not written at the orders of, and under the control of, the *Great esoteric Brotherhood*. This means that the facts on which the book was based have a fragmen-

---

8. Fragments p. 204 [p. 289].

9. *Ibid.*, p. 323 [p. 451].

10. John iii: 3, ff.

11. Mark iv: 11.

12. Fragments p. 19 [p. 41].

tary character. In the esoteric realm, all fragmentary knowledge is a source of danger. The works of ancient writers, such as St Ireneus, Clement of Alexandria, and Eusebius of Cæsarea, who wrote about the heresies of the first centuries of our era, confirm this. We learn, for example, that certain gnostic schools, seeing the imperfection of the created world, and without searching for the reason for the existence of these imperfections, have, by a shortcut of thought, jumped to conclusions such as the feebleness of the Creator, His incompetence, or even His evil nature. Thus the incomplete is the true source of all heresies. Only what the Tradition calls the *Pleroma*, which means *Plenitude*, including *Gnosis*[13] in its totality, offers a guarantee against all such deviations.

---

13. Ephesians iii: 18–19; *Didachè, passim*; St Clement of Alexandria, *Stromata, passim*, etc.

PREFACE

Esoteric studies help us to make sense of the evolution of man and of human society. This explains the increasing interest these studies have aroused in cultivated circles. Yet, paradoxically, many Europeans who feel drawn to these researches turn their eyes towards the non-Christian Traditions: Hinduism, Buddhism, Sufism and others. It would certainly be exciting to compare esoteric thinking in these different systems, because the Tradition is One, and whoever delves deeply into these studies will not fail to be struck by this essential unity. Yet to those who desire to go beyond pure speculation, the problem appears in a different light. This unique Tradition has been and still is now being presented in multiple forms, each meticulously adapted to the mentality and spirit of the human group to which its Word is addressed, and to the mission with which this group has been charged. For the Christian world, the easiest way; the least difficult way to reach the goal, is to follow the esoteric Doctrine which forms the basis of the Christian Tradition. Actually, the thought of a man who has been born and formed at the heart of our civilization, be he Christian or not, believer or atheist, is impregnated with twenty centuries of Christian culture. It is incomparably easier for him to begin his studies starting from this environment, rather than to adapt to the spirit of an environment different from his own. Transplantation is not without danger, and generally gives hybrid products.

We might add this: that all the great religions which have issued from the one Tradition are messages of truth — *otkrovenié istiny* — yet each of them addresses itself only to a part of humanity. Christianity alone has firmly announced its œcumenical character right from the start. Jesus said *'and the Gospel of the Kingdom shall be preached in the whole world, for a testimony unto all nations.'*[1] The power of the prophecy of the Word, as expressed in this phrase, cries out after twenty centuries: the Good News, first taught to a restricted group of disciples, has since been effectively spread over all the earth. This prodigious expansion is due to the fact that the Christian Doctrine, in its perfect expression, aims at a general resurrection, while other doctrines, even though they belong to the Truth, essentially aim at individual salvation and are therefore only partial revelations of the Tradition.

Thus this teaching is fundamentally Christian.

The Christian esoteric Tradition is based on the Canon, the Rites, on Menology, and lastly on the Doctrine. The latter is an ensemble of rules,

---

1. Matthew xxiv: 14.

treatises and commentaries given by the doctors of the Œcumenical Church. These texts were in large part assembled in a collection called the *Philokalia*.[2] In addition to these *sources*, there are isolated writings by other ancient and modern authors, religious and secular.

Most of the writings of the *Philokalia* were intended for people who had already acquired a certain esoteric culture. One can say the same for certain aspects and texts of the Canon, including the Gospels. It must also be noted that, being addressed to all, these texts cannot take account of the abilities of each person. This is why Bishop Theophan the Recluse, in his preface to the *Philokalia*, insists on the fact that without help *nobody*[3] can succeed in penetrating the Doctrine. This is also why, together with written sources, esoteric science conserves and cultivates an oral Tradition which brings the Letter to life. Oriental Orthodoxy has known how to keep this Tradition intact by applying the absolute rule of Hermetism in each particular case. From generation to generation, ever since the time of the Apostles, it has led its disciples up to mystic experience.

If hermetism has provided a safeguard for nearly twenty centuries, it must be said[4] that circumstances have now changed. At the current point in history, as at the time of the Coming of Christ, the veil has been partially raised. Therefore, for those who want to advance beyond book knowledge, which never goes beyond the domain of information; for those who intensely seek the true sense of life, who want to understand the significance of the mission of the Christian in the New Era, the possibility will exist of initiation into this divine Wisdom, *mysterious and hidden*.[5]

We have turned to the Slavonic text of the scriptures each time the meaning given by other versions appeared to present certain obscurities. This is for two reasons. The first is that the translation into this language was made in an era still rich in sacred exegeses, where the spirit of the texts remained close to their original meaning. The second is the fixed nature of the language: the Slavonic languages, Russian in particular, remain very close to the old Slavonic language, the language which is still in use in the divine services of the Orthodox religion in the Slav countries.

---

2. The Russian edition was issued in 5 quarto volumes, published under the supervision of Bishop Theophan the Recluse by the Saint Panteleimon Monastery on Mount Athos.

3. Underlined in the original.

4. Fr. 'constater'.

5. I Corinthians ii: 6-8

As for the antiquity of the Slavonic text, one can say this: it is generally attributed to Constantine the Philosopher, better known under the name of St Cyril, and to his brother St Methodius, both learned Greeks from Salonika who knew the Slavonic language perfectly. So, arriving in Chersonese of Tauric, St Cyril found in the ninth century that the Gospels were already written in this language. It is, therefore, infinitely probable that they were written in a period when the forms remained alive — as stated by the Apostle St Andrew, who taught Christianity in Russia in the first century of our Era.[6]

The fixity of the language is an equally important element if one wants to go back to the original sense of a given text: it is known that the fixed nature of the Coptic language allowed Champollion, starting from the liturgic formulae of this language, to establish the equivalence between Coptic writings and Egyptian hieroglyphics. The old Slavonic language has remained alive and has undergone few modifications to the original: the ritual formulas in particular are strong evidence of this fact. That is why the Slavonic text of the New Testament, as well as writings of ancient authors translated into that language, have particular importance for the seeker today.

---

6. The Slavonic text is also frequently quoted in the following works: *Unseen Warfare*, translated into English by E. Kadloubovsky and G. E. H. Palmer, London, Faber and Faber Ltd., *Early Fathers from the Philokalia* and *Writings from the Philokalia* — same translators and publisher.

INTRODUCTION

Homo Sapiens lives immersed in his everyday life to a point where he forgets himself and forgets where he is going; yet, without feeling it, he knows that death cuts off everything.

How can we explain that the intellectual who has made marvellous discoveries and the technocrat who has exploited them have left outside the field of their investigations the ending of our lives? How can we explain that a science which attempts everything and claims everything nevertheless remains indifferent to the enigma revealed by the question of death? How can we explain why Science, instead of uniting its efforts with its older sister Religion to resolve the problem of Being — which is also the problem of death — has in fact opposed her?

Whether a man dies in bed or aboard an interplanetary ship, the human condition has not changed in the slightest.

Happiness? But we are taught that happiness lasts only as long as the Illusion lasts... and what is this Illusion? Nobody knows. But it submerges us.

If we only knew what Illusion is, we would then know the opposite: what Truth is. This *Truth would liberate us from slavery.*[1]

As a psychological phenomenon, has Illusion ever been subjected to critical analysis based on the most recent discoveries of science? It does not seem to be so, and yet one cannot say that man is lazy and does not search. He is a passionate searcher ... but he misses the essential; he bypasses it in his search.

What strikes us from the very beginning is that man confuses moral progress with technical progress, so that the development of science continues in dangerous isolation.

The brilliant progress that has come from technology has changed nothing essential in the human condition, and will change nothing, because it operates only in the field of everyday events. For this reason it touches the inner life of man only superficially. Yet from very ancient times it has been known that the essential is found within man, not outside him.

We are generally in agreement in thinking that humanity has arrived at an important turning point in its history. The Cartesian spirit which destroyed scholastic philosophy is now in turn being left behind. The logic of history demands a new spirit. The divorce between *traditional*

---

1. John viii: 32.

knowledge, of which religion is a trustee, and *acquired* knowledge, the fruit of science, threatens to make sterile the Christian civilization which in origin is so rich with promises.

Yet it is an aberration to believe that Science by its very nature is opposed to Tradition, and it must also be firmly stressed that Tradition does not include any tendency opposed to Science. On the contrary, the Apostles foresaw the prodigious development of science.

Thus the celebrated formula of St Paul: *Faith, Hope and Love*,[2] summarizes a vast programme of evolution for human knowledge.[3] If we examine this formula in relation to its context[4] we see that the first two terms are temporary, while the third is permanent. According to the Apostle it was appropriate to the epoch in which it was expressed,[5] and its significance has had to evolve with time. This has happened just as predicted by St Paul. Science[6], and knowledge[7] in a general way — called on to replace Faith and Hope, which defined the limits of what was accessible to the mentality of the epoch when he taught — have since then known extraordinary development. He therefore adds: '*Now that I have become a man, I have put away childish things.*'[8] This is how the passage from Faith to Knowledge is described. St Paul then specifies that this last, although necessary in evolution, is not a final state, as it is incomplete by nature. He adds that *when that which is perfect is come, that which is incomplete disappears.*[9] The perfect is Love, which unites in itself the accomplishment of all virtues, of all prophecies, of all mysteries, and of all Knowledge.[10] St Paul insists on this point and ends by saying: *seek after Love.*[11]

It is by the joint efforts of traditional science, based on Revelation, that is, on Faith and Hope, and of acquired Science, the domain of positive knowledge, that one can hope to fulfil the programme traced out by St Paul, and finally attain Love in its integral meaning.

One of the reasons for this book is to develop the postulates of traditional Science, so as to bring out their links with positive Science.

---

2. I Corinthians xiii: 13. The third word is definitely *Love* and not *charity*. The distinction is important. *Love* is a noumenal power, while *charity* is only a certain attitude that constitutes one of the many manifestations of Love. (Ed. Although charity is derived from 'caritas', the Latin word for love.)

3. Fr. 'savoir'.

4. *Ibid.*, 1–12.

5. 'Now' says St Paul, verse 13.

6. *Ibid.*, 9 ff.

7. *Ibid.*

8. *Ibid.*, verse 11.

9. *Ibid.*, verse 10.

10. I Corinthians xiii: *passim*.

11. I Corinthians xiv: 1.

The author is convinced that only the synthesis of these two branches of knowledge can now resolve the problem of man, and that on this solution depends the solution of all other contemporary problems.

According to the Tradition, human evolution, after a long prehistoric period, continues in a succession of three cycles: the Cycle of the Father, which history knows only incompletely; the Cycle of the Son, which is now reaching its end, and lastly the Cycle of the Holy Spirit, which we are now approaching.

Anthropology traces the emergence of *homo sapiens fossilis* back forty thousand years from the present epoch. Life was then characterized by the matriarchy which had sprung from the system of collective marriage. Fourteen thousand years ago approximately, with the emergence of *homo sapiens recens*, the regime of the *matriarchal tribe* gave place gradually to that of the *patriarchal tribe*, characterized by polygamy. That was certainly progress, even though this system was still marked by bestiality. In that system, women were in the condition of living merchandise, yet these ancient tendencies prevailed for a long time.

Aristotle bears witness, to this when describing the attitude of the well-to-do classes towards the question of woman. He says that they kept legitimate wives to beget citizens according to the law, courtesans for pleasure, and concubines for daily use. A concept like this leaves little place for Love.

Jesus introduced into human relations something practically unknown before Him. For the law of the jungle: *an eye for an eye and a tooth for a tooth*,[12] He substituted a new commandment: *that ye love one another*.[13] This produced a revolution in relations between man and woman: Love was introduced into social life. The 'merchandise' of previous times now obtained civic rights, although certainly not integrally nor immediately. Nevertheless, the principle of reciprocal choice in love was established. That was the emergence of *romance*.

The *romance*, by which Christian society expressed the principle of reciprocal choice, reached its climax in the Middle Ages. In spite of the decline it has known since then, and in spite of a current tendency to return to regressive forms of relation between the sexes, it still remains the avowed ideal of our society. Is it not exact, then, to speak of the death of *romance*? A revolution is occurring silently which will replace the *free romance*, distinctive mark of the Christian era, with the *singular romance*

12. Exod. xxi: 24; Deut. xix: 21; Lev. xxiv: 20.
13. John xiii: 34, xv: 12; I John iii: 11.

characteristic of the era of the Holy Spirit. Liberated from servitude to procreation, this romance of tomorrow is called on to cement the indissoluble union between two strictly polar beings, a union which will assure their integration in the bosom of the Absolute. As St Paul says: *'Nevertheless, neither is the woman without the man, nor man without the woman in the Lord.'*[14]

The vision of such a romance has haunted the highest minds for thousands of years. We find it in platonic love, the basis of the singular romance in the myths of the Androgyne man; of Orpheus and Euridice; of Pygmalion and Galatea... This is the aspiration of the human heart, which cries in secrecy because of its great loneliness. This romance forms the essential aim of esoteric work. Here is that love which will unite man to that being who is unique for him, the *Sister-wife*,[15] the glory of man, as he will be the glory of God.[16] Having entered into the light of Tabor, no longer two, but one drinking at the fount of true Love, the transfigurer: the conqueror of Death.

Love is the *Alpha* and the *Omega* of life. All else has only secondary significance.

Man is born with the *Alpha*. It is the intention of the present work to show the path which leads towards the *Omega*.

Boris Mouravieff

---

14. I Corinthians xi: 11.
15. *Ibid.*, ix: 5.
16. *Ibid.*, xi: 7.

GNOSIS

Volume One

FIRST PART

MAN

CHAPTER I

(1)

Positive philosophy studies man in general; abstract man. Esoteric philosophy concerns man as he is[1]: the investigator is the object of his own studies. Starting from the constatation that man is unknown, his target is to make himself known to himself — as he is, and as he might become under certain conditions.

The final object of positive science is the same in principle, but the efforts are diametrically opposed. Starting from the centre, positive science extends, specializes, and so diverges towards the periphery. At the limit each point forms a separate discipline. Esoteric science begins from the multiplicity and variety observed on the periphery accessible to our senses, and moves towards the centre. It tends towards a more and more general synthesis.

The method of esoteric science is the same as that of positive science: observation, critical analysis of the given observations, and rigorous deduction from the established facts.

In spite of this similarity of method, there is a difference of application due to the personal character of most esoteric work. This does not always permit demonstration of the results of specific life experiences, nor allow public debate on their validity. This is why we apply this method here with the same rigorous objectivity, but in the opposite direction: in positive science we admit a postulate if we cannot refute it; here we would refute something if we do not find facts or phenomena to confirm it.

(2)

In Western civilization the interior life of the individual, with all its richness, finds itself relegated to a minor role in existence. Man is so caught up in the toils of mechanical life that he has neither time to stop nor the power of attention needed to turn his mental vision upon himself. Man thus passes his days absorbed by external circumstances. The great machine that drags him along turns without stopping, and forbids him to stop under penalty of being crushed. Today like yesterday, and tomorrow like today, he quickly exhausts himself in the frantic race, impelled in a direction which in the end leads nowhere. Life passes away from him almost

---

1. Fr. 'l'homme concret'.

unseen, swift as a ray of light, and man falls engulfed and still absent from himself.

(3)

When we ask someone who lives under this constant pressure of contemporary life to turn his mental vision towards himself, he generally answers that he has not enough time left to undertake such practices. If we insist and he acquiesces, he will in most cases say that he sees nothing: Fog; Obscurity. In less common cases, the observer reports that he perceives something which he cannot define because *it changes all the time*.

This last observation is correct. Everything is in fact continually changing within us. A minor external shock, agreeable or disagreeable, happy or unhappy, is sufficient to give our inner *content*[2] a quite different appearance.

If we follow up this interior observation, this introspection, without prejudice, we will soon constate, not without surprise, that our 'I', of which we are so consistently proud, is not always the same self: the 'I' changes. As this impression becomes more defined we begin to become more aware that it is not a single man who lives within us but several, each having his own tastes, his own aspirations, and each trying to attain his own ends. Suddenly we discover within us a whole world full of life and colours which until now we had almost entirely ignored. If we still proceed with this experience, we will soon be able to distinguish three currents within that perpetually moving life: that of the vegetative life of the instincts, so to speak; that of the animal life of the feelings; and lastly that of human life in the proper sense of the term, characterized by thought and speech. It is almost as if there were three men within us, all entangled together in an extraordinary way.

So we come to appreciate the value of introspection as a method of practical work which permits us to know ourselves and enter into ourselves. As we gradually progress, we become more clearly aware of the real situation in which we find ourselves. The inner content of man is analogous to a vase full of *iron filings* in a state of mixture as a result of mechanical action. Every shock received by the vase causes displacement of the particles of iron filings. Thus real life remains hidden from the human being due to the constant changes occurring in his inner life.

---

2. Fr. 'contenu intérieur', linking with the author's use of 'content' later in the book.

Fig. 1

Even so, as we shall see later, this senseless and dangerous situation can be modified in a beneficial way. But this requires work; conscientious and sustained effort. Introspection carried out relentlessly results in enhanced internal sensibility. This improved sensibility in its turn intensifies the amplitude and frequency of movement whenever the iron filings are disturbed. As a result, shocks that previously were not noticed will now provoke vivid reactions. These movements, because of their continuous amplification, can create a friction between the particles of iron so intense that we may one day feel the interior fire igniting within us.

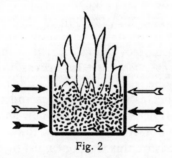

Fig. 2

This fire must not remain a harmless flare-up. Nor is it enough that the fire smoulders dormant under the ashes. A live and ardent fire once lit must be carefully kept alight by the will to refine and cultivate sensitiveness.

If it continues in this way, our state can change: the heat of the flame will start a process of *fusion*[3] within us.[4]

Fig. 3

3. Fr. 'soudure'.
4. Mark ix: 49; I Corinthians iii: 11–13; I Peter i: 7; iv: 12.

From this point on the inner content will no longer behave like a heap of iron filings: it will form a block. Then further shocks will no longer provoke interior change in man as they did previously. Having reached this point he will have acquired a firmness; he will remain *himself* in the midst of the tempests to which life may expose him.

This is the perspective before those who study esoteric science. But to reach the state which has already been described, we must from the beginning rid ourselves of all illusion about ourselves, no matter how dearly held; an illusion of this kind, if it is tolerated at the start, will grow en route, so that suffering and additional effort will be necessary in order to rid ourselves of it at a later date.

As long as man has not reached the point of *fusion*, his life will be in effect a factitious existence, as he himself will change from moment to moment. Since these changes will occur as a result of external shocks which he can almost never foresee, it will also be impossible for him to predict in advance the exact way he will change internally. Thus he will live subject to events as they occur, always preoccupied by constantly 'patching up' ('replastering'[5]). He will in fact progress toward the unknown, at the mercy of chance. This state of things, named in the Tradition *The Law of Chance*, or *The Law of Accident*, is — for man as he is — the principal law under whose authority he leads his illusory existence.

Esoteric science indicates the possibilities and the means of freeing oneself from this law. It helps us to begin a new and purposeful life; first to become logical with ourselves, and finally, to become our own master.

But to begin effectively on this way, one must first clearly see the situation as it is. A parable found in the most ancient sources permits us to get a clear picture of this, and so keep this condition in mind.[6] It is the parable of the *Coach*.

This image represents the characteristics of man by a coach. The physical body is represented by the coach itself; the horses represent sensations, feelings and passions; the coachman is the ensemble of the intellectual faculties including reason; the person sitting in the coach is the master.

In its normal state, the whole system is in a perfect state of operation: the coachman holds the reins firmly in his hands and drives the horses in the direction indicated by the master. This, however, is not how things happen in the immense majority of cases. First of all, the master is absent. The coach must go and find him, and must then await his pleasure. All is in a bad state: the axles are not greased and they grate; the wheels are badly fixed; the shaft dangles dangerously; the horses, although of noble race, are dirty and ill-fed; the harness is worn and the reins are not strong. The

---

5. Fr. 'replâtrage'.
6. Fr. 'à l'esprit'.

coachman is asleep: his hands have slipped to his knees and hardly hold the reins, which can fall from them at any moment.

The coach nevertheless continues to move forward, but does so in a way which presages no happiness. Abandoning the road,[7] it is rolling down the slope in such a way that the coach is now pushing the horses, which are unable to hold it back. The coachman, fallen into a deep sleep, is swaying in his seat at risk of falling off. Obviously a sad fate awaits such a coach.

This image provides a highly appropriate analogy for the condition of most men, and it is worth taking as an object of meditation.

Salvation may however present itself. Another coachman, this one quite awake, may pass by the same route and observe the coach in its sad situation. If he is not in much of a hurry, he may perhaps stop to help the coach that is in distress. He will first help the horses hold back the coach from slipping down the slope. Then he will awaken the sleeping driver and together with him will try to bring the coach back to the road. He will lend fodder and money. He might also give advice on the care of the horses, the address of an inn and a coach repairer, and indicate the proper route to follow.

It will be up to the assisted coachman afterward to profit, *by his own efforts*, from the help and the information received. It will be incumbent on him from this point on to put all things in order and, open eyed, to follow the path[8] he had abandoned.

He will above all fight against sleep, for if he falls asleep again, and if the coach leaves the road again and again finds itself in the same danger, he cannot hope that chance will smile upon him a second time; that another coachman will pass at that moment and at that place and come to his aid once again.

(4)

We have seen that the practice of introspection leads us very quickly to the constatation that our inner life changes at almost every instant. Man pretends however to have an orderly continuity of ideas, and to be consistent in his actions — because life requires him to give this impression. He cannot without great difficulty evade this necessity. His given word, agreed commitment and spoken vow bind him in spite of all the continual changes which he has just discovered within himself: changes which explain to him the underlying causes of his difficulties, of his inner and outer conflicts, and of the many failures which mark his life.

---

7. Fr. 'route'.
8. Fr. 'chemin'.

Man reacts as much as possible against this constant pressure of the difficulties and obligations which weigh him down. As for the changes within him, he generally compensates for these by instinctive reactions: a fixed attitude to each situation. He wants at all costs at least to appear logical with himself and master of his actions. Thus, whenever a stroke of luck or an unsuspected success happens to him, he tries to persuade his circle of friends — and indirectly to persuade himself — that he is not at all astonished; that he had predicted the sequence of facts a long time ago, and that all had been calculated in advance. In cases of failure he throws the blame on others, on events, and on circumstances in general.

It is because the friction between the particles of *iron filings* produces a disagreeable sensation in us that we feel the need to get rid of it. The movement of the *iron filings* stops when we find a solution and so ward off the shocks received. The discovery of a culprit will allow us this relief. As a result man appears to us to be constantly preoccupied with his interior patching up,[9] which in time becomes almost wholly automatic within him.

(5)

In this situation we must ask ourselves how we can define these inner changes? What it is that changes?

Speaking of himself, man says: 'I'. This is perhaps the most enigmatic and least defined term in human language. Speaking of his body, man treats it as a third person, which is correct. When he speaks of his Soul he again treats it in the same way as a third person. By this he affirms that he is neither body nor soul. Although it appears at first to be paradoxical, so common is this that it applies to the majority of human beings. Yet if man is neither body nor Soul, then what is Man?

What is this 'I' which he feels within himself — and to which he tries so hard to give at least a semblance of rational continuity?

It is, properly speaking, nothing but the particles of iron filings, whose relative position one to another changes all the time, and which in their ensemble represent our 'I' within us. This 'I' is not constant; it takes on a multitude of different aspects, yet it is this same 'I' with which man as he is born on Earth evolves in life.

Not only is this same 'I' neither constant nor permanent, but it is also multiple, since each of the three men who co-exist within man, and of whom we have spoken, is equally a composite subject. As this is so, our 'I' is the ensemble of a multitude of little 'I's, each relatively autonomous and

---

9. Fr. 'replâtrage'.

8

with a tendency to act in its own way. Such is the nature of the 'I', *legion*, as it is put in the Gospel.[10]

If we come back to the question: 'What is man?' we can now give a precise answer: it is the *Personality*. In other words it is Mr. X identifying himself with that psychic organism which resides within him and which offers nothing stable, or at least very little stability; which changes in reaction to impressions received, whether agreeable or disagreeable — and even in response to physical shocks.

Jesus said: '*Whosoever smiteth thee on thy right cheek turn to him the other also.*'[11] But who can do this? Only he who has dominated the bestial and instinctive reactions within him and who has consequently mastered the mechanical movement of the iron filings. What prevails in primitive man is '*an eye for an eye and a tooth for a tooth.*'[12] The purpose of this (Gospel) formula is to protect the particles of iron filings from ungoverned reaction: to remain ones own self in a state of unruffled inner calm after having received a slap on the cheek. Turning the other cheek is only possible to a being who is truly master of himself. The Scriptures offer a number of examples which illustrate the urgent necessity that man should become master of himself.

(6)

To reach this it is necessary for us to study the structure of our Personality. Here, as everywhere else, Knowledge[13] leads to power.

Let us return once again to the image of the three men who co-exist within man. In reality, three main currents act in our mental[14] life: intellectual, emotional[15] and motor-instinctive. Although not clearly delineated, for reasons we shall see later, these divisions correspond to our thoughts, our feelings, and to our senses and sensations.

The centres of gravity of each of these three modes of our mental[14] life are situated in the brain, the heart and the loins: but this description must not be taken too literally. Whenever an impulse is received by or emanates from one of these three centres, the other two, although they take part in it, generally adopt a passive attitude. This happens in such a way that the one who is in command at any particular moment speaks in the name of the Personality in its ensemble, and therefore represents the man as a whole.

---

10. Mark v: 9; Luke viii: 30.
11. Matthew v: 39; Luke vi: 29.
12. Exodus xxi: 24; Deut. xix: 21.
13. Fr. 'Connaissance'.
14. Fr. 'psychique'.
15. Fr. 'émotif'.

Further on, this state of things will be examined in detail. For the moment let us try to fix these ideas by means of a diagram which will be completed gradually as our studies continue, and will serve as a progressive instrument for this work.

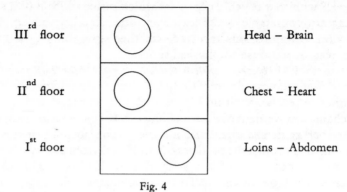

IIIrd floor   Head – Brain

IInd floor   Chest – Heart

Ist floor   Loins – Abdomen

Fig. 4

These three centres, which represent the three currents making up our mental[16] life, each have a double function: reception and expression.[17] From this point of view the system is admirably conceived; each centre in its own domain perfectly meets the needs of man's inner and outer life.

Let us bear in mind that the theory of the functions and locations of the mental[16] centres is merely a convention in the sense that these are centres of gravity. We think mainly with the head, but not exclusively. It is the same with our hearts, in which we locate our emotional centre. The motor centre governs instinctive life as well as movement and all mental[16] activity: its action is thus distributed[18] throughout the body. For reasons which will become clear later, however, we locate this on the 'first floor', which corresponds to the loins and abdomen.

(7)

The human Personality, this ever-changing ensemble[19] of iron filings, is not destined to be inactive. The opposite is true; the mental[16] body is an organism created[20] to play a predetermined role, but it is not generally employed for this purpose. The reason for this is that we use it as strangers,

---

16. Fr. 'psychique'.

17. Fr. 'manifestation'.

18. Fr. 'répandue'.

19. Fr. 'ensemble': used throughout the book to describe a combination whose constitution and/or structure remains changeable — a 'mixture', not a compound.

20. Fr. 'conçu' - from v. 'concevoir'.

without knowing it, without having studied it, and without having understood it.

For each one of us, esoteric studies start precisely with the study of the content, structure, and functioning of the Personality.

Let us define accurately the mental functions of the three centres:

— *The Intellectual Centre* registers, thinks, calculates, combines, researches etc.;
— *The Emotional Centre* has for its domain the feelings as well as refined sensations and passions;
— *The Motor Centre* directs the five senses, accumulates energy in the organism through its instinctive functions, and with its motor functions governs the consumption of this energy.

The motor centre is the best organized of the three centres. While the other two centres are neither complete nor organized before the gradual growth and development of the child, the motor centre is fully functional at conception. It is thus the most mature and the best organized. It is also, so to speak, wisest, although it does make mistakes.

Conversely, the other two centres place us in the most grave difficulties. They are anarchistic, often overstepping each other's domain and the domain of the motor centre in such a way that the latter becomes disorganized.

In fact, we have neither a pure thought nor a pure feeling: nor are our actions pure. Everything in us is mixed and even entangled, often by all sorts of *considerations* which either come from the intellectual centre, tarnishing the purity of our feelings by its calculations, or from the emotional centre, which clouds the calculations of the intellectual centre.

Because of this, unless we have first deeply studied the structure of our Personality, it is impossible to create any order in our mental[21] life or to make it emerge from its state of continual anarchy and its profound senselessness. It is by this study that the searcher can go on to regulate and tune this organism.

There is no other way to reach the goal except by working on oneself by self observation.

---

21. Fr. 'psychique'.

CHAPTER II

(1)

Simple ideas are the most difficult to grasp. They escape us because the extreme complexity of our minds makes us complicate everything. It is only simple ideas and formulæ that matter in life.

Let us now consider the relation between these notions: to *know*, and to *understand*.

We can know without understanding, but we cannot understand without knowing. It therefore follows that *understanding* is *knowing* to which something imponderable is added. We are touching on a problem which is simple but at the same time can raise great difficulties.

We pass from *knowing* to *understanding* to the measure that we assimilate *knowledge*. The capacity for assimilation has its limits: man's capacity to *contain*[1] understanding differs from person to person.

This problem concerns what we call the *being* of a person. It is one of the basic notions of esoteric science. It has several facets. In the terms that concern us here, *being* is demonstrated by a person's capacity for assimilation.

Knowledge is widespread everywhere. However, it is external to us. Understanding is within us.

If we pour the contents of a bottle into a glass, the latter can only contain an amount equal to its capacity. Any more will overflow. That is exactly what happens with us. We are only capable of understanding within the limits of our capacity to contain understanding within our *being*.

Jesus said to His disciples: '*I have yet many things to say unto you but ye cannot contain them now.*'[2]

To be able to evolve, in the esoteric sense of the term, we must above everything else constantly seek to enhance our *being*; to raise its level.

(2)

The Gospels do not use specialized terminology. That is one of the reasons for their popularity: they are accessible to all. The Christian Esoteric Tradition follows their example and tries to avoid specialized vocabulary: this would cause additional difficulty in following a path

---

1. Fr. 'contenir': in the sense of 'ability to contain': man's 'capacity to contain' understanding is both finite in amount, and can vary, as the volume a glass can contain is fixed for a particular glass but can vary from one glass to another.

2. John xvi: 12. Taken from the Slavonic text, which uses the word 'contain' instead of 'bear'.

which is already difficult enough. The scriptures start from the principle that if we take the trouble to ponder them deeply, *everything* can be expressed without having to refer to neologisms. Nevertheless, it is necessary to define clearly the meanings of the words used.

In the first place, we must specify what the Tradition means by *Consciousness*[3] and its derivatives. In modern language as well as in philosophical literature we attribute varied meanings to the word consciousness; it is sometimes qualified by additional attributes. We find, for example, expressions such as 'super-consciousness', 'cosmic consciousness', etc.

In esoteric science we attach maximum significance to the term *Consciousness*: that which touches the divine plane. Bishop Theophan the Recluse, one of the most fully authorized commentators, said: '*The way to perfection is the way to Consciousness.*'

He therefore does not attribute the current meaning to the word 'Consciousness'.

We do not possess *Consciousness*. What we call consciousness is only one of its derivatives, but it is all that is accessible to man as he is born of woman.[4]

All in all there are four levels of consciousness: Consciousness — called 'absolute' — and its three derivatives:

_____   ●   Absolute Consciousness
_____   ●   Consciousness of the real *I*
_____   ●   Waking consciousness
_____   ●   Subconsciousness

Fig. 5

Starting from the bottom we have in the first instance subconsciousness. This is the twilight consciousness which we have for example during sleep, where it controls the organism without being interrupted. This subconscious direction of certain functions of our bodies continues during the waking state.

The domain of subconsciousness is vast and very little about it has been studied. We sometimes treat it as if everything that does not enter waking consciousness is in the subconscious. We not only attribute the reflexes and the general functions of instinctive life to it, which is correct, but also the lightning ideas which come from higher spheres and which we call by vague terms such as: *intuition, sixth sense* etc., which is erroneous. The reason is that we consider waking consciousness, clear consciousness as it is sometimes called, to be the peak of consciousness.

3. Fr. 'conscience'.
4. Matthew xi: 11.

Esoteric science however distinguishes two levels[5] of consciousness higher than waking consciousness. We do not have these by right of birth, nor do we acquire them by normal education or instruction. But they can be reached as a result of special efforts properly directed.

The first higher level is that of *self consciousness*: alternatively called the *consciousness of the real 'I'*. Above that, there is the level of *Consciousness* — in the full sense of this word.

From bottom to top we can define the four levels in other terms, as follows :

1) Subconsciousness is the twilight consciousness of the body. Its force does not depend on the cultural level of the individual. We often find that elementary or primitive beings have a much stronger consciousness of their bodies than intellectuals.

2) Waking Consciousness is the daytime consciousness of the Personality. Putting pathological cases aside, its scope and its amplitude[6] develop with the cultural development of the individual: it is the *subjective* consciousness of 'I'.

3) Consciousness of the real 'I' is the consciousness of the *Individuality*, otherwise described as *objective* consciousness of the individual 'I'.

4) Consciousness is absolute consciousness: the consciousness of the Absolute.

(3)

We shall return to the question of *Consciousness* further on, when we are better armed to sense and understand the true meaning of this word. As for the *consciousness of the real 'I'*, we can now form a certain idea of this, even in its passive form. We know it as the only *permanent* point which exists within us, hidden behind our ever changing personality; always dragged along by the torrent of our thoughts, our feelings, our passions or sensations, which pass through it and involve the whole man in unpremeditated acts which he himself would later condemn. This permanent point is the impartial *Referee* within us who judges our own acts; the *Referee* whose soft voice is often obscured by inward uproar or by events. Although weak and passive, this evanescent form of the consciousness of the real 'I' is always just and *objective*.

The doctrine of sin and of our responsibility for our acts would have no meaning if, when we come face to face with temptation, the consciousness of the real 'I' did not give us a warning of danger.[7] On the other hand, it is this presence within us which makes it possible for us to evolve

---

5. Fr. 'niveaux'.

6. Fr. 'ampleur'.

7. That is why we cannot say that man who is not yet esoterically evolved, *exterior* man, may be regarded as free of responsibility (cf. P. D. Ouspensky, *Fragments*, p. 19 [p. 41.]).

esoterically[8] in the deepest sense which, as we have already seen, is evolution towards *Consciousness*.

Because the real '*I*' does not manifest itself in man as he is born except in passive form, this inner *Judge* does not pronounce his verdict except where the personality itself submits its acts for his evaluation.

(4)

In modern life, contact with the real '*I*' is rather exceptional. Man, however, pretends to be '*I*', as if able to act at the level of consciousness appropriate to this '*I*' whose attributes he would possess: attributes such as ability to judge the consequences of his acts, the constant exercise of a will of his own, the ability to do, and a bearing appropriate to a being who is consistent with himself.

An objective examination of facts would be enough to belie these pretensions. Let us consider, for example, the way we commit ourselves to undertakings. It is clear that they are not always kept. If they are respected, it is often at the price of struggles within ourselves.

In reality, we do not act at the level of consciousness appropriate to the real '*I*', but at the level of waking consciousness, which belongs to the '*I*' of the Personality. We identify ourselves with this '*I*' no matter what facet it presents. Its instability thus models our attitudes. At a given moment, a little '*I*' or a group of little '*I*'s that compose the Personality decides on something, and acts. Then it makes way for another little '*I*', or for another group of little '*I*'s, which disapproves of the action taken and of its consequences. The changes caused by the entry on the scene of different combinations within the Personality can sometimes be so radical—especially if we have acted under the influence of a particular passion, of a violent feeling, or on the basis of erroneous calculation—that it appears to us as if a foreigner had acted in our place. We do not recognize ourselves in most of these decisions, which we bitterly regret.

(5)

There is thus a considerable gap between what man generously attributes to himself, that is, the qualities of the real '*I*', and what is properly his. Yet to reach the level of consciousness which corresponds to this real '*I*' is in the realm of possibility, of hope, as the Apostle Paul has said. But before what he pretends he already possesses can become his,

---

8. Nothing could be born from nothing. There must be a seed for a plant to be born: Matthew xiii: 31; Mark iv: 31; Luke xiii: 19.

man must carry out a considerable amount of conscious work upon himself.

(6)

As long as man remains sure of himself, despite all the evidence, the more he is still satisfied with himself, the more he continues to live in the absurd and inconsequential, taking his desires and illusions for reality. He must pass through a serious bankruptcy and a moral collapse,[9] both of which he must constate and accept without seeking to patch them over.[10] It is only then that we start to search, and only then that we discover the reasons for working on ourselves, and only then do we acquire the necessary strength to do so. This is true for all the world. There is only one exception: that of the *just*, for whom such work is a joy; as they are just, it is not necessary for them to constate such a bankruptcy. But who among us is just? Who, even, is of good faith?

In one way or another we are all corrupted. Even though everyday experience shows us the contrary, man thinks of himself as being of a certain importance. This opinion is the consequence of a deficiency in our judgement. In fact, we are all in the same boat. Even though they are different, for each one of us the algebraic sum of our qualities and of our defects is nearly the same. We must not be under false illusions: the amount of this sum is not large. It is an infinitesimal, and as such tends towards zero, which is Death.

To create a *unity* from this 'infinitesimal', based on latent faculties we pretend to actually possess, is what esoteric science expects of those who study it. It considers them at the start as sick people to which the principle proclaimed by Jesus applies: '*They that are whole have no need of a physician, but they that are sick.*'[11]

(7)

The problem of making a unity of oneself, starting practically from nothing, brings us once again to examine the question of *being*, but in a slightly different way. It acts, to use the language of the Alchemists, by a *transmutation*, a transformation of our factitious existence — whose value is no more than potential — into real existence. This happens through realization of that potential. It acts by progressively raising the level of

---

9. Fr. 'écroulement moral'.
10. Fr. 'sans tentative de replâtrage'.
11. Matthew ix: 12; Mark ii: 17; Luke v: 31.

our *being*. This work is to be done in stages according to a definite programme.

We recognize four distinct levels of *being*, correlated with the four levels of consciousness: a higher level of *being* and three lesser ones.

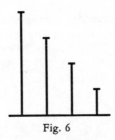

Fig. 6

As with consciousness, the higher level of *being* rests upon lower levels. The lowest of all levels belongs to every living body, but extends over a wide scale of values. Certain animals, especially among the higher mammals, touch the next higher level, that of humans.

Thus, for example, most mammals can and do have *representations* of objects and phenomena, a function which properly belongs to the lower level of human waking consciousness. But they can go no further; they do not have the faculty of generalization by which man forms his notions.

The third level of *being*, which corresponds to the consciousness of the real '*I*' is that of esoterically evolved men, properly called *alive*: that is, of those who have acquired permanent, unshakeable real '*I*'. Lastly the fourth level belongs to the perfect or complete man: he who has arrived by his esoteric development at the summit of evolution possible within the conditions of our planet.

(8)

The question of *being* is closely linked to the problem of power. We have already indicated that a man who has nothing within him but an unstable, changeable and factitious '*I*' has not — and can never have — any continuity of ideas or of behaviour. That is why he cannot *do*.

We have already established the relation which exists between the notions: *to know* and *to understand*. It is now the time for us to establish the relation between the notions: *knowledge* and *savoir-faire*.[12] We can easily understand from what has already been said that there is no possibility of passing directly from *knowledge* to *savoir-faire*. We generally explain the failure of our attempts to act as due to lack of will. That is not correct. It is

---

12. Tr. Here the French text gives 'savoir et savoir-faire': 'savoir' translates as 'knowing'; 'savoir-faire', already part of the English language, refers to 'doing'.

neither the will nor, to be more accurate, the intensity of desire which is lacking in these cases; to be precise we lack *being*, which would allow us first to *understand* the knowledge we have acquired, and so obtain the *power* that gives access to *savoir-faire*. The chain would be presented as follows:

| (passive form) | (active form) |
| *knowledge — being — understanding* | *being — understanding — savoir-faire* |

The acquisition of *knowledge* is relatively easy, as we have said. It is the acquisition of *being* which is substantially more difficult. But it is precisely *being* that leads us towards understanding, and from this towards *savoir-faire*. This formula remains the same in every sphere and domain.

CHAPTER III

(1)

W e find the Personality between the body and the Soul.[1] Though tied to both, it is generally more attached to the former. We have also constated that the 'I' of whom we speak every day corresponds to the Personality, known by our name.

The question that faces us next is how we may know[2] what the Personality is in itself. We certainly feel it within us. We are aware of its attitudes, its desires, and its actions; but we are not at all able to represent it.

Thinking about oneself evokes a certain image; of a clothed body, or a face which strives to be dignified and charming. This image is only a reflection of the Personality. If we want to discover the latter, we have to penetrate more deeply, and only introspection would permit us to discover its true face. Introspection leads us to discover that there exists a sort of little 'nebula'[3] within us. This is insubstantial, or almost so, but is gifted with the capacity for experiencing and thinking, for feeling emotion, and for action. An exercised and sustained attention permits us also to constate that this 'nebula' is mobile: it is sometimes found in the brain, and sometimes it descends to the heart and sometimes to the solar plexus. After a violent impression is made — for example after some great terror — it can move downward through the whole body to the feet. In such cases, everything goes on as if it had abandoned the general direction of the body, which it governs when it is situated in the brain,[4] in order to act on a local plane only, in reflexes of a very elementary nature. Once the emotion has passed, this 'nebula' normally re-ascends to a place in the higher part of the head. We then say that the person has come back to himself.

Contemporary man however, worrying more about the question of appearances[5] than about that of being, caught up in circumstances, always absent from himself — or falling during his hours of idleness into a drowsy satisfaction — can no longer feel the pulsation of life within him. To make such fundamental discoveries, he must make efforts, must exercise, and must practise inner observation.

---

1. Fr. 'Ame'.
2. Fr. 'savoir'.
3. '*Kloube*' in the Russian texts of the Tradition.
4. Fr. 'dont elle dispose lorsqu'elle se situe dans le cerveau'.
5. Fr. 'paraître'.

(2)

The Personality depends on the physical body much more than we generally admit. A localized and somewhat severe pain is sufficient to relegate all our generous ideas and all our refined feelings to the background of consciousness. On the other hand, when some person is capable of mastering his pain and continues to carry out his work in cold blood, such an attitude is considered heroic, for such behaviour reveals an exceptional character.

The intimate dependence of the Personality on the physical body, in which it resides and functions, leads logically to the conclusion that one must act through the latter to discover it, study it, and finally act on it. That is why all mental[6] exercises require physical training. The principle is general; its application nevertheless varies and depends on the method of the esoteric teaching. In the present essentially psychological method, physical training is reduced to the absolute minimum, but we cannot altogether do without it. We shall limit ourselves now to giving sufficient information — if followed — to enable us to resolve the first problem of physical training: to find the most suitable body posture for these mental exercises. Millennia of experience show that only a single posture meets this need. Leaving details aside, the posture must place *the head, the neck and the spinal column in one single straight line—and this line must be vertical*. Except in certain special cases which will each require other precise instructions, this rule must be strictly observed whether we are standing or sitting. Before we begin the mental or psychological exercises, we must discover this posture and familiarize ourselves with it. For Westerners who exercise at home, the most practical way is to sit on a hard seat 25 to 35 centimetres high, legs crossed, preferably right over left, palms flat and facing downward on the knees. This is one of many variants of that posture traditionally called the *posture of the sage.*

Here are some complementary indications: the muscles must be completely relaxed, the head high and the shoulders naturally pushed back, the waist curved in such a way that, viewed in profile, the spinal column would present a slight convexity directed forwards. The eyes can either be opened or closed; at the start it is preferable to leave them closed, because if they are left open without special training, they tire very quickly and interfere with the exercise. We must strive to reach this posture daily and regularly. Regularity of training, and the choice of a fixed time to practise, are the necessary conditions. *Tendencies accentuate themselves,* says an esoteric law; and again: *a rhythm increases results tenfold.* Yet one must not proceed too quickly. That is why another traditional maxim says: *'make haste slowly'.*

---

6. Throughout this chapter, 'mental' translates the French 'psychique'.

Once these conditions have been fulfilled, this posture must be practised in the morning before breakfast, initially for a maximum of two or three minutes. The duration must be prolonged slowly but progressively, always subject to the express condition that one must be able to maintain complete immobility, eyes included, during the whole exercise.

Here a question arises: What criterion[7] will let us know the moment when we have found the *posture of the sage*?

The answer in simple terms is: a feeling of restfulness. A quarter of an hour holding the correct posture gives a sensation of being rested that many consecutive hours of sleep cannot give.

Once the posture has been found, and not before—an operation which, depending on the individual, may demand weeks or months—we can start the exercises whose aim is to obtain a feeling of the 'nebula'.

It must be made clear that the *unit of measure* of time is individual and varies, particularly with age. This basic unit for each person is the interval between two heartbeats when the body is at rest. One must acquire the interior memory of this unit, of this heartbeat, because the rhythm of esoteric exercises is always regulated in accordance with it.

The first exercises are done in the following manner: inhale during four heartbeats, hold your breath for four heartbeats, then exhale similarly during four heartbeats. This movement must be executed harmoniously, without sudden changes. A shiver may appear; constant persistence in these exercises will eliminate it at a later time. It is the same if great distress appears. On the other hand, if we feel somewhat ill, even if it is nothing but a slight cold or fever, the exercises must be interrupted.

As for the result, it varies in its appearance in each individual case: with some it is acquired almost immediately; with others, at the end of a long period of training. But he who achieves the result easily can lose it just as easily, while he who reaches it by means of sustained work will possess it firmly.

(3)

The first sensation of the 'nebula' generally comes during the third phase of the exercise, that is, during exhalation. One feels it passing through the larynx, and all along the thyroid gland. The sensation is agreeable. Afterward, if the 'nebula' can be felt from the top of the head down to the heart and beyond, the student will know that he has taken a big step forward.

---

7. Fr. 'moyen de contrôle'.

Feeling the 'nebula' within oneself is already much, but it is only the first step. We have said above that, with certain qualifications, it is the Personality which makes itself felt within us in this way. On the mental plane, the 'nebula' thinks, feels, acts and changes constantly, yet a direct sensation of it gives a hazy impression of a cloud-like mass of amorphous character. This impression is false.

The personality is an organism. As such, it has a structure. But we miss this structure because we neither know[8] nor study it. Our attention is constantly being held by exterior facts and events, and by the mechanical reactions which they provoke within us.

The first attempts at internal observation have already led us to distinguish three foci of mental life, represented by the three centres (Fig. 4). It must be understood that these three centres are not physical points or organs, located in exactly determined places in our bodies. They are more in the nature of *centres of gravity* for each of the three currents of our mental life. Even this is not an altogether exact definition. For example, the motor centre takes an active part in all physical and mental movement. When thought initiates movements within us, the motor centre is present and regulates the motor element of the phenomena. It is the same for feelings, passions, sensations etc. Thus a discovery made by the intellectual centre with the aid of the motor centre, is immediately communicated to the latter, then transmitted to the emotional centre, where it provokes corresponding reactions. That transmission can also take place in a different order. That is how Archimedes, transported with joy by the discovery of the principle which bears his name, ran around the town of Syracuse shouting: *'Eureka!'*: thought; emotion; movement. That shows that the three mental centres which embrace, regulate and express the life of our Personality, and also constitute its structure, are not autonomous.

Persistent introspection will later allow us to constate that each one of the three centres is divided into two parts: positive and negative. Normally these two parts act in conjunction with one another: for they are in fact polarized as are the double organs of the body, which duplicate the same function or participate in the same work at the same time; our arms for example. That division of the centres, a reflection of the universal polarization, allows them to establish *comparisons*: to consider both sides of problems posed to them. The positive part of each centre looks — one might say—to the head, and the negative part to the tail of these problems. The centre as a whole constructs an appropriate synthesis and draws its conclusions, inspired by the constatations made by each of the two parts.

---

8. Fr. 'connaissons'.

An example is the process of critical analysis. It is therefore totally erroneous to consider that the names of these parts indicate a beneficent or harmful role depending on whether they are positive or negative. These terms do not imply any value judgement—any more than the constatation of positive and negative charges upon elementary particles.

If we consider the functioning of the motor centre, we can perceive that these parts are inseparable one from the other, in their structure as well as in their action. With certain reservations we can say that the positive part of this centre corresponds to the ensemble of the instinctive functions of the psycho-physical organism of man, and its negative part to the motor functions. In other words the motor centre is in the full sense of the word the manager of our bodies: it must equilibrate the energies that it accumulates by its positive part with those that are consumed by its negative part.

This symmetry—this polarity—is to be found in the two other centres.

Constructive and creative ideas are born in the positive part of the intellectual centre. But it is the negative part that evaluates an idea, that takes its measure, so to speak. It is on the basis of this functional polarity that this centre, as a whole, judges.

It is the same with the emotional centre, the action of the negative part opposes the positive part, which at the same time completes it, for example permitting the centre as a whole to distinguish the agreeable from the disagreeable.

We can nevertheless misuse the faculties of the negative parts. This negative abuse is a real danger. The case is obvious as far as the motor centre is concerned, yet here physical exhaustion acts as a control, intervening to stop excessive consumption of energy. When it comes to the other centres, the misuse of the negative parts takes much more insidious forms, which entail more serious consequences for our minds[9] as well as our bodies. That is how the negative part of the intellectual centre nourishes jealousy, afterthoughts, hypocrisy, suspicion, treachery, etc. The negative of the emotional centre receives all the disagreeable impressions and serves as a vehicle for negative emotions, for which the keyboard is very large, ranging from melancholy to hate. We shall have occasion to go deeper into the problem of negative emotions. Their destructive role is generally unknown, but represents one of the major obstacles to esoteric evolution.

---

9. Fr. 'psychisme'.

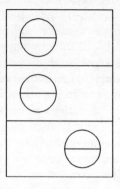

Fig. 7

The structure of each centre is not limited to two divisions: positive and negative; each half is further divided into three sectors. This is done in such a way that if the previous diagram were completed in this way it would appear as shown below:

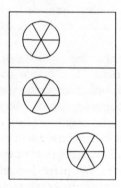

Fig. 8

In every centre there is therefore as much on the positive side as on the negative; one sector of each possesses the characteristics of that centre in a pure state. In the intellectual centre are sectors which are purely intellectual — positive and negative; in the emotional centre sectors which are purely emotional — positive and negative; in the motor centre sectors which are purely motor — positive and negative. Beside the pure sectors we find composite sectors which are, so to speak, the representatives of the two other centres. In their ensemble the sectors are:

For the intellectual centre:

1) pure intellectual
2) emotional-intellectual   } positive and negative
3) motor-intellectual

For the emotional centre:

1) pure emotional
2) emotional-intellectual   } positive and negative
3) emotional-motor

For the motor centre:

a) positive part

1) pure instinctive
2) instinctive-intellectual
3) instinctive-emotional

b) negative part

1) pure motor
2) motor-intellectual
3) motor-emotional

There are in all eighteen sectors, which in their ensemble form the structure of the Personality.

Thanks to this system, none of the three centres — pathological cases excluded — can act in a purely autonomous manner. Through the sectors representing the two other centres, the whole system moves in unison. It goes without saying, however, that the participation of two centres in the work of another is always coloured by the latter's character.

As we can see, the system of the centres is complex but answers perfectly to all needs. It allows us to perceive all the psycho-physical elements of the Universe, to react to the impressions so received, to reach concepts, and to proceed to complex operations.

(5)

Study of the structure of the Personality allows us to deal with a problem which plays a big role in esoteric science, that of human types. If it is true that every man in some way represents a unique factor in the universe, it is no less true that human types repeat themselves. Human types recur even more often than is commonly believed. In fact, there are not many of them, but only three basic types.

These types are distinguished by the preponderance in the Personality of one or the other of the three mental centres: the man who is predominantly intellectual; who thinks, calculates and researches; the man who is emotional above all; who is sentimental, artistic, romantic; lastly the man of action. In the Doctrine we name them as follows:

— *man 1* — is he whose mental centre of gravity abides in the motor centre;

— *man 2* — is he whose centre of gravity resides in the emotional centre;

— *man 3* — is he whose centre of gravity resides in the intellectual centre.

Man as he is born of woman must belong to one of these three fundamental types, to which all of humanity belongs, regardless of race, caste or class. This is a law of Nature. It is not given to men to escape from it and to change at whim from one type to another.

We shall see however that other types exist, superior to the three fundamental types. But apart from quite exceptional cases, man cannot belong to one of these higher types by right of birth. Their creation is the outcome of a long process of gestation to which Jesus alluded while talking to Nicodemus, when He said that man must be born anew. To rise to these levels one must make continuous and sustained conscious efforts in accordance with rules established millennia ago by esoteric science.

CHAPTER IV

(1)

The *exterior* man[1] has three 'I's: the 'I' of the body (physical), the 'I' of the Personality (mental[2]), and potentially the real 'I' (spiritual). Theoretically, the real 'I' should have assumed the responsibility for commanding the whole system. But since the fall of Adam, the real 'I', in its aspect as the inmost heart,[3] has been relegated to the background of consciousness, dominated by the mental[2] 'I' of the Personality. The latter, who commands by default, so to speak, lacks unity. Changing, floating, multiple, he can only act in a disorderly manner. Thus the 'I' of the body, who should normally obey the mental[2] 'I', frequently imposes his own purposes upon the latter. The usual example of such domination is that of adultery, due to sexual attraction without any spiritual ties.[4]

In reviewing in our lives different examples of the connections between the three 'I's, we would certainly profit by meditating once again on the symbol of the *coach*, which offers many analogies in this vein, all of them profoundly instructive.

(2)

In the waking state we employ the 'I' of the Personality. During sleep, we lose awareness[5] of this 'I'; the 'I' of the body then takes its place.[6] Of course, the purely physiological functions have a continuity of character. It is only when man sleeps, that is to say when the mental[2] 'I' has vanished and does not interfere any more in the activities of the 'I' of the body, that the latter can act on its proper plane, knowingly[7] and without hindrance.

It is the motor centre which serves as the organ of manifestation for the 'I' of the body[8]. As for the mental[2] 'I', the 'I' of our Personality, this normally expresses itself through the emotional and intellectual centres. In the majority of cases it uses these centres in an improper manner, and it

---

1. Mark iv: 11.

2. Fr. 'psychique'.

3. Fr. 'for intérieur'. Translated as 'conscience' or 'inmost heart' depending on context.

4. Not to be confused with the calculated exploitation of sexual attraction by the intellectual centre of the Personality in order to attain definite goals.

5. Fr. 'connaissance'.

6. We should note here that the 'I' of the body does not completely disappear even in states such as lethargy, anæsthesia or coma.

7. Fr. 'à bon escient'.

8. We shall see further on that it is not the only one to fulfil this function.

equently intervenes in the functioning of the motor centre. The immediate result of this state of things is the illogicality of our mental[9] life, because the 'I' of the body competes with the 'I' of the Personality. The latter, being multiple has not — and cannot have — any logical continuity either in its ideas or its actions. Man thus spends his life swinging from action to reaction and from reaction to action.

The broken[10] succession of our lives is well known. Often it forms the complex tissue of the works of novelists and dramatists. In the Tradition, in this context, we often evoke the image of three men co-existing in each man: one who thinks, another who feels,[11] and a third who acts.

We can describe their interference[12] in domains that are not properly theirs; interferences which in different situations can be natural or unnatural, salutary or harmful. Unnatural interferences are always harmful and are the cause of a large part of our interior and exterior conflicts. Such interferences, sometimes mild but more often violent, are aggravated still more by the fact that the centres, because of their division into sectors, can never act in an autonomous manner, although each one of them claims to impose itself upon the others. Thus the stronger the action taken by one of the centres, the more powerful the mechanical compulsion[13] suffered by the other two — pathological cases excluded.

(3)

The 'I' of the Personality is composed of a considerable number of little 'I's, forming different groups which take turns at ruling our attitudes and actions. How then can we reconcile this chaotic state with the continuity it provides, even if only apparently, to our mental[9] life? Three elements are found to form the basis of this apparent continuity:

— our name;
— experience, as fixed by memory;
— the faculty of lying to ourselves and to others.

The *name* we bear corresponds to the 'I' of the Personality, that is to say to the ensemble of the particles of iron filings, regardless of the relative positions they occupy. After adolescence a man's name also represents his image of himself in his waking state.

He sometimes attaches to this an ideal image of himself: an image of what he aspires to be or to become.

---

9. Fr. 'psychique'.
10. Fr. 'décousu'.
11. Fr. 'éprouve les sentiments'.
12. Fr. 'immixtion'.
13. Fr. 'l'entraînement mécanique'.

That is why he holds on to his name as he would to a life-raft.[14] In effect, everything that exists has a name; without a name one cannot imagine any existence, mental[15] or physical, real or factitious.

In the case of man, his name and his Christian name cover the ensemble of what we can define as his own universe—in its material elements as well as its imaginary ones. He often considers these latter to be real.

Memory is a direct function of the *being* of the individual. The higher the level of *being*, the better the memory and the greater its capacity to contain. Loss of memory, which causes the notion of the name and the ensemble that is attached to it to be forgotten, makes a madman out of a normal man: the sense of continuity is no longer present.

The *faculty of lying* is the third element in our factitious life. It helps substantially to give it a semblance of continuity. We can easily realize the role played by this faculty of lying if we imagine what our existence would come to if this possibility were taken away. Life would become impossible, due to the shocks and conflicts which we would have to face. In this way, lies serve as *buffers*,[16] like the buffers of railway carriages which soften shocks. It is this faculty of lying which makes our lives less of a battle, and contributes greatly to the impression of continuity life gives us. We are brought back once again to the fact that we attribute to ourselves faculties which we do not possess — except as possibilities for development: we pretend to be truthful because telling the truth and living a truthful life are possibilities which can become real; but they can do so much later, after we have worked hard and long upon ourselves. In the meantime we are condemned to lie. Whoever denies this only testifies to our difficulty in facing the truth.

(4)

We must linger a while on the question of lying, a question of great importance to which we must return more than once. The faculty of lying is a function of our imagination, a creative faculty. Before we create anything we must imagine what it is we wish to create. This gift belongs only to humans. Animals never possess it.

It is thanks to this gift of imagination, a divine gift, that we have the faculty of lying. We lie for different reasons, wishing generally to ameliorate situations which seem to us unbearable or difficult to accept. Lies thus open the way for mechanisms of rationalization or of justification, which are ways of 'patching up'. We shall see further on how the entangled behaviour of persons round about us provokes many shocks, creating

---

14. Fr. 'planche de salut'.
15. Fr. 'psychique'.
16. Fr. 'tampons'.

difficult and sometimes insoluble situations of human relations, veritable *Gordian knots*. It is thus in the utmost good faith that we resort to lies.

This being so, the attitude of the esoteric Doctrine towards lying is clear and realistic. It does not require us to stop lying from the start, because nobody can carry out such a resolution. However, if man cannot stop lying to others, the same cannot be said as far as he himself is concerned. He is therefore asked to stop lying to himself—and this in a definite way. This requirement is absolute, and we can easily understand why. The objective of esoteric work is the march towards *Consciousness*, which means towards *Truth*. It would be a *contradictio in objecto* to try to approach the truth while continuing to lie to ourselves or to believe in our own lies. We must therefore eliminate any attempt to lie to ourselves: on this point no compromise can be tolerated, no excuse admitted.

But while in our present condition we cannot live without lying to others, we must at least be conscious of our lies.

There is, nevertheless, another recommendation which we can make in this domain. In the ensemble of our lies to others, tolerated esoterically, we must exercise ourselves to distinguish between those lies which are indispensable or inevitable, those lies which are simply useful, and those which are not. The Doctrine asks those who study it to fight energetically against those useless lies.

It is only by training of this nature that we shall progressively be able to master the rooted tendency to lie which exists within us. Every attempt to hurry things, so far as lying to others is concerned, though it be a noble attempt, is doomed to early failure. We live in a world which is immersed in lies and moved by lies. It is to be noted that the Decalogue, which imposes observable commandments on man, does not forbid him from lying except in a small sector of human relations; that of bearing false witness, and also in situations where he is already badly predisposed to someone.[17]

(5)

It is also necessary to guard against a variant of the habit of lying to ourselves, one which we commonly adopt from early childhood and against which we must fight by every means. This variant is widespread because at first glance it appears to us to be a positive attitude. Such an attitude can normally be adapted easily to any case; used in spoken language or in writing; in mundane conversation, or in a thesis for a doctorate, it is betrayed by the phrase: *'yes but...'*. This in itself does not imply any harm when it is used. On the contrary, such usage is helpful and even indispensable in discussions, controversies and pleadings — where we

---

17. Deuteronomy v: 20.

resort to it quite frequently. However when applied to ourselves and for our own benefit, with the aim of softening a shock, or rediscovering our inner peace after we have sinned, or excusing our actions or faults, this idiom crystallizes within us over a period of time to create a true *auto-tranquillizing mechanism*. It is to be noted that the effects of this mechanism are not to be compared with 'sang-froid', or the ability to answer well and quickly, or those of inspirations[18] from consciousness. On the contrary, it is a true mechanism of mental anaesthesia, founded on a refined and disguised lie. It sows hypocrisy in man towards himself.

This *auto-tranquillizer*, like all other moral buffers, must be destroyed.

(6)

Let us now return to the study of the 'I' of the Personality. It has been established that this 'I', as it is, is shifting *sand*. As used in the Gospel,[19] the image of sand and that of *legion* are both very near reality. For what we take to be our 'I' is, in fact, a mixture of a number of little 'I's. In the Personality each little 'I' or group of little 'I's enters the scene according to circumstance. There are many possible combinations between these 'I's, but their number is limited: it can be calculated.

We have seen that, according to the Tradition, man possesses three mental[20] centres, each divided into six sectors. This raises the number of the Personality's various organs of consciousness to eighteen. Every little 'I' is nothing but a fractional consciousness of the Personality, that is to say, of the 'ensemble' of the mental[20] 'I', which for the moment thinks of itself in that way. Applying algebraic calculations to the possible combinations of three, two and one which can arise from the three centres and their eighteen sectors, we find that the number of these combinations amounts to nine hundred and eighty seven.

This fractional form of consciousness betrays the deficient state in which the Personality is generally found. Let us say for the moment that this fractional consciousness that arises in man is one aspect of these many possible combinations of sectors which at every moment play a part in the receipt of impressions and in the expression of desires, feelings and opinions.

These groupings generally occur in threes or twos; it is rather rare that one sector alone participates in a mental[20] state. As long as the fusion of the particles of iron filings has not occurred, these nine hundred and eighty seven possible combinations of the centres and their sectors give birth to an equal number of partial states of consciousness of the Personality. Each

---

18. Fr. 'éclairs de la conscience'.
19. Mark v: 9; Luke viii: 30.
20. Fr. 'psychique'.

affirms itself as — and at that moment thinks of itself as — the complete 'I'. We must bear in mind that we are dealing here with these little 'I's of whom we have talked many times before.[21]

The various combinations incessantly made and unmade within us by the little 'I's weave the fabric of our lives; their outcome is harmful. This life, the iron filings in the vase (Fig.1), keeps continually modifying itself in an anarchistic way. It is dominated by outside events, and lacks the interference of a pre-established plan by which it may attain a premeditated goal. This reminds us of the phenomenon of wave interference or white-caps,[22] which we can graphically represent by intertwined sinusoids.

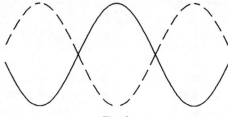

Fig. 9

This phenomenon results in a draining exhaustion which can lead a man to death. Later, we shall see the problem from a different point of view, which will better explain the cause of ageing and death. From the esoteric point of view, *death is bankruptcy*.[23] The friction between the iron filings which occurs in our everyday lives is not intense enough to kindle an interior fire sufficient to transfigure the whole *being* — which would permit him to vanquish Death. Such friction is however more than enough to totally exhaust the reserve of vital forces and so bring on death. It is to such cases, among others, that the words of Revelations apply:

'I know that thou art neither cold nor hot: I would thou wert cold or hot. But because thou art lukewarm, and neither hot nor cold, I will spew thee out of My mouth. Because thou sayest, I am rich and have gotten riches and have need of nothing; and knowest not that thou art a wretched one, and miserable and poor and blind and naked: I counsel thee to buy of me gold refined by fire that thou mayest become rich; and white garments, that thou mayest clothe thyself, and that the shame of thy nakedness be not made manifest; and eyesalve to anoint thine eyes, that thou mayest see.'[24]

---

21. Some psychologists have reached objective findings which are, in fact, quite close to the number we have calculated. Thus Sheldon and his co-workers have gathered, by empirical methods, 650 *traits of character* which have been commonly admitted (cf. Guy Palmade, *La Caractérologie*, Presses Universitaires de France, Paris, 1953, p. 91).

22. Fr. 'houppée'.

23. Fr. 'la mort est une faillite'.

24. Rev. iii: 15–18.

CHAPTER V

(1)

The formation of the three mental[1] centres in the Personality is not synchronous with their development.

The *motor centre* is already highly developed in the newborn. Its *positive instinctive* part grows and forms itself while still in the mother's womb, beginning at conception, and continuing throughout pregnancy in such a way that at birth it functions at its normal rhythm. After this it will no longer be subject to qualitative change. On the other hand, the *negative motor* part of this centre is much less developed. It can be said that if the instinctive part of the newborn functions at around 75% of its normal output, the percentage for the motor part only reaches 25%, and this almost totally devoted to the internal processes of the body. Throughout growth, before and after puberty, this part of the motor centre not only develops quantitatively, but qualitatively. In addition, all the *savoir-faire* of the bodily 'I',[2] from the time the infant takes his mother's breast until he performs the most complex movements, must be complemented at every step[3] by qualitative development. This development continues throughout life.

The *emotional centre* in the newborn is characterized by its purity. As long as the child has not learned how to lie, he retains the marvellous faculty — proper to this centre — of spontaneously discerning the true from the false over a very wide range of experience. With time, education, and all that is instilled in the child, this centre is deranged and this faculty lost, to be found again only much later as a result of esoteric work, special exercises, and sustained efforts. It must also be noted that the emotional centre in the newborn is generally much less developed than the motor centre, and that commonly during the life of man 1, 2 or 3, *exterior* man, it does not develop like the two other centres.

Although education[4] is a major preoccupation of families and public authorities, the emotional development of the child is almost totally left to chance. In our contemporary civilization, this leads to an extraordinary impoverishment of our affective lives. Even in the eighteenth century, the Abbé Prévost notes:

---

1. Fr. 'psychique'.
2. Fr. 'moi physique'.
3. Fr. 'en chaque cas'.
4. Fr. 'l'instruction'.

'There are few people who know the full force of the different movements of the heart. The vast majority of men are only sensitive to five or six passions, in the circle of which their lives are passed and which define the boundaries of their imaginations. Take away love and hate, pleasure and pain, hope and fear, and *they will feel nothing*'.

He further added:

'But persons of a nobler character can be moved in thousands of different ways. It seems that they can receive ideas and sensations which surpass the ordinary norms of nature.'[5]

The development of the emotional centre is the principal object of esoteric culture. We shall see later that it is only through this centre that man can find the key which will open the door to give him access to a higher life.

The *intellectual centre* is in an embryonic state in the newborn. It goes through an intensive development which continues for the length of life, very often taking hypertrophied form in our civilization.

Man's shaping is almost exclusively the shaping of his intellectual centre through instruction, personal experience, and analytical or constructive work, whether original or compilatory.

(2)

The intellectual centre in the child is a tabula rasa. It can be compared to a system of gramophone discs which have not yet been recorded. The system is vast, well regulated, and provided with a mechanism — that of association — by which any disc arriving at its end automatically releases a second, the contents of which are related to the first. A record which turns as someone speaks can similarly provoke in us — again by association — the release of an equivalent record. In general this is how dialogue is born and sustained.

This procedure is mechanical. We can easily observe this in any conversation between a number of persons who know each other slightly. Such an interchange necessarily falls to an elementary level of the most banal interests: weather, political news, or the city. We hear these records being played, turning continually and passing from one person to another, each with their faces congealed in a grimace which — we commonly agree — gives evidence of an amiable attitude.

The recording continues practically forever, as the disc library is vast and the recording apparatus very sensitive. When a person speaks, it is generally easy to distinguish whether his records are playing or whether he speaks from some deeper part of himself. In the latter case, he uses a pictorial, rustic and sometimes awkward language; in the former he speaks in a singing tone of voice. It is important to make these observations upon

5. Abbé Prévost, *Histoire du chevalier des Grieux et de Manon Lescaut* (Payot, Paris, 1926) pp. 96–7.

ourselves, in order to be able to constate such variations of speech. One moment it is 'I' who speaks then, unnoticed, it is no longer I; a recording from the past begins to play in me. A curious thing: once a record has been started, it is almost impossible to stop it before it has run through its content.

There are discs which we should carefully preserve, while others should be re-recorded. A special series of discs sometimes concerns the techniques of one's work. Everyone in his everyday work unconsciously creates a collection of such discs, which he uses for the needs of his profession.

Beside these recordings are others whose contents are without sense: they do not correspond either to needs or facts. This category includes for example anecdotes and what seems to the speaker to be witty conversation.

Interior observation of this phenomenon would reveal a whole repertoire of such records. A discovery like this would offer us the opportunity of working to control the release of a particular type of recording, and so try to eliminate it completely.

For that, we must first start to distinguish these from useful discs which have some purpose. This is done by analysis of their contents, and by the inner 'taste' which causes them to be played, as well as by the characteristic intonation that they give to the voice. Thereafter, we must try to catch the exact moment of their release. It is in that precise moment — we shall see later on why this is so — that it is possible to control these recordings and eliminate those which are useless.

(3)

Experience confirms the evidence that the child identifies himself with the 'I' of the body. The Personality is found to be obedient to this 'I' and still very underdeveloped. The proof of this is that he speaks of himself by evoking his own name, which is an attribute of the Personality. He speaks of himself in the third person, exactly as an adult who identifies himself with his personality treats his Soul as a third person. The Soul is as much of a stranger to the *exterior* man as the Personality is to the child, but this is not true of his body, even though he treats it in the third person. Indeed, although less apparent, the obedience of the Personality to the 'I' of the body frequently continues in adults.

Having become conscious of this bondage, someone who devotes himself to esoteric practices seeks to overcome it. He may have recourse to dangerous processes to attain this end. Thus it happens that certain esoteric Orthodox, Muslim and Hindu techniques make the mistake of using mortifications which are excessive and surpass the limits of good sense. We forget that the body is the horse which we are called upon to ride[6] for the

6. Fr. 'chevaucher'.

whole of our lives; an instrument which cannot be replaced. Certainly it must be trained, disciplined and kept in its place, which is to be obedient; but it is nonetheless true that it must be suitably cared for and maintained. The result to seek in this domain is always a state of discipline which compromises neither health nor vigour.

We must tune the instrument which emits discordant sounds, not cut the strings to stop the cacophony.

(4)

The formation of character occurs at the same time as the growth and development of the mental[7] centres in man. We have seen that the Personality is made up of little 'I's, each in turn based on[8] one of the possible combinations of the centres and their sectors. These little 'I's form the iron filings which under certain circumstances — *friction* and *fire* — can be radically transformed by what we have called *fusion*: this is when the character of man can be considered to be finally formed. It is only then that the following ideal qualities are acquired: firmness in man; gentleness[9] in woman. These are then gained not momentarily — only until a new storm — but in permanent form, although always coloured by the given qualities of the individual[10] nature. As long as the *fusion* is not complete, what we call the character can be compared to a tent erected on a sandy beach, open to winds and tempests. In reality, this character represents — in the ensemble of the small 'I's — a grouping of a number of them having in common certain factors such as: innate disposition; education; training; common or personal interests[11] on every level of consciousness, especially the sub-consciousness, and lastly accidental associations. Such groupings can be constituted on very different bases, and the strength of the bonds uniting the little 'I's can make a fragile federation out of them, or may constitute a partial fusion between them. The latter can be produced in different ways: either in the form of an annular or lateral *crust*, or in the form of *lumps*.

Fig. 10

Fig. 11

---

7. Fr. 'psychique'.
8. Fr. 's'affirme'.
9. Fr. 'douceur'.
10. Fr. 'personne donnée'.
11. Fr. 'attractions'.

In the first case, the character shows a certain degree of constancy but is rather superficial both in form and in appearance. This situation[12] is not uncommon in Anglo-Saxons and generally among Germans. Such a nature in man has principles, but essentially it is rather too pragmatic. In the second case the orientation of character is more rigid. This case occurs more frequently among the Latin[13] peoples. With time, this type of character has turned towards the cult of formal logic and the formation of a Cartesian spirit.

The third category is no longer characterized by the formation of a single group of particles amongst[14] the little 'I's, but has two groupings, like *lumps* in the middle of a fluid mass.

Fig. 12

Such cases are often found among the Slavs and the people of the Near and Middle East. The presence of two groupings instead of one simply tends to make the ensemble of the Personality more fragile and excessively concerned to defend the individual's personal interests.

On the other hand, this structure makes him 'bilateral', therefore more objective and consequently more understanding.

When there are two *lumps*, one constituted by little 'I's of an emotional character and the other by little 'I's of an intellectual character, if an interior or exterior shock occurs, close collaboration is established between these two groupings. For a time they form a single block. The character becomes particularly firm for that period; capable of taking decisions or keeping up a heroic fight. In ordinary conditions the character of these human groups is such that interest, adventure or money do not constitute a sufficient stimulus to break the equilibrium between the two *lumps* and provide the impulse to work for complete *fusion*. They must always be magnetized by some disinterested motive: ideas, beliefs, doctrines, devotion, trust etc. Occasionally the formation of two *lumps* has a negative result: man then becomes hesitant, incapable of taking a decision as he always finds as many arguments in favour of abstention as of action. Russian literature offers more than one example of human types of this class, particularly in the novels of Dostoevsky. The simultaneous crystallization of two *lumps* in the

12. Fr. 'cas'.
13. Fr. 'romanité'.
14. Fr. 'au sein'.

mass of little *'I's* can provoke a split in the Personality. There even exist cases of formation of three *lumps*, but these are classified as pathological cases, and deep examination of these does not enter into the scope of the present study. It is sufficient to note that generally the formation of three *lumps* and more leads to complete dissolution of the Personality.

The Emperor Alexander I of Russia[15] offers a classical example of Personality schism.

(5)

Let us now examine the position the Personality of the adult occupies in relation to the real *'I'*, our innermost self; that supreme, equitable, impartial but passive *judge*. We can represent this relative position in the figure below:

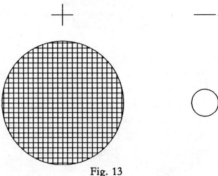

Fig. 13

The circle on the left represents the *'I'* of the Personality—the ensemble of the little *'I's*—which is in fact a *Non-I*. The circle on the right is the real *'I'*. In man 1, 2 or 3, the Personality dominates. It is the Personality which acts, while the real *'I'* who, since the fall of Adam, occupies a very passive position in man, must bear the consequences of those acts. The Personality follows its own goals and acts as it likes, often transgressing against the principles and maxims of the real *'I'*. This observation permits us to grasp

---

15. Third Emperor of the Holstein-Gottorp dynasty. Son of a half-madman (Paul I. assassinated); grandson of a degenerate (Peter III assassinated); great grandson of Charles-Frederick, Duke of Holstein-Gottorp, an alcoholic. The reports of contemporaries of Alexander are very strange. Thus, Lagerbjörk, Swedish ambassador, said of him: 'the Emperor Alexander is as subtle as the point of a needle, sharp as a razor, false as the surf of the sea'. We should also recall the words of Napoleon: 'It would be difficult to have a brighter mind than Alexander, but I am convinced that he is missing a part therein and it is impossible to find out which one it is.' Lastly, N. K. Schilder, the best biographer of the Emperor, said that: 'it was usual for him to have two ways of thought for everything'. Alexander hated all people who had guessed the state of his personality, of which he was undoubtedly aware. He hid this duality, but always ended by the most complete negation of what he professed, as he did of his most sacred ideals.

the profound meaning of the words of the Apostle St Paul: '*I do not do what I will and I do what I hate*.'[16]

This is the situation of any man who goes through life in ignorance of his latent faculties, that is to say, of real Life.

His factitious existence is only a *loan*: it is temporary and ends with death, according to the divine word: '*for dust thou art and unto dust shalt thou return*.'[17]

What is the sense and purpose of such an existence? We cannot find an exact answer to this question until we examine it in a large context—that of the life of the Cosmos. We shall then understand the meaning of human life, and its objective 'raison d'être' *in relation to the economy of the Universe*. On the other hand, looked at from the individual point of view — subjectively — such an existence seems absurd. Great minds have always seen this and clearly said it. Pushkin cried: '*Marvellous gift, useless gift, life, for what purpose were you given to us?*'

Here we are touching on the great problem of Death. The more man identifies himself with his Personality, the less he thinks of death. Contrary to all evidence as he sees everything die all around him, man has no spontaneous feeling of his mortality. Though gifted with fertile imagination, man can conceive of his own death only with difficulty. An effort is needed in order to come to the idea of one's own death, and to create its image. All man can imagine in this respect is to evoke the image of his own corpse: he can never exclude from this representation the observer who contemplates this image. This fact is known, and certain authors have seen it as proof of our immortality. There is in this a fragment of truth. Without his being aware of it, the mental effort of representing his own death detaches man a little, unaccountably not only from identification with his own body, but also from his Personality — so that he identifies himself, partially and for a few instants, with his real 'I'. Otherwise, the latter remains neglected, generally forgotten somewhere in the deepest parts of our waking consciousness — which is the consciousness of the 'I' of our Personality, accompanied by the consciousness of the 'I' of the body.

This exercise is useful and even necessary. In Esoteric Orthodoxy, it is imposed on students together with the *prayer of Jesus* as a daily exercise, under the title of *remembrance of death*. Death is the only *real* and unique event which happens to us without fail. In other words, constantly bearing in mind the idea of death approaching nearer every day is a concrete means of facing an implacable reality — before which all the joys and all the worries of the Personality fade. It is thus that one learns that in effect: '*all is vanity and torments of the mind*.'[18]

---

16. Romans vii: 15.
17. Genesis iii: 19.
18. Ecclesiastes i: 14; ii: 17. Quoted according to the Slavonic texts.

(6)

The situation is without outcome as long as man, regarding himself as a Personality, identifies himself with his relative consciousness, making the aims and the interests of the latter his own. For *'broad is the road that leads to perdition'*.[19]

But where then is: *'narrow is the gate and strait the road that leadeth unto Life?'*[20] Our brief examination of relations between the Personality and the real 'I' shows where we must search for the answer. Whoever seeks escape from this factitious existence — who has measured its vanity — must concentrate his efforts on this point. All hope is here.

(7)

Starting from these constatations, esoteric science no longer views man as *a given fact*,[21] but as a *possibility*. It indicates that the biological, psychological and moral growth and development of the *exterior* man stops spontaneously at a certain level. It is true that in every field man continues to act and even to act in a constructive manner on the higher levels[22] of his waking consciousness — and especially in his profession: he can make discoveries; he can render substantial services to society; *but as he is, he can no longer raise the level of his being.* As a result of this, the process of degeneration immediately acts without relenting: it starts with the physical body, and leads to ageing and then to death.

The *narrow road leading to Life* offers the possibility — which is real — to reverse[23] the situation represented in the previous figure (Fig. 13). This is done by introducing a continuous and *permanent attachment* between the Personality and the passive real 'I', so as to render the presence of the latter constant in the field of action of the Personality. Then, with time and according to the intensity of efforts, the situation can undergo a complete change: the more[24] the real 'I' — like the *grain of mustard seed*[25] — takes root in the mental[26] life which was until then dominated by the Personality, the more the latter is subjected, little by little, to the will of the *judge*. Identifying himself with it, man will rediscover his real 'I' in all its integrity and permanence. *For him*, life then loses its factitious character, to become

---

19. Matthew vii: 13.
20. Matthew vii: 14.
21. Fr. 'donnée'.
22. Fr. 'plans'.
23. Fr. 'renverser'.
24. Fr. 'au fur et à mesure'.
25. Matthew viii: 31; Mark iv: 31; Luke viii: 19.
26. Fr. 'psychique'.

logical and factual. This new condition can be represented by the figure below, which shows an essential difference compared to the previous one:

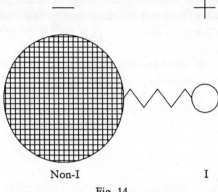

Non-I   I

Fig. 14

The permanent link which must be introduced between the Personality and the real 'I' is *esoteric Knowledge*.[27] The knowledge and savoir-faire that it permits us to acquire represent the *philosophers' stone* of the medieval mystics. They are capable of provoking in man the *transmutation* to which he aspires.

The great difficulty — which makes this road narrow and painful — consists in the fact that for the Personality this transmutation results in the loss of its dominating position: it must bow and submit. What makes the problem even more difficult is that the Personality must accept the new situation in advance; more, it must aspire to it; must wish for it ardently. As we have already said, the real 'I' remains in a passive state in the *exterior* man. For the Personality, the prospect of the emergence of that 'I' and its permanent presence in daily life entails the loss of free choice, and it reacts sharply. In the best cases this reaction is not continuous but is revealed by reactions which may become dangerous. This is the effect of the arrogant pride[28] of the Personality, which wants to continue to assert itself as supreme authority. We can now better understand that to successfully enter the narrow path — that is, esoteric work — the man-Personality must accept in advance (the need) to pass through moral bankruptcy.[29] As long as he is self-satisfied, he must be considered *rich* according to the Gospel, and we already know that it is '*easier for a camel to go through a needle's eye, than for a rich man to enter into the kingdom of God*.'[30]

---

27. Fr. 'Connaissance'.
28. Fr. 'orgeuil'.
29. Fr. 'faillite'.
30. Matthew xix: 24; Mark x: 25; Luke xviii: 25.

In the discovery of this road lies the true meaning of our lives: this wonderful gift, otherwise useless according to Pushkin. This gift gives us a possibility. We are called by the voice of our innermost heart[31] to realize this gift. But to succeed we must work ceaselessly, for fear of not succeeding in time. One must work, says Jesus, '*while it is day: the night comes when no man can work.*'[32]

If we keep the image of death constantly in our minds, we will appreciate with bitter regret the value of each lost day.

31. Fr. 'for intérieur'.
32. John ix: 4.

CHAPTER VI

(1)

W e now stand very close to the domain of esotericism proper. The Apostle St Paul said: *'Make sure that nobody makes prey of you by philosophy or by mere deceit, depending on human tradition derived from elements of nature and not according to Christ — for only in Him the whole fullness of the Divinity lives bodily. Only in Him is all complete, since He is the source and the power of it all.'*[1]

This passage is important. In it the Apostle establishes a fundamental distinction between positive philosophy on the one hand, based on the speculations of what he calls *carnal intelligence*;[2] on a tradition which is purely human in origin, and on the other hand the higher knowledge[3] whose unique source, he says, is Christ. For St Paul, carnal intelligence is none other than that of the Personality — dominated in cultured circles by an education which is predominantly intellectual. In spite of all its refinements in the art of reasoning, this intelligence cannot go beyond the limits of agnostic rationalism. Enclosed within this circle, human reason does not know[4] and will never know[3] what lies beyond these limits: *'ignorabimus'*, says R. Virchow.

This distinction between the human knowledge[3] accessible to our Personality and higher knowledge[3] coming from the divine plane stands out in a very striking manner when we compare the following texts of St John the Apostle. The affirmation: *'No man hath seen God at any time'*[4] seems to be in flagrant contradiction to the words of Jesus, quoted elsewhere by the same evangelist: *'If a man love Me, he will keep My word: and My Father will love him. And We will establish a dwelling in him.'*[5] And in Revelations: *'Behold I stand at the door and knock, if any man hear My voice and open the door, I will come unto him and will sup with him and he with Me.'*[6]

We can find many similar quotations from Holy Scripture to give weight to these texts, but we need only go back to the definition given by St Paul the Apostle of these two kinds of knowledge, which apparently have no common measure: *'Now the animal man receiveth not the things of the Spirit of*

---

1. Colossians ii: 8–10. From the Slavonic text.
2. *Ibid.* 18.
3. Fr. 'savoir'. 'Know' and 'knowledge' throughout this chapter translate 'savoir' and its derivatives unless annotated otherwise.
4. John i: 18.
5. *Ibid.* xiv: 23. Cf. I Corinthians, iii: 16 — 'Know you not that you are the temple of God, and that the spirit of God is dwelling inside you?'
6. Revelations iii: 20.

God: for they are foolishness unto him; and he cannot know them, because they are but spiritually judged. But he that is spiritual, on the contrary, judgeth all things, and he himself is judged by no man.[7]

The agreement between these texts permits us to affirm that the Apostles made a fundamental distinction between two different kinds of knowledge: the first relative, limited, knowing nothing about the second, and that second absolute, unlimited, encompassing the first. St Paul the Apostle attributed the first to the man he called *animal*, the other to the man he called *spiritual*.

What is meant by these two species of human beings? Is there no way by which the *animal* man can become a *spiritual* man?

We can also say that these texts confront us directly with the problem of the essential difference in quality between human wisdom and divine wisdom. What is left is to know if it is possible to be initiated into this divine wisdom, and how — or at least how to begin to approach it.

(2)

We have seen that the real 'I' rarely manifests in man, and in general does not do so unless the Personality asks him to. His attitude is similar to that of a Judge who remains in his court without seeking to pronounce sentence; whose passive attitude is opposed to the Personality's active attitude. We have also seen that if we introduce the bond of *esoteric knowledge* between the Personality and the real 'I', their reciprocal positions can very gradually become reversed. The real 'I' then becomes active and the Personality, as well as the 'I' of the body, submit themselves entirely to the real 'I', who becomes the undoubted and absolute master.

This reversal of the situation is characterized particularly by an inversion of man's attitude towards his own desires. Previously he *willed for that which he yearned for*; from now on, he *will yearn for what he first wanted*.

The more he progresses in esoteric knowledge, the more the seeker objectively constates within himself the undeniable realization of that change. The more he advances on this way, the deeper and more extensive the change becomes. Conversely, whenever the seeker constates such a phenomenon within himself, he will know he is progressing and be able to measure his progress.

(3)

Let us now examine through which organs the real 'I' manifests in man, and how one can widen and intensify its manifestation.

---

7. I Corinthians ii: 14–15.

Beyond the three mental[8] centres of the Personality — which from now on will be called *lower centres*—we have within us two other higher centres, independent of the physical body and of the Personality. In ensemble, these two higher centres truly represent our Soul, of which our current language speaks in the third person. Their presence in our innermost heart, and the rarity of the impartial and objective messages that we are able to receive through the medium of these centres, give us our impression of the real *'I'* as a Judge residing in his courthouse. But we shall see in an instant that this aspect of the real *'I'* is not unique. Far from it; the doctrine of the higher centres will not only resolve the apparent contradictions in the texts quoted above, but it will also help us penetrate the meaning of a number of other obscure points in the Holy Scriptures, in the Tradition, and in life. What is even more important; it will allow us to understand ourselves better.

While the lower centres in the *exterior* man are not fully[9] developed, the higher centres are perfect and work at full capacity. But as we are, we cannot receive more than a negligibly small part of their communications. The reason for this is that man views himself as nothing but Personality. This illusion has as its immediate effects, pride, egocentricity and egotism. These form a kind of screen, only allowing the most rudimentary messages from the higher centres to pass, although their communication continues non-stop. They *knock at the door*; but it is for us to *hear the voice* and *open*.

(4)

If we leave the picturesque language of St John, we can say that the deficiency of our lower centres is the reason why we do not receive the communications of higher centres. We have already seen that the motor centre is the only one of the three lower centres which functions almost normally. This is important: because this centre plays a part in all our mental activity, we must use it to achieve our esoteric ends. Its incomplete development hinders it from fulfilling this role, so we must educate it. In the same way the intellectual centre must be constantly awakened by all sorts of shocks and impulses. Being the slowest of the three, it has a natural tendency to drowsiness and inaction. Goethe used to say; *'Man is weak, he falls asleep all the time...'* The higher stages in the education of the intellectual centre, as with the motor centre, are achieved by appropriate esoteric exercises which are a necessary complement to theoretical study.

Among the lower centres, the emotional centre is worst off. In our civilization — as we have already observed — it generally receives neither

8. Fr. 'psychique'.
9. Fr. 'intégralement'.

rational education nor systematic training. Its formation and development are now left to chance, since religious education today has been largely intellectualized and rationalized. All sorts of *considerations* dictated by worldly wisdom and mundane vanity; the habitual practice of lying — especially to ourselves — and hypocrisy, from which no one is totally exempt, imprint dangerous distortions on the emotional centre. Frequently struck by a feeling of inferiority and by the need for compensation, its usual motivation; accustomed as it is to judge and to criticize everybody and everything; surrendering itself to a strangely voluptuous enjoyment of negative emotions; this centre becomes unrecognizable. It degenerates to the point where it becomes the *instrument of destruction* of our *being*, which it accelerates on its way towards ageing and death.

The two higher centres work much faster than the lower centres. Of the latter — as we have already said — the slowest is the intellectual centre; the motor centre is slightly faster, but the fastest of all should have been the emotional centre if it were not in that deranged state of which we have just spoken. It generally works in slow motion, at the same pace as the motor centre.

(5)

The schematic arrangement of man, when completed by including the higher centres, appears as follows:

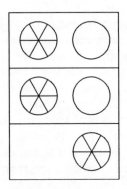

Fig. 15

The higher emotional centre is to be found at the level of the heart, and the higher intellectual centre at the level of the head. Their functions are different. In the Tradition they are sometimes called the eyes of the Soul. Thus, St Isaac The Syrian said: '*While the two eyes of the body see things in an identical way, the eyes of the Soul see differently: one contemplates the truth in images*

46

and symbols, the other face to face.'[10] In other words, messages received through the higher emotional centre can be translated into pictures or language, but they always take the form of images or symbols. This is the case, for example, with the Book of Revelations. In its ensemble this text is unintelligible if one studies it only by means of the lower centres. To grasp its true sense, it must be read with the help of the higher emotional centre. It is thus that it was revealed to St John on the island of Patmos, and it is only thus that we can understand this most important communication. It is true that the 'I' of the Personality can read it, but he will only understand a very small part of it; the grandiose meaning of these magnificent visions will remain hidden from him. As for communications received through the higher intellectual centre, they are of such a transcendent nature that there is no way in which they can be translated into human language.

We do not register the messages of the higher centres, which are ceaselessly working in us at full capacity. This is not only because our lower centres are under-developed, but also because they are not equilibrated. We must therefore apply ourselves to stimulate the growth of the Personality within us, and to equilibrate and regulate the work of our three centres. By the intensive practice of self-observation,[11] we must try hard to distinguish the work of each centre within us, then the work of their two parts, and lastly of their sectors. So we enter within ourselves.

If by appropriate exercises we can succeed in completely developing and perfectly equilibrating our lower centres, we shall be able to establish a permanent tie with our higher centres. Such a tie will be established gradually, starting from the lower emotional centre. The further the latter is purified and developed, the better it will acquire its normal rhythm. This is what will allow contact with the higher emotional centre. Later on, through the latter, it will make contact with the higher intellectual centre.

As no direct link exists between the lower intellectual centre and the higher intellectual centre, the intellectual culture which is the almost exclusive basis of our education cannot lead us to higher levels of consciousness. In spite of the refinement of his intelligence, no matter how extensive or deep the knowledge[12] he acquires, *exterior* man remains enclosed within the circle of reason. Escape is possible only via the heart; that is why the cultivation of our emotional life dominates the attention, the pre-occupations and the obligatory efforts demanded by esoteric teachings. However, if a purely intellectual culture, rational and positive, cannot lead us directly towards the higher planes of Life, one must not think that it is useless. From the esoteric point of view, it retains its full value, and will

---

10. *Philokalia*: St Isaac the Syrian, 82nd/72nd sermons.
11. Fr. 'l'introspection'.
12. 'connaissance'.

be of great help when *Individuality* is formed within us. But we have to begin at the beginning, that is to say, with the training of our hearts and the refinement of our emotional lives. On this point Theophan the Recluse, an authority on this matter, has been quite categorical. He said: '*There, neither dignity nor erudition would be any help.*'

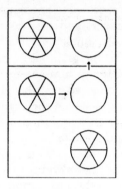

Fig. 16

Access to the higher emotional centre is access to the level of consciousness of the real, individual 'I'. Access to the higher intellectual centre raises us to the level of Consciousness — that is, to participation in the universal 'I', through the *interior communion* it permits. This is the end of all possible evolution for man under terrestrial conditions. But what a tremendous prospect. The Apostle St Paul says this about it: '*And we know that to them that love God all things work together for good, to them that are called according to His purpose. For whom He foreknew He foreordained to be similar to the image of His son, that He might be the firstborn among a multitude of brethren.*'[13]

To sum up: our higher centres are two divine sparks: one issues from the other: the higher emotional centre — spark of the Son — and the higher intellectual centre — spark of the Father in his consubstantial aspect of the Holy Spirit. We should now better understand the profound meaning of the texts quoted at the beginning of this chapter, as well as the essential difference, described by St Paul, that exists between human philosophy and human tradition on the one hand, and the esoteric Tradition on the other.

If we now seek to encapsulate in one idea the path we have to walk from birth to the summit of esotericism, we can conceive it as the evolution of the 'I', always taking new forms without annihilating the old.

13. Romans viii: 28–29.

There are four levels of the 'I' which correspond to the four levels of *being* and of *consciousness*:

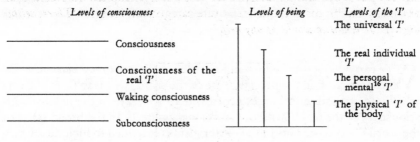

Fig. 17

Gabriel Derjavine defines this evolution in his famous formula: '*I am worm, I am slave, I am king, I am God.*'

(6)

W hat has been said above should lead us to ask ourselves what is the meaning and mission in evolution of the Personality; this fine and complex organism which nevertheless is a '*Non-I*'; with which we identify ourselves and from which we should be able to detach ourselves at the price of particularly painful efforts.

We must remember that it is since the fall of Adam that the spiritual man, having become an animal man, has lost contact with his higher centres, that is to say, with the *Tree of Life*, by giving pre-eminence to his lower centres, that is, to the *Tree of Knowledge*[14] *of Good and Evil*. Nevertheless, by means of the Personality and of its three centres, we possess within us — in either embryonic or developed state — all the elements of which the Universe is composed, which the Orthodox Tradition calls the 'World'. These elements are represented by corresponding parts of our Personality.

As he gradually acquires mastery and control of his Personality, man, with the aid of this complex instrument, succeeds in Knowing[15] the Universe in all its parts — and in establishing conscious and organic links with it. This occurs according to the principle of Plato which says that: '*Like can neither be grasped nor understood except by like.*'

This is the objective meaning and place of the Personality in the evolution of the 'I': by a kind of *conscious identification* which is the fruit of appropriate exercises of concentration, he who seeks will succeed in Knowing[15] the exterior '*Non-I*' by means of the interior '*Non-I*', that is

14. Fr. 'connaissance'.
15. Fr. 'connaître'.
16. Fr. 'psychique'.

to say, by means of his Personality. This procedure, to which we shall return later, will give him access to powers. '*Try to penetrate inside the inner cage and you will see the outer cage, (the Universe), for both are one.*'[17]

(7)

We can now better understand and define the notion of *esotericism*. By esotericism, in the precise sense of the word, we mean facts and acts which are accessible to higher centres, that is to say, to the field of consciousness of the real 'I', and of Consciousness itself. In the broad sense of the word the accepted notion of esotericism is extended to include the two steps that give access to this field: it first embraces *exotericism*, characterized by discarding belief in the Personality as of permanent value, and then *mesotericism*, which is the first stage of approach to the real 'I'. In the following figure these three degrees of esotericism are drawn as three concentric circles outside which the '*wilderness*'[18] is found: that zone where *exterior* man lives in subordination to his Personality.

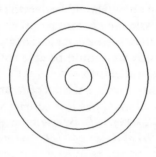

Fig. 18

Seen in perspective, the previous figure would appear like this:

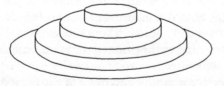

Fig. 19

Let us now examine from the practical point of view how man can reach esotericism; by what means he can work towards the aim of establishing

---

17. *Philokalia*: St Isaac the Syrian, 2nd/30th sermons.
18. Fr. 'brousse'.

permanent connections which will make it possible for him to evolve. The problem is treated in the Tradition by the help of the diagram below. In esoteric teaching this figure could be said to be *the most important*. It incorporates a multitude of ideas; far more than the comments we are about to give. That is why we must return to it often and meditate upon it.

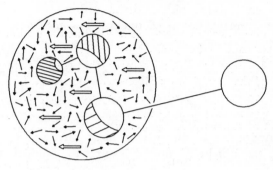

Fig. 20

The black arrows represent influences created within life by life itself. This is the first variety of influence by which man is surrounded. These are called 'A' influences. We will notice that they are distributed almost equally over all the surface of the circle of life. As in the case of all radiant energy in nature, their effect is inversely proportional to the square of the distance; thus man is subject most of all to arrows influencing him from those immediately around him. He is pulled every instant by the way they act at that moment.

The influence of the 'A' arrows on *exterior* man is imperative; driven, he wanders in the circle of his life from birth to death, following a broken line which is sometimes subject to dangerous changes of direction.

The ensemble of 'A' influences forms the *Law of Chance* or *Law of Accident*. Man is subject to its rule, yet if we examine the figure more closely we will perceive that each black arrow is counterbalanced, neutralized in some other part by another arrow equal in force and dia-metrically opposed, so that if we had left them to effectively neutralize each other the resultant force would have been equal to zero. This means that in their ensemble the 'A' influences are illusory in their nature, although the effect of each one of them is real, so that *exterior* man takes them for reality.

The white circle represents the *esoteric Centre*, located outside the general laws of life.

The white arrows represent influences called 'B'. These influences are thrown into the turmoil of life and originate from the esoteric Centre. Created outside life, these arrows are all oriented in the same direction. In their ensemble they form a sort of magnetic field.

Since 'A' influences neutralize each other, 'B' influences actually constitute the only reality.

The small circle with the shaded lines represents man, who in this figure is taken in isolation. The oblique shaded lines signify that the nature of *exterior* man is not homogeneous: it is mixed.

If man spends his life without distinguishing between 'A' and 'B' influences, he will end it as he started, one could say mechanically, driven by the *Law of Accident*. However, according to the nature and the intensity of the resultant forces to which he is subjected, it can happen to him to make a brilliant career, in the meaning the world gives to this expression.

Yet he will come to the end of his days without having either learned or understood anything of *Reality*. And *earth returns to Earth*.

In life, every being is subjected to a sort of competitive test. If he discerns the existence of the 'B' influences; if he acquires a taste for gathering and absorbing them; if he continually aspires to assimilate them better; his mixed inner nature will slowly undergo a certain kind of evolution. And if the efforts which he makes to absorb the 'B' influences are constant and sufficient in force, a *magnetic centre* can be formed within him. This *magnetic centre* is represented in the diagram by the small white space.

If this centre once born in him is carefully developed, it takes form, and in its turn will exercise an influence over the results of the 'A' arrows which are always active, deflecting them. Such a deflection may be violent. In general it transgresses the laws of *exterior* life and provokes many conflicts in and around man. If he loses the battle, he emerges with the conviction that the 'B' influences are nothing but illusion: that the only reality is represented by the 'A' influences. Slowly the *magnetic centre* which had been formed within him is reabsorbed and vanishes. Then, from the esoteric point of view, his situation is worse than the one he had started with, when he was just beginning to discern the 'B' influences.[19]

But if he emerges a winner in this first struggle, his *magnetic centre*, consolidated and reinforced, will draw him to a man having a 'C' influence stronger than his own, and possessing a stronger *magnetic centre*. And so on in succession, the last man being in connection with another having an influence 'D', who will be his link with the Esoteric Centre 'E'.

Henceforth in life, that man will no longer be isolated. He will certainly continue to live as before under the action of the 'A' influences, which for a long time will continue to exercise their power over him; yet little by little, thanks to the effect of the influence of the chain 'B'–'C'–'D'–'E', his *magnetic centre* will develop. To the measure of its growth, the man will escape the dominion of the *Law of Chance* and enter the domain of *Consciousness*.

---

19. This is the example pointed out in the parable of the unclean spirit and the empty house. Matthew xii: 43–45. Cf. Hebrews vi: 4–8; II Peter iii: 17.

If he reaches this result before his death, he can say that his life was not lived in vain.

(8)

Let us now examine a different version of the same diagram:

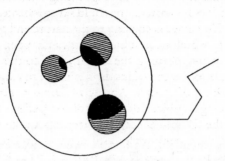

Fig. 21

This second figure, with black *magnetic centres*, represents the situation where man deludes himself and, believing he is absorbing 'B' influences and making the necessary selection all the while, he in fact absorbs 'A' influences, those of the black arrows that are in some way parallel to the white arrows of the 'B' influences. This will put him into contact with people who possess *magnetic centres* of the same nature: who are themselves duped or who dupe others, and who have no direct or indirect link with the esoteric Centre.

(9)

A last remark. What guarantee can man have that he will not dupe himself and that he will not fall into the latter situation? The answer is simple. The purity of the *magnetic centre* must be scrupulously maintained from the start and all through his evolution.

(10)

Let us repeat once more that the comments given about this diagram are not exhaustive. Other comments are still possible, and those who persevere in studying the doctrine are urgently invited to meditate on this image so as to go still deeper.

If they do, they will become aware that this figure includes a whole series of laws of human life, which are treated in the Gospel in the form of parables, images and allusions.

CHAPTER VII

(1)

We shall now examine the changes produced, in that mental[1] organism we have called the Personality, as a result of the appearance and growth of a *magnetic centre* within us. In a general way, one can say that the radiance of this centre will assist in efficiently perfecting the development of the lower centres. Under its banner,[2] relations between the three centres will be radically modified, and this will strongly influence a man's life. In turn, this will lead to certain repercussions in his relations with those around him.[3]

We have seen that the system of sectors is such that the three centres are permanently interdependent. As a result, every movement of one or other of them automatically leads to a response in[4] the other two. Because of this, as long as the mental[1] life of the individual is composed solely of various combinations and movements of the lower centres, man can neither have a pure thought, nor a pure feeling, nor can he take any final[5] decision. Because of the way these mechanical ties operate, everything is mixed up within him. Certainly the *response* of the other centres does not have the same strength of movement as the centre where an action originates. Nevertheless, in ordinary circumstances man cannot ignore[6] them. This phenomenon, accompanied by a varied amount of under-development and derangement in the centres and their sectors, is the cause of the doubts and inner conflicts in which man struggles so often. In addition, these bundles of mechanical ties have a specific significance, playing a positive role in the mental[1] life of the individual. Taken in ensemble, they constitute the organ—or better still the instrument—of *morality*. Given that, in *exterior* life, the voice of the real 'I' is weak and rarely heard, man, almost constantly identified with the 'I' of the Personality, can and often does act without taking the words of this secret[7] voice into account, even if he repents later. In practice, under these conditions, the mechanical ties between the three centres are the only brake on his ungovernable greed.

This moral instrument is moulded to fit the traditions of milieu and family. It is shaped from birth onwards by education. Clearly, without

---

1. Fr. 'psychique'.
2. Fr. 'égide'.
3. Fr. 'entourage'.
4. Fr. 'replique des'.
5. Fr. 'nette'.
6. Fr. 's'en débarrasser'.
7. Fr. 'intime'.

this instrument, the organization of social life in all its forms is unthinkable. Yet because of its nature, it cannot guarantee good and equitable human conduct; to ensure its own existence in times of peace, human society has always been obliged to have recourse to constraint and the application of penalties: necessary remedies, since morality will never be strong enough to curb the extreme and anarchistic tendencies of the Personality. The latter, in effect, lacks that kind of consciousness that the practical studies of religion describe as the *fear of God*.[8]

(2)

In view of the above, we can easily understand that morality is not identical to Consciousness.[9] The former is a kind of substitute, not based — like authentic Consciousness[9] — on spontaneous, simple and direct judgement, but on an ensemble of *considerations*. Among these, race, civilization, the times, class, the environment, and single or multiple personal motives, all play their role. Thus the notion of what is moral changes as a result of variations in the elements that form it. So we can distinguish the morality of a cultivated man from that of a savage, the morality of Roman society from that of the Middle Ages, and the latter from that of our present times. We must not believe, however, that morality *progresses*, becoming ever better with the passing of time. From the esoteric point of view, the notion of progress as we habitually understand it has no absolute value. The fruit of the efforts of Personalities who are themselves shifting sands, progress does not in itself give any guarantee of permanence. Our experience of recent wars and revolutions has given us irrefutable proof of the extreme fragility of everything which until the XIXth century — at least among civilized peoples — was seriously considered to be the unshakeable foundation of human morality.

The mechanical ties between the centres can be represented very schematically, as shown on the following page (Fig. 22).

In *exterior* man, these ties are normally sufficiently solid to function throughout a lifetime. Nevertheless, under the conditions of our feverish and somewhat unbalanced modern life, these ties, particularly the one between the intellectual centre and the emotional centre, are somewhat slack. Sometimes we even observe them to be severed. For the individual, this rupture results[10] in the loss of all notion and sense of morality.

---

8. Job xxviii: 28; Psalms cx: 10; Proverbs i: 7, ix: 10; Eccles. xii: 13. We must warn the reader here that throughout the present text, the numbering of the Psalms follows the Slavonic text of the *Bible or Books of the Holy Scriptures of the Old and New Testaments*, 1762 edition (see bibliography).

9. Fr. 'conscience'.

10. Fr. 'entraîne'.

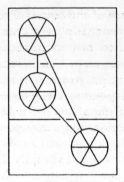

Fig. 22

Alteration of these ties, relaxation or even disappearance, produces a whole series of psychological phenomena. The process is essentially characterized by a hypocrisy which becomes more and more pronounced; it culminates in the complete rupture of these ties, making the man an amoral person.

(3)

We have said that the emergence of the *magnetic centre* can provoke a profound change in the mental organism. Having reached a certain degree of growth, this centre establishes direct ties — no longer mechanical but conscious — with each of the three centres, as shown by the diagram below:

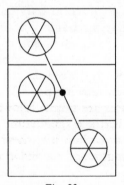

Fig. 23

When these new ties are sufficiently consolidated they replace the old ties, which fall away. From now on, man regains the capacity to have pure thoughts and pure feelings, no longer adulterated[11] as a result of the

---

11. Fr. 'mélange'.

mechanical interdependence of the centres. From this point, each cent
will be able to work independently[12] but under the strict control of the
magnetic centre, which ensures their coordination.

Thus, acting on our *moral nature*,[13] the emergence and growth of the
magnetic centre will result in progressive replacement of the elements of
this moral nature by corresponding elements of Consciousness. We then
stop being the victims of impulsive movements, and our reactions to
impressions and shocks become more and more reflective and conscious.
However, one must not think that such a radical transformation of both
inner and outer life can come about abruptly. Excluding very rare exceptions, which concern the *just*[14] by nature — this evolution seems a long
process, an uninterrupted combat with a series of successes and falls. More
than once, he who searches will fall into crises of discouragement; more
than once it will seem to him that he is being driven beyond the limits of his
own life; he will sometimes feel crushed under the burden of the tests[15] and
difficulties against which he will be pitted during his search. This can be
understood when we know that esoteric science in its teaching goes far
beyond simple information. Its purpose, in fact, is nothing less than the
transformation of the very being of those who study it, a concern completely
outside the scope of positive science. Because it generally deals with those
of the *unjust* who nevertheless aspire to the light, it calls on them — in the
words of St Paul, to: '*Put off the old man, and put on the new man, that is being
renewed unto knowledge after the image of Him that created him.*'[16] In every case
where esoteric science offers *all*, it demands *all* in return. One must pay all.
It is impossible to reach the *True* by the path of lies or hypocritical games,
because in this case we seek to *be*, rather than to *appear to be*.[17] It is at this
level of ideas that one must search for the underlying meaning of the fearful
story of Ananias and Saphira that St Luke told in the Acts of the Apostles.[18]

(4)

This is how things appear, seen from below: from the point of view of
the Personality, which acts on the maxim: '*This is mine and so is that*'. A
sage once said that God smiles when He hears man reasoning in such a
way. Seen from above, things can be viewed in a totally different light. The

---

12. Fr. 'isolément'.
13. Fr. 'nature morale'.
14. Fr. 'juste', righteous or 'just'.
15. Fr. 'épreuves'.
16. Colossians iii: 9–10; Ephesians iv: 22–24.
17. Fr. 'paraître'.
18. Acts v: 1–11.

Personality of the *exterior* man is mortal. Consequently, all the values to which it normally aspires are temporary: are indeed *lent* to him. Being perishable, they are therefore illusory.

Esoteric science indicates the path towards the *permanent*. To reach the latter, man is asked to detach his heart from the perishable, which drags him towards the abyss. According to the words of Jesus, it sells him *pure gold* — which he cannot recognize — against his false money which he thinks authentic. Man, afraid of being duped, hesitates and so suffers. In this we find the origin of the great misunderstanding (that recurs) when human life is taken in a personal way. The whole of the Gospel is here. It is addressed to those who aspire to Life.

'*If any one wants to ignore it let him ignore it*' says St Paul.[19] He will be excluded from the *narrow way*, to fall back into the *broad way* which — as we know — will lead him toward Death.

Now, and only now, can we better understand the sense, as well as the absolute necessity of the indispensable requirement common to all religions and to all esoteric traditions: *humility*.

Let us first define the notion of *pride*,[20] its opposite. In the esoteric sense *pride is the affirmation by the Personality of his primacy in relation to the real 'I'*. In *exterior* man, such an attitude is natural. If he succeeds in life, that will confirm him in this attitude. But the esoteric law is explicit. God says: '*I stand at the door and knock.*'[21] Meaning that every man is always kept under permanent pressure coming from the esoteric Centre in the form of 'B' influences.[22] However, man must *open the door* by his own efforts; in other words, he must discern and assimilate these influences, then the Personality, surmounting its proud nature, must bow[23] to and accept the primacy of the real 'I'. It must do this in advance by an act of faith and of hope, *not knowing exactly where it will lead*.[24] We are therefore invited to 'put our trust in God'.[25] This is the role of humility as the *sine qua non* condition for any practical[26] esoteric work. From this we will be able to grasp the meaning of the old maxim that: '*God resists the proud, but is gracious to the humble*'.[27] Never must we understand this in a metaphoric sense. The Personality which habitually commands in man, together with the 'I' of the body, must bow in front of the real 'I' and give him homage.

---

19. I Corinthians xiv: 38.
20. Fr. 'orgeuil'.
21. Revelations iii: 20.
22. Cf. Fig. 20, Chapter VI.
23. Fr. 'se plier'.
24. Hebrews xi: 8.
25. Fr. 'faire crédit'.
26. Fr. 'constructif'.
27. James iv: 6; Proverbs xxix: 23; I Peter v: 5.

To reach that, the great obstacle to be overcome is described thus: Illusion, thinking it is reality, takes Reality for illusion.

The power of Illusion acts in man particularly by means of his sexual centre, or more exactly, at its expense. Ignoring the ties between the

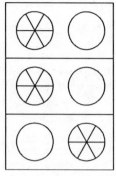

Fig. 24

centres, man's complete structure appears as follows:

The sexual centre is analogous to the higher centres: it is indivisible, does not have a negative part, and is not divided into sectors. But the lower intellectual centre or the lower emotional centre — or both together — can usurp part of its energy. This produces negative phenomena, among which we list confusions between the unreal and the Real, as well as all the many manifestations of intransigence.

If we resist such tests,[28] the 'I' of the Personality will be more and more frequently displaced to reside in the *magnetic centre*. Conversely, the more that 'I' remains in this (magnetic) centre and identifies itself with it, the more the growth of this centre will progress.

When the *magnetic centre* finally takes shape, it establishes an undisputed authority over the three centres of the Personality. He who was man 1, 2 or 3 becomes man 4. Throughout this stage of his evolution such a man will have the task of recognizing the mode in which each of these three mental[29] centres is functioning, assigning its proper role to each of them, and equilibrating them. This is how the *magnetic centre*'s growth is perfected and how its development commences. The latter is a function of conscious efforts to develop the lower centres up to their limits. The further this development is continued, the more the *magnetic centre* absorbs the lower emotional centre, at the same time identifying itself more and more with the higher emotional centre. Once the three lower centres are fully developed

28. Fr. 'à l'épreuve'.
29. Fr. 'psychiques'.

and equilibrated, the *magnetic centre* once and for all[30] identifies itself with the higher emotional centre, dragging with it the lower emotional centre which it finally absorbs. From now on the lower emotional centre, with the *magnetic centre*, will form an integral part of the higher emotional centre.

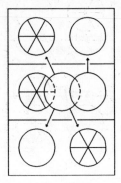

Fig. 25

This union[31] realized, he who has carried out this work on himself will become man 5.

In contrast to men 1, 2 or 3 who are called *exterior* men, men 5, 6 and 7 are *interior* men.[32]

By establishing a link between the higher emotional centre and the higher intellectual centre, man 5 will become man 6, after which all that will be left for him to do is to consolidate the results. This consolidation is the last stage of esoteric evolution.

The tasks for each stage of evolution can be defined as follows:

— Man 4 — to recognize the existence of the three lower centres, make them grow and develop to the limit, and regulate their functioning;

— Man 5 — to acquire new faculties and powers;[33]

— Man 6 — to develop the faculties thus acquired to their utmost limits;

— Man 7 — to consolidate the results obtained.

This consolidation is obtained by the sublimation of sex.

---

30. Fr. 'définitivement'.
31. Fr. 'jonction'.
32. Romans vii: 22.
33. These are the gifts of the Holy Spirit, I Corinthians xii; xiv, *passim*.

When we consider the completed figure of man (Fig. 24), we must keep in the back of our mind that the same figure from a slightly different angle will appear as follows:

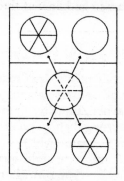

Fig. 26

This is the schema of a man who has become complete and immortal in accordance with the meaning of the words of St Paul: '*We shall not all die but we shall all be changed.*'[34] The higher emotional centre, now placed in the centre of the figure, has absorbed the lower emotional centre. The significance of the dotted lines in this—as well as the link with the sexual centre —will be explained later.

(5)

Men 1, 2 or 3, driven by the energy of the sexual centre freely flowing through the three centres, make do with the provisional '*I*' of the Personality, an unstable '*I*'; changing; illogical with himself; leading[35] a factitious existence. The situation is completely reversed when — crossing the stage of man 4 successfully — the dedicated searcher becomes an *interior* man: 5, then 6 and finally 7:

— Having become man 5, he becomes permanently[36] conscious of his *real 'I'*;
— Having become man 6, he attains permanent *Consciousness*;
— Having become man 7, he is liberated by obtaining a true *Will.*

'*I*'—*Consciousness*—*Will* constitute the triple objective of esoteric science, and these are the reward for efforts made consciously by the searcher.

---

34. I Corinthians xv: 51.
35. Fr. 'implique'.
36. Fr. 'il accède d'une manière permanante'.

Here ends the esoteric evolution possible to man in the conditions of terrestrial humanity.

It is by this evolution that animal man can overcome Adam's Fall, can become a spiritual man, and so be initiated into divine wisdom.

(6)

An important note: In spite of the strict requirement for humility we must not fall into the other extreme and go so far as to neglect our mental 'I', despise or ill-treat him. Equally, we must not neglect, despise or ill-treat our bodies by submitting them to excessive mortifications. All we have to do is to give them the value which is properly theirs, and stop attributing to them supreme authority or the qualities of the real 'I'. At the same time we must fight by every means against the spirit of self-complacency, knowing that the 'I' of the Personality is only a *provisional* 'I'; itself perishable. If we obstinately identify ourselves with this, we reaffirm that we are still subject to the *Law of Accident* and that we are in fact steadily walking on the path toward Death.

Without going to such an extreme, we must treat our Personality — the provisional 'I' — and our body in which it lives, as a good horseman treats his horse. It is in looking after this 'I' — while training him — that we will be able to travel the long path which leads to our goal. And before each effort is made we must measure our forces. The horse does not know where the horseman is going, he alone is responsible for both.

SECOND PART
THE UNIVERSE

CHAPTER VIII

(1)

Parallel to the study of man, we have seen that esoteric science studies the Universe. In this way it guards against separating man from his organic context. It envisages man within the ensemble of life on Earth; an element of the planetary world gravitating around the Sun, one of the stars of the Milky Way, our world, born inside the manifested Absolute, Who assures its existence and its subsistence.

The fact that man by his actions is more and more inclined to isolate himself from the Earth — walking on soles of shoes, travelling in cars, trains or planes — ends by creating in his subconsciousness the idea that he is separate from Nature. Yet in spite of all the machines created or to be created he will never cease being an integral part of Mother Earth, because everything in the Universe is living, and forms part of an ensemble. This is the underlying reason why it is necessary to study the Universe while studying man.

The Orthodox Tradition considers the Universe to be a living being. Origen, in *The Principles*, compares it to an immense organism, the Soul of which is God. This conception has been conserved almost intact in the esoteric Tradition; we find it expressed in an abridged way in the liturgical prayer and responses called the *Great Ektenia*.[1]

Of old this conception was shown in a diagram; starting from God as the Soul of our Soul, and gradually reaching to God Who contains within Him everything that exists. This diagram is made up of twelve concentric circles: starting from the centre, these represent the elements given in figure 27.

This double conception of the unique God — as the Soul of our Souls, and as God embracing the Universe created by Him — is characteristic of esoteric Orthodoxy. We also find it in the Gospels and the Apostles, but it generally passes unnoticed. We have already mentioned it, while quoting St Isaac the Syrian about the identity of the internal and external cages.[2]

In connection with the preceding we could quote the speech made by St Paul in Athens. St Luke reports it in the following words:

...All the Athenians, as well as the strangers living with them, did not find pleasure in spending their time, except in saying or listening to something new. Paul, standing in the middle of the Areopagus said:

---

1. Ektenia – Russian for litany.
2. *Philokalia*: St Isaac the Syrian, 2nd/30th sermons.

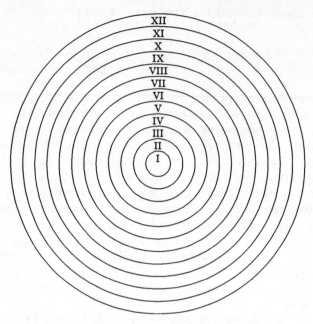

Fig. 27

I. God, Soul of our Soul	VIII. Our planet
II. Soul	IX. Our solar system
III. Man	X. Milky Way, our Galaxy,
IV. Room	our World
V. House	XI. All the Worlds, like and
VI. City	unlike
VII. Country	XII. God who encompasses all

'Athenians, in all things I perceive that ye are particularly pious. For as I passed along, and observed the objects of your worship, I found also an altar with this inscription, *To the unknown god.*

'What therefore ye venerate without knowing; I have come to announce to you.

'The God that created the Universe and all things therein, he being Lord of heaven and earth, does not dwell in temples made with men's hands; nor does He require to be served by men's hands, as though He needed anything, seeing He Himself gives to all life, and breath, and all things.

'He has made all men *issued from the same blood,* to dwell on the whole surface of the earth, having pre-determined the duration of times, and the boundaries of their habitations.

'That they should seek God, though He is not far from each one of us. Would they not have felt Him? Would they not have found Him? For by Him we live, by Him we move, by Him we exist.'[3]

---

3. Acts xvii: 21–28. Translated from the Slavonic text. The italics are the author's.

(2)

The astronomical world which we observe from our planet appears as it does because we see the body of the Universe from the inside. We do not view it in its ensemble because our observations are made and interpreted on our own scale,[4] infinitesimal in relation to the ensemble. What misleads us is the distances between the stars, which are foci of living matter, and particles of the universal organism. Seen in an internal perspective they appear immense, yet the density of the Universe in its ensemble is analogous to that of our bodies. Man in the Universe resembles a micro-organism in the human body. If we could become microbes, we would see our bodies from within — similar to the starred skies full of galaxies which would be our organs. On the other hand, if we could become immense and see the Universe on its own scale,[4] we would see it as a living body. This is the effect of the *Principle of Relativity*.

(3)

What then is the meaning of human life in this Cosmos as we know it? Man's existence has two main purposes:

— as an element of the universal organism, it serves the aims of the latter;

— as an isolated individual, he can pursue his own aims.

To better understand why and how these two objectives are bound together, let us take an example:

The position of man in the Universe is analogous to that of a cell in the human body. Each cell is a part of an organ which, in its turn, is an element of a group of organs that assures proper accomplishment of some definite function of the organism.

From this point of view, let us examine the lot of a cell in our bodies. It is subject to two categories of laws. To simplify, let us say that it is placed under the rule of two laws.

The first keeps the cell in its place. In esoteric science we call it the *General Law*. The second leaves a certain liberty of action for the cell, and is called the *Law of Exception*.

The first law, which is conservative, ensures that the organ of which this cell is a part accomplishes its function with no impediment. To this end, the first condition is that during their lives the cells which compose the organ fulfil the role given them. This law obliges these cells to remain in their own places, to complete their work, and to dedicate their lives to it.

---

4. Fr. 'échelle'.

It is evident that if this law did not keep the cells of the body within the limits of each organ, if it did not oblige them to fulfil their function, the latter would not be able to exist. Thus this law is beneficial; by ensuring the existence of the organs, it permits the whole body to endure.

We know, however, that the total removal of certain organs of the body is compatible with survival. In the current state of our knowledge it even seems that removal of some of them leads to no serious functional inconvenience. Even more; the organism tolerates partial resection of some organs without compromising the roles played by the latter in the general economy. This shows that the disappearance of a few cells, an infinitesimal part of an organ, goes unnoticed: its functioning is not impaired. As the essential role of the *General Law* is to watch over continuity of function, this disappearance passes unnoticed by it. Therefore it places no further obstacles. Symbolically, one can say that cells which escape from this law now enter the domain of the *Law of Exception*.

This escape of a few cells is a phenomenon which occurs constantly. All our cells from the epidermic to the nervous are constantly renewed according to different and variable rhythms. In addition to this renewal from within, there are also disappearances, compensated or not compensated for by new units.

Up to this point, the analogy with what happens to man because of the *General Law* and the *Law of Exception* could be taken as complete.

But it stops here, at least as regards the present state of our knowledge. In this activity of life, of migrations and of cellular death, there is no justification for thinking that the passage from the *General Law* to the *Law of Exception* results from any conscious actions of the cells.

For man it happens differently.

As a cell of humanity, man forms part of organic life on Earth. This life in its ensemble represents a very sensitive organ of our planet, playing an important role in the economy of the solar system. As a cell of this organ, man finds himself under the influence of the *General Law*, which keeps him in his place. In fact, this law leaves him a certain margin or tolerance. It allows him some *free movement* within the limits it sets. Within these boundaries, which are very limited objectively although subjectively they appear vast, man can give free rein to his fantasies and his ambitions. Without going too far into the definition of these limits and detailed description of the components of this *General Law*, we can say as an example that one of those factors is hunger: the servitude of working to assure our subsistence. The chain: sexual instinct; procreation; and the care of parents for their children, is another factor. The esoteric maxim that applies to this aspect of life is conceived thus: *carnal love is necessary for the general good*. Lastly, fear in its many forms constitutes the third group of factors in question. On the whole, the permitted margin for *free movement* tolerated by the *General Law* is limited by something best described in a term less scientific than colourful: bourgeois happiness. Careers in every branch of human activity; fortune; family; love; honours etc.; all are subject to the *sine qua non* condition of unconditional if only subconscious acceptance of the inevitability of *Death*.

As long as man accepts the principle of the final annihilation of his Personality without a fight, he can carry on in life without attracting the increasing pressure of the *General Law* upon himself.

The case is totally different if he struggles to surpass the limits which it imposes. He then runs against the action upon him of this Law and its derivatives. It acts simultaneously on several planes: physical, mental and moral. Its action on the moral plane is conceived by man, since time immemorial, in the form of a personification: *the Devil*.

In the orthodox Tradition demonology occupies a considerable place. We find there practical constatations, fine and profound observations on the highly sophisticated and insidious forms that the *Devil*'s action takes in very varied circumstances, in which it goes as far as using the good faith of humans for its own ends.

We will also find precious advice, based on accumulated experience over the ages, which is particularly helpful to students of esoteric science; because once the first positive results are obtained those students will unmistakably run up against the active opposition of the law and the *game of the Crafty One*.

It must be realized that in placing himself under the aegis of the *Law of Exception*, man goes against the *General Law*, which he is even called upon to overthrow, if only on the individual scale. He must not forget — under penalty of 'surprise attack' — that salvation depends on victory over the *Devil*, which as we have said, is the personalized moral aspect of the *General Law*. This is so even though this, being a cosmic law, is naturally a divine law. One must not be afraid, as the *Law of Exception* is also a divine law:[5] in choosing it, man continues to serve the interest of the whole, but differently and in an incomparably more efficient manner. During his fight against the first law, he is subject to tests that often take the form of temptations. In orthodox Doctrine deep studies are devoted to this theme. As stated above, they contain precious advice of a practical nature, details of which we cannot cover in this present work. We are however permitted to draw attention to the indirect nature of diabolical action. If, aiming straight towards his goal, which is liberation and salvation, the seeker successfully overcomes the obstacles and by this shows proof of a strength that would permit him to defy the authority of the *General Law*, the latter will begin to act upon him indirectly, generally by the mediation of his near

---

5. One must not forget that Jacob fought for a whole night against the Angel, overcame him and received the surname of *Israel* from him; this means: '*who fought against God*,' or '*strong against God*.'

ones if they do not follow the same path: this action occurs on the moral plane, and often takes emotional forms appealing to his most noble, generous and disinterested sentiments: to his charity; his obligations; his pity. It impels him down blind alleys, insinuating that he will thus be returning to his duty, that by so doing he will go on walking in the right path, etc. This will clarify the profound saying of Jesus that: '*A man's worst enemies are those of his own household*.'[6]

(4)

Let us now repeat, because it is important, that esoteric work is by its nature a revolutionary work. The seeker seeks a change of state: to overcome Death and attain Salvation. This is the goal given to this work by the Scriptures and by the Apostles. As St Paul says: '*If ye live after the flesh, ye must die*.'[7] But do not forget what else he says: '*We shall not all die, but we shall all be changed*.'[8]

The man who lives passively under the first law, insensibly and without being aware of it — even as an excellent citizen — involves himself in '*The broad way that leadeth to destruction*;' he who chooses the *Law of Exception* takes: '*The narrow road that leadeth unto Life*.'[9]

(5)

Starting from the Absolute as the initial focus of life, the Universe comprises a vast scale of elements, spreading in many branches to the outer *crust*; the *epidermis*, represented by the ensemble of the satellites of all the planets.

Before we start the study of the structure of the Universe, it would be better to summarize the conditions of Creation. Orthodox Tradition teaches that the Universe was created by a *sacrifice of God*. We shall understand this postulate better if we consider that it differentiates between the state of *manifested* Divinity and that of *unmanifested* Divinity — which is therefore limitless and free from all conditions.

God's sacrifice is *Self-limitation* by manifestation. What are the conditions of this limitation? They are three in number: the Universe is created in *Space*, in *Time* and then in *Equilibrium*.

---

6. Matthew x: 36.
7. Romans viii: 13.
8. I Corinthians xv: 51 — already quoted.
9. Matthew vii: 13.

The three fundamental conditions of Creation manifest in the Universe in the form of three basic principles of life: the static, dynamic and neutralizing principles.

Anything in creation can be analysed and studied in the light of these three principles, which appear in a way analogous to that described while talking about the conditions of creation of the World. They apply uniformly to all levels of the Cosmos.

If we take the creation of an enterprise as an example, we would be able to say that first the idea must be conceived as possible, the project studied, and plans drawn up. All this is based upon the Static principle. Then we pass on to realization, in accordance with the Dynamic Principle. Each principle acts in the manifested world according to an appropriate law, which will be studied later.

In practice, an enterprise created in this way risks collapse if the directors do not take into consideration the third principle, that of Equilibrium, and carefully apply it to their creation. The *principle of Equilibrium* must be followed from the first studies of the project, all through realization of the latter, and must be strictly adhered to during the whole course of the enterprise. In a very general way we can say that the promoters — in whatever branch of human activity — must primarily maintain equilibrium between the efforts which the enterprise requires for its creation, and the means at their disposal for that realization. If we deal with scientific studies — and this applies equally to esoteric studies — we must also maintain equilibrium, but in a different manner: in this case, the plan for the studies must correspond to the nature and structure of the object studied.

(6)

In talking about the creation of the Universe, it is necessary to mention the notion of *Eternity*. We generally have an erroneous idea of this. Habitually, we portray Eternity to ourselves as a prolongation of Time to infinity. Eternity is not Time; it is, so to speak, perpendicular to Time. It follows that it is not infinite, but limited: the Tradition places the end of Eternity and the end of the World together. We thus praise God in His pre-eternal state. In the *kontakion* of Christmas we sing:

> The Virgin this day gives birth to the Pre-existent,
> And cavern Earth brings forth the Inaccessible,
> Angels and shepherds sing praises,
> As the Magi walk with the star,
> For us is born the boy child, the pre-eternal God.[10]

10. Translation from the old Slavonic Text.

As for the end of the World, we portray it to ourselves in the form of the *Accomplishment*, which, according to the words of Jesus, is the *Announcement* of accomplished works and facts.

(7)

Two of the three fundamental principles of Creation, *Space* and *Equilibrium*, offer no danger for the created Universe. It is not the same where *Time* is concerned. Being a dynamic principle which underlies all action — including creation and every realization — it implies the certainty of final annihilation for everything created. In this connection, we may remember the myth of Chronos devouring his children.

To palliate this menace, by the action of Time, the divine Wisdom introduced a device to avoid the immediate destruction of the created world . This acts through one of two laws, the basis of which we shall study in the following chapters, in their principles; their working; and their effects. For the moment it will be enough for us to say that, thanks to this artificial law, the forward flow of Time is closed off into cycles, and this eliminates its destructive effects — of course within certain limits. So Time will not work in straight lines but 'turns' in a curve.

These cycles close and repeat themselves. Thanks to this cyclic action, the Universe itself and all the elements of which it is composed can endure. Every element follows its own cycle. The Ancients were well aware of this law; their philosophy never admitted straight lines; it was based on the cyclic principle.

(8)

Let us now try to give a general picture of the structure of the Universe. Here are the elements of what we call in esoteric science the *Ray of Creation*, more rarely called the *Cone of Creation of the World*.

We can draw its figure in the following manner. *Earth* has the *Moon* for a satellite. That is the limit; the last rung of Creation, after which there is nothing. The moon — like the satellites of the other planets — has no satellite for itself.

Directing our sight towards the centre, we find that the Earth is part of the *planetary World* which gravitates around the *Sun*, the master of our system. The *Sun* is one of the many stars of the galaxy known by the name of the *Milky Way*, a system to which the whole of the solar system belongs. We know that the Milky Way is not unique of its kind. In the sky we can detect other galaxies similar to ours, and we can equally suppose that there are other worlds that would not resemble it. These large units in their

72

ensemble constitute *All the Worlds*: the whole content of the Universe, which gravitates around what we call in the Tradition the *Central Sun*: the Absolute, that is to say, God manifested.

The figure looks as follows:

— Absolute

— All Worlds

— Our World – The Milky Way

— The Sun

— The Planetary World

— The Earth

— The Moon

Fig. 28

We shall continue to use this diagram. It is quite convenient for developing and clarifying our reasoning. We must not forget that it represents only one ray of creation, not the whole Universe. Nor must we forget that the Universe as a whole is analogous in its structure to a tree where, starting from the root — the Absolute in our figure — a whole series of branchings extends out to the foliage, of which one leaf would be analogous to the moon in our *Ray*.

If we want to construct a figure that would be closer to reality, we must locate all the levels of figure 28 one inside the other, including them all inside one large circle, which would represent the Absolute — in whose bosom lives all that exists — embracing the whole.

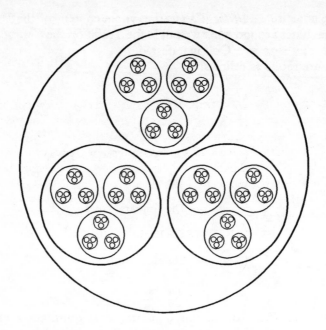

Fig. 29

Note: For technical reasons graphic representation in this figure stops at level 5.

CHAPTER IX

(1)

We have described the three basic conditions under which the Universe was created. We shall now study the two fundamental laws that rule over all that exists and lives, at all the steps[1] of the created Universe. The first of these laws conditions the existence of everything that fills the Cosmos, whether it be beings, objects, or events.

The second fundamental law rules over every action and every movement, particularly the process of life in all its forms, up to the most subtle and most intimate movements of thought and feeling.

These two fundamental laws are omnipresent and all-penetrating: nobody and nothing can escape them.

(2)

In esoteric science the first law is called the *Law of Three*. Its definition explains its name:

Definition: *All that exists, exists as a result of the converging action on the same point at the same time of three forces: passive, active and neutralizing.*

We will note that the three forces reflect the three basic conditions of creation of the Universe, of which we have already spoken. As such, they represent the manifestation, inside the created Universe, of the three conditions of creation as conceived by the non-manifest Divinity in the pre-existence of the world. The *passive force* is a derivative of the *static* condition: Space. The *active force* is a derivative of the *dynamic* condition: Time. Lastly, the *neutralizing force* ensures the maintenance of Equilibrium in all the Universe, on every plane, and at every step.[1]

Naturally, as they are forces, these three forces are active. Their names express the role that each of them plays in the co-operation which gives birth to the particular phenomenon being considered.

Seen from that angle, life in the Universe is nothing but a perpetual process of creation in every domain, on every plane, and at every step.[1] In addition, for each event, large or small, important or insignificant, an act analogous to the First Creation of the entire Universe is reproduced, with all proportions maintained; in this act, as we have said, the three forces act as a replica of the three conditions which conceived the created Universe before its manifestation.

---

1. Fr.' échelons'.

The classical example which the esoteric schools give to represent the play of the three forces is bread. To make bread we must have flour, fire and water. In this example, flour is the conductor of the passive force, fire of the active force, and water of the neutralizing force.

Here we must make it clear immediately that the substance which serves in one case as conductor for the passive force, may in other cases be the conductor for the active force, and in a third situation, a vehicle for the neutralizing force.

Let us examine these alternations in another classical example, that of the conception of a child. The woman appears here as a passive force, the husband as the active force, and carnal love as the neutralizing force: if these three conditions are present, conception becomes possible. If we pass from the carnal plane to the moral plane, we see that the situation is reversed. It is the woman who acts — or is rather called to act — being the source of inspiration as the active force, whereas man — when co-operation on this plane is fertile — figures as the passive force. In the same way that on the physical plane the woman bears the fruit of love through her pregnancy, brings it into the world, nourishes it, and educates it, on the moral plane it is the man who conceives the inspired idea or, fertilized by the woman, develops it inside him, and lastly brings it into the world in the form of some work, or more generally in the form of a creation.

The primordial character of the passive force can be illustrated by numerous examples. Let us take the case of a purchase: the offered merchandise constitutes the passive force; the need or desire of the purchaser intervenes as active force, and the price paid for the object acts as neutralizing force. In a more general manner, the offer intervenes as passive force, demand as active force, and payment as the neutralizing force.

That the passive force is a force, and as such possesses an active character, is demonstrated quite clearly, particularly on the psychological plane; active as it may be, feminine seduction represents the passive force in love novels. Where the third or neutralizing force is concerned, it often escapes our observation—either due to the bipolar character of our minds, or because of its own nature—which can in many cases leave it unobserved. It also sometimes plays the role of catalyst—far less conspicuous than the binding tie which is the most fundamental role of the neutralizing force.

According to the way the three forces act through matter, the Tradition makes the following distinctions:

When a substance serves as a conductor for the *passive force*, we call it *Oxygen (O)*; when it serves as a conductor for the *active force* we call it *Carbon (C)*; when it serves as a conductor for the *neutralizing force* we call it *Nitrogen* (Azot) *(N)*. When considered independently from the forces of which it is the conductor, the substance is called *Hydrogen (H)*.

I f the junction[2] of the forces remains sterile, this means that in the esoteric sense their co-operation was not complete.[3] The fault could arise from one of the three forces, from two of them, or even from all three. Analysis in the light of the law in question can greatly assist in determining the one or many causes of failure. For example, with the same good flour, the bread can be bad or inedible if we have added too much water—or not enough — or if the flame was weak or too high.

The last constatation allows us to grasp the sense and effect of a subsidiary law of the *Law of Three*. We see that with the same flour — the passive force in our example—we can experience failure due to a defective sharing of the active force (Fire), of the neutralizing force (Water), or of the two together. This would lead us to the conclusion that the action of the active and neutralizing forces must be regulated in accordance with the content of the passive force, which influences the reaction here as the stable element; a mathematical *constant*. The passive force contains all the *possibilities* for creating the phenomenon, while the active force intervenes as the *realizer*, and the neutralizing force as the *regulator*, of the relations between the two other forces, determining the dosage for both in an optimal way. This explains and justifies the fact that pre-eminence in the phenomenal world is attributed to the *passive force*.

Let us note here that this pre-eminence is a direct result of conditions at the first Creation. To pass or cross from the non-manifested state — a *monopolar* one, concentrated on the unique consciousness of *Self* within which the Divinity remains before the Creation of the World—the *first Idea* which makes[4] the Divinity come out of the state of non-manifestation to become manifest, is necessarily that of the *You*. This idea, conceived by the divine sacrifice of Self-limitation, has Love, a neutralizing force, for third force. In language accessible to humans, St John expressed it by saying: *'For God so loved the world that He gave His only Son, that whosoever believeth in Him should not perish but have eternal life.'*[5] We can see that, in itself, the attitude of the manifested Absolute is regulated in accordance with the passive force — the World: the universal *You* envisaged as an *object* of His solicitude.

Thus, from the beginning of Creation, the divine existence becomes bipolar, Love being the neutralizing force which sustains relations between the universal *'I'* and the universal *'You'*.

---

2. Fr. 'concours'.

3. Fr. 'intégrale'.

4. Ed. Although a correct translation of the French, the English word 'makes' has overtones of compulsion that do not apply here and would in fact be a serious theological error.

5. John iii: 16.

It is important to look for and find many examples of the action of the *Law of Three*. This should not only be done to convince ourselves of its validity, but also to accelerate the re-education of our intelligence on an esoteric basis.

We know that the structure of the lower intellectual centre is bipolar. This structure is perfectly adapted to that of what in the orthodox Tradition is called the 'World'. This 'World' consists in ensemble of the 'A' influences of which we have spoken earlier (Chapter VI, figure 20). It is the world in which we live, which appears to the human Personality as the only reality, but is in fact relative or even illusory. We have examined the figure showing the 'A' and 'B' influences, (Fig. 20) and as we have already stated, all the 'A' arrows have counterparts which neutralize them. This symbolizes the creation of the world, starting from *Zero*, by division into two groups of forces, equal in power and diametrically opposed in direction.

The bipolar structure of the intelligence, an exact counterpart of the structure of the 'World', allows man to study and recognize all the 'A' influences, to orient himself in their immediate and furthest field of action, to apply his abilities to it in order to search, calculate, combine, intervene, act and even to create within the limits of the field of action of these influences.

We know, however, that this 'World' is, in fact, illusory; that the 'B' influences represent the only imperishable reality in life. Has not Jesus said: '*Lay not up for yourselves treasures upon the earth, where rust and worms consume, and where thieves break through walls and steal. But lay up for yourselves treasures in heaven, where neither moth nor rust doth consume and where thieves do not break through walls nor steal.*'[6]

It is well understood that it is a question here of two worlds which interpenetrate each other: the world constituted by the ensemble of 'A' influences – 'earth'; and the esoteric world – 'heaven', formed by the 'B' influences.

By studying the play of the three forces attentively, the searcher will train himself to recognize the action of the 'A' and 'B' influences, and distinguish between them. This is one of the essential elements of that re-education of which we spoke earlier.

(4)

Let us, however, be very careful not to give the distinction between 'A' and 'B' influences too narrow an interpretation. 'A' influences act through the *General Law*, and therefore conform to the Divine will. We already know one reason for their being: to serve the interests of

---

6. Matthew vi: 19–20.

the Ensemble. Yet let us not forget that everything is relative. He who studies esoteric science must not naively oppose 'A' influences. That would only succeed in bringing catastrophe. This was Don Quixote's instructive experience — so wrongly understood. 'A' influences play a positive role in the economy of the Universe. They combine with devastating force to oppose anyone who tries to attack them directly in their ensemble. The task of the seeker is different. Instead of trying to annihilate the 'A' influences, or to carve out a path between them for himself by his exploits, while continuing his esoteric education, he should instead escape their grasp.

It is important to understand that we can never attain this goal by our own forces. It is by absorbing 'B' influences — divine influences from a higher level,[7] which are consequently more powerful—and by putting full trust in them, as well as by giving proofs of capacity and devotion, that we shall be liberated from the dominion of these 'A' influences — which are ruled by the *General Law*, assisted by the *Law of Accident*.

He whose efforts are crowned with success—who attains higher levels[8] of *being*—is immediately utilized to share in the management[9] and growth of a given level[10] of the lower forces of the Cosmos.

In general he will have to accomplish — as a mission — a task in the domain of the 'A' influences. Above all, this work will require study of the bipolar world. Intelligence is the only tool we possess with which to achieve this end. This is its real reason for being, as well as the reason why its structure exactly reflects the world of the 'A' influences. This instrument thus allows man, in accordance with Plato's principle, to grasp and know[11] the *similar by the similar*.

Knowing[12] this, the student of esoteric science must guard against falling into the extremes expressed in some teachings; he must neither despise nor neglect his intellectual faculties. The intelligence must be developed and sharpened up to the limit of what is possible, and thought must become sharp as the point of a needle. But it must not be forgotten that the Personality, in spite of its complex structure and its many abilities, is nothing but an instrument, whose functioning remains purely mechanical. It is for this reason that in esoteric matters it does not know,[13] and will never know anything with certainty. By its nature agnostic, and concerned with phenomena, it is limited by form and function to three dimensions. It

---

7. Fr. 'niveau'.
8. Fr. 'niveaux'.
9. Fr. 'gestion'.
10. Fr. 'échelon'.
11. Fr. 'connaître'.
12. Fr. 'Sachant' – *from* 'savoir'.
13. Fr. 'sait'.

is incapable of exceeding these boundaries, but sincerely takes the world of 'A' influences as the only reality.

(5)

Knowing about the *Law of Three* allows us to be fully aware of the complex structure of the *Ray of Creation* (Fig. 29).

At the start, the Absolute assumes the first aspect of His manifestation. He is One, and the three forces reside united within Him. This is the traditional doctrine of the *Holy Trinity, consubstantial and indivisible.* Seen from below upwards, the Trinity is allegorically called the *summum bonum,* which crowns the Universe, then conceived as a *Pyramid.*

The three forces of the Absolute, the three *Hypostases* of the Trinity, endowed with autonomous will, but interdependent, create the phenomenal Universe and everything it contains. At the first step[14] they create the *Worlds.* These *Worlds,* whose existence is no longer consubstantial, since they are separate, depend directly and entirely on the will of the Absolute, the three forces of whom they maintain in a state of disjunction.

Created by these three disunited forces, these *Worlds* are yet continually penetrated by the three forces in a consubstantial state proper to the Absolute in His manifest state.

Aiming at the development of the *Ray of Creation* from above to below, creation still follows the same process. Each world is created by the three forces proper to it, and is equally subordinated to the authority of the forces that rule over the preceding steps,[15] from which it issues.

Each of these creative forces represents a group of laws of the same order, and these laws will condition the world belonging to a particular step,[14] and make it perform its function. This allows us to complete figure 28 by means of a scale,[16] which will represent the number of groups of rectifying laws all along the *Ray of Creation* (Figure 30 opposite):

Such a hierarchy of laws is none other than a hierarchy of competence and power.

Descending from step[14] to step, until we reach the *crust* of Creation, the will of the Absolute penetrates everything and all beings in the Universe— down to the most primitive organisms, and still further, to the most inert matter, which the Tradition designates by the term *stone.*

---

14. Fr. 'échelon'.
15. Fr. 'échelons'.
16. Fr. 'échelle'.

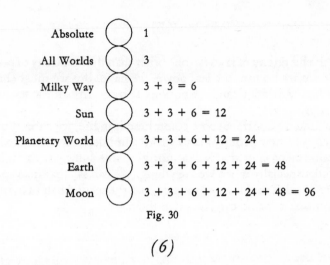

Absolute	◯	1
All Worlds	◯	3
Milky Way	◯	3 + 3 = 6
Sun	◯	3 + 3 + 6 = 12
Planetary World	◯	3 + 3 + 6 + 12 = 24
Earth	◯	3 + 3 + 6 + 12 + 24 = 48
Moon	◯	3 + 3 + 6 + 12 + 24 + 48 = 96

Fig. 30

(6)

What is the significance of the numbers in the preceding figure? They represent the conditions or forces of Creation; in other terms, the laws or more exactly categories of laws under which each step[17] of the *Ray of Creation* is placed. Unity belongs only to the Absolute, and this number *1*, indivisible although it contains the consubstantial Triad, represents and means the *liberty* of God. All that proceeds from Him progressively loses its liberty, meaning that it is found to be subject to a number of laws — or categories of laws — which becomes greater and greater. A being making his way through the *Ray of Creation* from the Absolute to the Moon would be more and more bound; we, who are on Earth, are bound by 48 groups of laws, a number which is in itself enormous. For *exterior* man we must add to these 48 groups of laws — under the influence of which the Earth pursues its existence — the laws relative to organic life on Earth, with other laws resulting from human society, and the organs and cells of that society: races, castes, families etc. We live in a 'wilderness' of laws and that is the reason why in spite of a certain forward impetus, our lives run up against all sorts of obstacles. Salvation consists precisely in progressive liberation from subjection to this large number of laws. In each case, although one must not trample over these obstacles, one must at least go around them. Esoteric science also says: *'We cannot fight against the laws which tie us by successively attacking each of them; by this procedure we will never attain anything.'* We might perhaps need a thousand consecutive lives to get the required result in this way. We must therefore evade this state of things in its ensemble, and then there is a chance. What is it? We will discover in the following chapters.

---

17. Fr. 'échelon'.

(7)

Since the hierarchy of laws is none other than the hierarchy of power, the more we are bound, the less power we have. But we must change the way in which we understand the notion of power. In esoteric science, *power means liberty*.

Every time we contract some commitment in life, we submit ourselves voluntarily to a new group of laws which administers the domain in which this commitment is made. We do not give this sufficient thought, often none at all, especially when we are young. We can say that man spends the first half of his life making agreements, and the second half of his existence asking himself how he can live with them.

(8)

The initial creative force, the neutralizing force that ties the universal *You* to the Absolute '*I*', is *Love*. Although always identical in essence, this force of Love penetrates the whole Universe from top to bottom—and vice versa—taking different form at each step[18] of Creation. St John said clearly: '*God is Love.*'[19] Inversely we could say: *Love is God.* The apostle concluded: '*He that loveth not, has not known God.*'[20] *Love*, a divine Hypostasis, manifests in the Universe as the force of renaissance and perpetual renewal.

(9)

The life of the Universe is organized according to a strict and perfect order. All that appears to be disorder or anarchy, looks this way to us because of our deficiencies in perception and judgement. The major part of the 'B' influences evade us. Yet in the economy of the Great Universe, each being or phenomenon has its place. Each, knowingly or unconsciously, serves in the attainment of a precise goal.

These are the essential characteristics of the first divine law, the *Law of Three*.

---

18. Fr. 'échelon'.
19. I John iv: 8.
20. *Ibid.*

CHAPTER X

(1)

We have established that, in the World created by the play of the three forces, the *Law of Three* reflects the three fundamental conditions of Creation: static, dynamic and equilibrium. We could never stress the importance of this law enough. Everything that exists in the Universe, in fact or in potential, exists only by grace of the combined action of these three forces.

We shall now study the second fundamental law: the *Law of Seven*. This law applies neither to the creation nor to the existence of things and phenomena in space, but to their evolution in Time. It concerns the action of all types[1] of movement on all planes at all the steps[2] of Creation.

To understand the *Law of Seven* better, and to realize its importance, we must examine another aspect of the problem. We have seen that while he lives in such a jungle of laws, the only chance man has is to put himself under the authority of the *Law of Exception*, an esoteric law which permits him to escape from the *ensemble* of 'A' influences whose action in the external world strikes our inner world directly. As an *action*, this evasion also falls under the empire of the *Law of Seven*.

In accordance with this law, as we shall see in a moment, every action is subject to one or more changes in direction and as a consequence is in principle doomed to failure. However, by analyzing the action of the *Law of Seven*, we shall grasp the character of these deviations, and their necessity from the objective point of view. We shall learn how it is possible to combat these deviations and continue in a constant direction in pursuit of our goals.

(2)

The nature of the *Law of Seven* and its objective necessity result from the destructive character of Time, the second condition of Creation. By virtue of this principle, everything which is born or created — man included — is doomed to annihilation. The Universe itself ever since its creation has also been threatened with annihilation through the action of Time. It has been necessary ever since to face up to this danger. The *Law of Seven* represents the means by which the destructive action of Time is to a certain measure neutralized.

---

1. Fr. 'catégories'.
2. Fr. 'échelons'.

A movement cannot be dissociated from its duration. As all action is either an exterior or an interior movement, every action takes Time. The *Law of Seven* consists precisely in the fact that any movement, once launched, undergoes a deviation at a certain moment and then, after going a certain distance in the new direction, another deviation, then yet again. If the initial impulse is strong enough, by its last deviation after tracing a Hexagon the movement comes back to the point where it started. Thus, under the influence of the *Law of Seven*, every action generated in the Universe unfolds in cycles (Fig. 31).

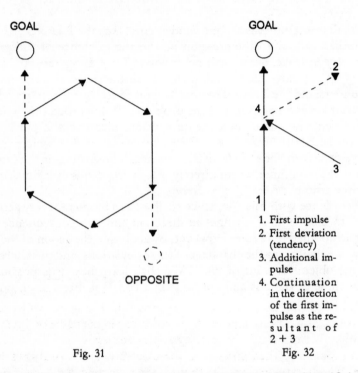

Fig. 31

1. First impulse
2. First deviation (tendency)
3. Additional impulse
4. Continuation in the direction of the first impulse as the resultant of 2 + 3

Fig. 32

While the *Law of Three* is a natural law, the *Law of Seven* is artificial. If it does not neutralize the destructive action of Time completely, it at least moderates it by imposing successive curvatures on every action or movement to close them into cycles. In the beginning, Time itself will be found to curve, deviating from a straight line so that it closes off into a great Cycle which encompasses all subordinate cycles. Because of the *Law of Seven*, annihilation does not occur in the first cycle, nor in following cycles until the force of the initial impulse is exhausted. In the meantime, the law makes it possible to revive any movement which is losing its energy and its speed, by imparting supplementary impulses to it at opportune moments and points (Fig. 32).

The Great Cycle, which circumscribes Time from the first impulse of divine manifestation until the *Accomplishment*, that is, the end of the World, is conceived in the Tradition as *Eternity*. Eternity, as we have indicated previously, is thus not infinite. Like any other created thing, it is limited. It embraces all Manifestation, and contains in itself the accomplishment of all possibilities and of all promises.

The curvature of Time—the result of the *Law of Seven*—makes even this return to its point of departure after circumscribing the polygon of Eternity. Thus considered, as we shall see later, Eternity has a certain *duration*, of the order of 2.10^{15} earth years. These considerations on the curvature of Time and of all movement — including any physical, mental or moral action whatever its nature — permit us to give a definition of the *Law of Seven*.

Definition: *Any movement that begins in a given direction undergoes a deviation at a certain moment.*

Conversely: *For a movement going towards a definite goal to continue without deviation in the same direction, it is necessary to impart to it adequate additional impulses at specific moments and points.*

Corollary: *If left to itself, by the third deviation a movement which follows a definite direction is found to be going in the diametrically opposite direction.*

These are the essential characteristics of the *Law of Seven*.

(3)

In human activity on the moral plane, the above corollary is found to apply at every moment. How much blood has been shed in the name of the Son of God who preached Love? How much cruelty, violence and imprisonment has been imposed by revolutions in the name of liberty and fraternity? We can multiply these examples endlessly.

At the moments when they occur, these deviations almost always escape notice. We continue to imagine that we are following the same direction though, without realizing it, we are insensibly led to take the opposite direction. At that moment our action on the moral plane automatically receives a new impulse, which comes from the reaction of those around to the original impulse. The more vigorous it is, the more 'avant-garde', the more 'revolutionary', the stronger the reaction by the *principle of Equilibrium*. In this way the movement in the opposite direction, called in common language the *reaction*, has such unexpected force that it sometimes pushes the promoters of the initial action back to well behind their point of departure. That is almost always the case with political doctrines.

To *consolidate* the first success, the second impulse must allow its *exploitation*. History gives many examples of the necessity of this second impulse: where it has been lacking after battles are won, the war has often been lost.

We must point to another effect of this law. We have seen that one must pass by two consecutive deviations to reach a direction opposite to the initial movement. This means that to maintain the initial direction of a movement, and ensure the success of an enterprise, one must foresee two consecutive additional impulses.

(4)

To take a step forward in the study of the *Law of Seven*, and so understand why it was given this name, we must take a look at the relation between *matter* and *energy*, and also at the nature of the cyclic movements that characterize them.

Contemporary positive science has established the close relation between matter and energy, a fact known to esoteric science since time immemorial. Today, it is no longer an impudence to say that matter is only a static form of energy — whose nature is above all dynamic. Certain phenomena which have been known from time immemorial already allowed clear perception of that notion: *spherical lightning* or the fireball, for example, which possesses certain characteristics specific to matter, such as volume and colour. But the state of knowledge in the past century did not allow productive study of this phenomenon; it remained relatively unnoticed due to its rarity. The recent progress of positive science has led to the rediscovery, if not in every detail[3] at least in part, of ancient traditional knowledge, particularly in the field of the relations of matter–energy. Traditional esoteric science envisages the manifestation of all energy as a form of cyclic vibratory movement. It further teaches that matter is composed of a relatively restricted number of *nuclei* of different qualities, and is analogous in nature to *spherical lightning*. These nuclei are animated by cyclic vibratory movements of varying frequency and amplitude. Here the Tradition introduces a notion of density which is applicable to energy as well as to matter. Finally, it establishes the law according to which: *the density of matter and the density of vibrations are inversely proportional.*

Always in accordance with that traditional teaching, the quantity of *nuclei* in matter, nuclei which to be precise are matter itself, is minimal. The volume occupied by an object, whatever it may be, is filled by what we call the very fast *traces of motion*: movement of a limited number of nuclei. All depends on the density of these movements and their speed. The

---

3. Fr. 'intégralement'.

heavier and more sluggish the vibrations, the larger the number of nuclei needed to constitute a body, and vice versa. We know that speed of movement is capable of modifying the physical characteristics of matter. For example, when we rotate a light piece of paper on a spindle at five to six thousand revolutions per minute, it becomes capable of sawing a piece of wood. At this frequency our piece of paper appears as a disc, although it is in fact square. If we increase the speed of rotation much beyond that mentioned above, the disc, as it turns, will take on for our senses the characteristics of a solid object at rest. We would then be able to touch the sheet of paper, without the risk of having our hands sawn off.

In the light of this theory the structure of matter appears analogous to that of the Universe, which we observe 'from the inside', with the rotation of the star systems. We have spoken of this already (Chapter VIII, p. 67) and have said that if — by reducing ourselves to the proportions of an infinitesimal being—we were able to observe our bodies from inside, as we observe the body of the Universe, we would perceive nothing different. The structure of the Universe is strictly uniform on every scale,[4] with reservations due to the application of the *principle of Relativity*.

(5)

The Tradition considers all movement as an acceleration or reduction of vibrations of the same order. It rejects the idea of stability, since everything that exists does so as a result of movement, and is found in a perpetual state of movement. The same body can accomplish — and generally does accomplish — several movements at the same time. Thus our planet Earth is animated by a great number of motions, of which twelve are considered primary. As to our satellite the Moon, it is endowed with about a hundred. On the mental[5] plane, and even on the physiological plane, we can often observe an ensemble of opposed components in one and the same pattern of movement: one part progresses, the other regresses; nothing can properly be said to be stable. From the esoteric point of view, stability is unthinkable; it is fiction. The only stability which may be admitted is *stability in movement*: this phenomenon is of the first importance, as it is this which has permitted the creation of matter as we know it, in its three forms.

4. Fr. 'échelon'.
5. Fr. 'psychique'.

We will now look at the action of the *Law of Seven*, in movements in which vibrations increase. In this case, the consecutive deviations we have spoken of at the beginning of this chapter will create a discontinuity. This discontinuity intervenes in the propagation of all movements, though they can and do seem to us progressive and uninterrupted. In this context, let us examine the musical octave, whose structure perfectly reflects the *Law of Seven*.

By *octave*, we mean the doubling of vibrations. The musical scale[6] is located between the limits of an octave, and comprises seven tones and five half-tones. The missing half-tones are positioned as indicated by the arrows in the following figure:

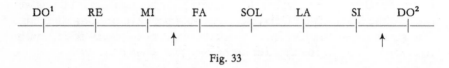

Fig. 33

The first is found between the notes MI and FA, and the other between SI and DO². Let us now see the way the vibrations progress, which, as we have said, occurs discontinuously. The following diagrams show this discontinuity, expressed in fractions and whole numbers on the one hand, and in the curve of discontinuity of a musical octave, on the other.

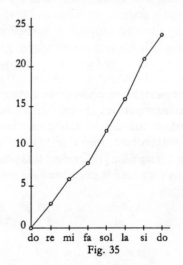

DO 1 — 24 ₃
RE $9/8$ — 27 ₃
MI $5/4$ — 30 ₂
FA $4/3$ — 32 ₄
SOL $3/2$ — 36 ₄
LA $5/3$ — 40 ₅
SI $15/8$ — 45 ₃
DO 2 — 48

Fig. 34

Fig. 35

---

(7)

We have said that every existing phenomenon exists in Time, and that consequently it is movement. All movement, as a function of Time, takes place under the dominion of the *Law of Seven*; otherwise under the *Law of Octaves*. The action of the Absolute, who created the Universe—the existence of which is assured on every level[7] by the *Law of Three*—is itself also developed in Time according to the *Law of Seven*.

The *Ray of Creation*, in its progress from the Absolute to the satellites of the planets—to the moon in our case—must necessarily follow a descending sequence of the octave. In the Tradition, it is called the *Great Octave* or the *Cosmic Octave*. It is a *descending* octave:

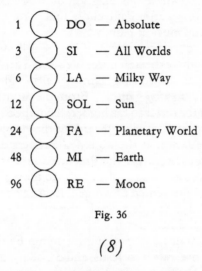

1	DO	— Absolute
3	SI	— All Worlds
6	LA	— Milky Way
12	SOL	— Sun
24	FA	— Planetary World
48	MI	— Earth
96	RE	— Moon

Fig. 36

(8)

The esoteric teaching, formerly reserved for the initiated only, was known not only in the Orient but also in the Occident. We can see the evidence of this by analyzing the names of the notes of the musical scale,[8] established, as we know by, Guido of Arezzo, an Italian Benedictine (*c*.995–1050). To do this, he utilized the hymn to St John the Baptist, composed two centuries previously by Paul Diacre or Warnefrid, a historian of Lombardy (740–801). The latter was a secretary to the king of Lombardy, Didier, and after that lived at the court of Charlemagne, then in that of Benevent, to retire finally to the monastery of Monte

---

7. Fr. 'échelon'.
8. Fr. 'gamme'.

Cassino, where he ended his days. The hymn to St John the Baptist goes like this:

UT queant laxis
R Esonare fibris
*MI*ra gestorum
*FA*muli tuorum
*SOL*ve polluti
*LA*bil reatum
*S*ancte *Johannes*[9]

We see that this hymn was composed by Paul Diacre in hermetic form. Such a procedure was always favoured in esoteric teaching. Comparative study of the diagram of the *Great Octave*, and the hymn of Paul Diacre, leaves no doubt that he knew this diagram quite well. So did Guido of Arezzo who, two centuries after Paul, chose that hymn amongst all others to introduce it into the musical gamut.[10]

We can even see for ourselves why Paul Diacre utilized the syllable *UT*, instead of *DO*, to designate the first note. We should carefully note that he conceived this hymn as an *ascending* gamut,[10] although the *Great Octave* naturally represents a *descending* gamut.[10] From the meaning of its content, this hymn tends from the lower to the higher, from the coarse to the fine, in other words, from the human plane toward the divine plane. But he stops, without reaching the latter, at the note *SI*, consecrated to St John the Baptist. Let us say in passing that the Precursor enjoys a very particular veneration in the Tradition, and is placed above the Apostles. On certain Byzantine icons he is represented as winged, having two heads, one quite normally placed on his shoulders while the other, which is similar, is severed and bloody, and he bears it with his own hands on a platter.

If Paul Daicre had wanted to prolong his hymn by one more line, he would have had to consecrate it to Jesus, and consequently to start it from the syllable *DO*. But he did not do that. His eminently human gamut,[10] having begun with man as he is, *born of woman*[11] in all his imperfection, could obviously not start with *DO*, which really stands for *Dominus*. He chose the syllable *UT*, from the word *Uterus*, the organ of gestation, precisely in order to underline that imperfect condition which is as common to all the devout as to all men, in order to direct them on the track of St John, of whom Jesus said: '*Verily I say unto you, among them that are born of women there hath not arisen a greater than John the Baptist.*'[12]

---

9. This is the translation of that hymn: 'That your trusting believers may, with all the sinews of their soul, sing of the marvels of your life, to purify their soiled lips (of sin), O St John.'

10. Fr. 'gamme'.

11. Matthew xi: 11.

12. *Ibid.*

Thus, *UT—Uterus*—symbolizes the door of birth according to the flesh and *SI*, the door of the *second Birth*, according to the Spirit, without which *man cannot see the kingdom of God*.[13] The ascending gamut of Paul Diacre thus comprises an *octave of regeneration*, going from birth on earth to birth in the heavens.

That is the explanation of this hymn, closely conforming to the sense of the mystical traditions of the past.

(9)

An exhaustive examination of the names of the notes that form the musical octave shows direct correspondence with the notes of the *Great cosmic Octave*, as can be seen from the following diagram:

1	◯	DO	— God. The Absolute manifest. The central Sun	*DO*minus
3	◯	SI	— Starry sky. Ensemble of all Worlds	*SI*dereus orbis
6	◯	LA	— Our Great World; the Milky Way	*LA*cteus orbis
12	◯	SOL	— The Sun	*SOL*
24	◯	FA	— The Planetary World, to which antiquity attributed direct influence on our destiny	*FA*tum
48	◯	MI	— Earth, our imperfect world, under the mixed rule of Good and Evil	*MI*xtus orbis
96	◯	RE	— The Moon, ruler of human fate according to the Ancients	*RE*gina astris

Fig. 37

(10)

Let us return to the problem of *matter—energy*, to clarify the question of atomic structure as it is understood by esoteric science. We have seen that the first manifestation of energy appears in the form of a cyclic intra-atomic vibratory movement. This movement, animating a certain number of nuclei, forms *matter*. If we can say in effect that these moving nuclei form *matter*, then we must not forget that they themselves consist of energy in a static form. Conversely, *energy* is no more than matter taking dynamic form. The disintegration of the atom gives a clear example of such a transformation. On the other hand, we have named spherical lightning as an example of the concentration of dynamic energy in the form of nuclei.

---

13. John iii: 3.

This process is the converse of the first, and can be compared to the phenomenon of atomic fusion.

We have also mentioned that the structure of matter is subject to the *principle of Equilibrium*, and that its density is inversely proportional to that of the internal vibrations which animate it. This serves to introduce into our studies the notion of the *atom*, as described in the Tradition. According to the classical definition, the atom is that particle of any element which is said to be simple; which can be divided no further if it is to keep all those chemical properties which determine the various ways in which it combines with other bodies. Esoteric science has a different notion. Here it is:

Definition: *The atom is the smallest particle, the last division of any given substance which integrally conserves all its properties: physical, chemical, mental and cosmic.*

We can see that this definition is closer to that of the *molecule*, even though it also goes beyond that.

We therefore recognize atoms of various compound bodies as well as the atoms of those elements which chemistry considers to be simple. For example, (there is) an atom of water, an atom of air etc... In correlation with the cosmic properties of the atom thus defined, esoteric science recognizes various *Orders of Matter*, classified according to the density of the typical atoms that correspond to every level[14] of the *Great Octave*. Given this conception, it does not in principle admit any opposition between *Matter* and *Spirit*. If we oppose one to the other, it is as a convention for simple convenience, in the same way that astronomy continues to utilize Ptolemy's system for its practical aims, while pertinently aware that it is the system of Copernicus that more exactly reflects reality. From the point of view of esoteric science, which is in principle monistic, *all is matter* in the manifest world. Matter is a manifestation of energy, which is no more than a form of Spirit. In a hymn which has been preserved in Orthodoxy, the attributes of the Holy Spirit quite clearly show this form of thought:

> King of Heavens, Comforter
> Spirit of Truth, *Omnipresent*,
> *All Filling*,
> Treasure of Saints,
> Dispenser of Life,
> Come and abide in us,
> Purify us from all pollution
> And save our souls, O good one![15]

---

14. Fr. 'échelon'.

15. Translated from old Slavonic, with author's italics. The author notes that this concept of the Holy Spirit is represented in the form of Fire (Acts ii: 3) and is analogous to *Agni* in Hinduism. We should also note that in Greek the terms *spirit* and *air* are homonyms (*pneuma*), as are the terms *spirit* and *breath* (*doukh*) in old Slavonic.
Fr. 'ô Bienheureux'.

This said, we can understand that only the atom of the Absolute is really simple and consequently indivisible: here a single nucleus of Energy-Spirit vibrates at maximum intensity. It is the lightest atom; in esoteric science its matter-density is taken as *unity*. Then, coming down the *Ray of Creation* step by step, the vibrations progressively lose their speed. It follows that, at each successive note of the *Cosmic Octave*, the constitution of the atoms will require more matter: the atoms become more and more heavy and inert. As we shall see hereafter, the typical atoms of each level reflect the form of Creation in accordance with the *Law of Three*, as described above (Chapter IX, p. 81, Fig. 30; Chapter X, p. 89, Fig. 36), in such a way that the density of these typical atoms follow the notes of the *Great Octave*, and can be represented by the figure on the following page.

Positive science only considers four of the seven levels of cosmic matter: it studies the level of the Earth integrally; a large proportion at the level of the Moon, and in gradually lesser proportion the levels of the Planetary World, and the Sun. As yet it does not possess any means of perceiving or knowing the three higher levels. The atoms of the Planetary World — as defined above — already appear in some way hypothetical. As for the Sun, we know very few things concerning that star. But the progress of positive science has placed us today on the eve of important discoveries in this field, as in our knowledge of our satellite. We will be surprised to learn that, objectively, the Sun has an altogether different appearance from the one we perceive, and that the Earth, seen from the Moon, appears altogether other than what we make of it.

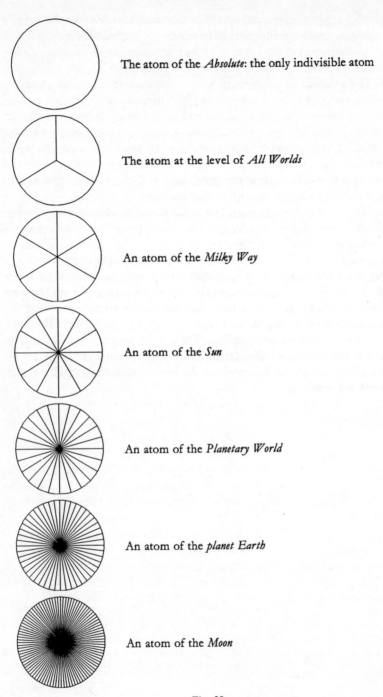

The atom of the *Absolute*: the only indivisible atom

The atom at the level of *All Worlds*

An atom of the *Milky Way*

An atom of the *Sun*

An atom of the *Planetary World*

An atom of the *planet Earth*

An atom of the *Moon*

Fig. 38

CHAPTER XI

(1)

The *Law of Seven* is a general law, which governs all categories of motion, conscious or mechanical, that occur in the created Universe. This means that every movement or creation develops through a gamut.[1] In each gamut, this natural progress is subject to deviation. It slackens and sometimes stops at the intervals between DO and SI, and between FA and MI. This is the deeper meaning of the notion of *Destiny* as understood by the Ancients.[2] According to them, Zeus himself did not escape its rule. In fact, the actions of the Absolute in his creative work, which follow the *Ray of Creation*, are also subject to this law. Like every creative work, this action follows a descending gamut. For the will of the Absolute to pass to the stage of manifestation, and then descend through every step of the *Ray of Creation*, down to the final point which is RE, the Moon, it was and still is first necessary to fill the interval between DO and SI. Then it is necessary to neutralize the tendency to deviate, caused by the sudden slowing in its progress between FA and MI.

The first interval is filled by the will of the Absolute. In fact, by His creative will, which manifests at this point as a conscious effort, giving the first impulse to a premeditated and predetermined creation. This creative force, as we have already said, is *Love*. As for the interval between FA and MI of the *Great Octave*, it is equally filled by the will of the Absolute, but no longer directly, as in the first case. This will acts here in the second degree, but always as a creative force of Love. It appears at this stage on a lower plane,[3] corresponding to the interval we are talking about. This complementary outpouring of forces, in its place and at a cosmic moment, allows that first creative action to continue its development without impediment.

The two diagrams that follow reflect, on the one hand the *plan of Creation* (Fig. 39), and on the other hand its *application* (Fig. 40).

Technically, in the execution of the cosmic plan, the transmission of creative energy across the second interval is realized by the introduction of an *auxiliary lateral Octave*, which starts from the Sun: the SOL of the *Great Octave*. With the creation of the Planetary World, the SOL of the *Great Octave* begins to resound as the DO in this *lateral octave*.

---

1. Fr. 'gamme'.

2. Tr. A study of mythology should clarify for the reader whether the ancients in their use of the notion of destiny actually referred to these intervals, or simply revealed in this word the inevitability of change for everything in time.

3. Fr. 'plan'.

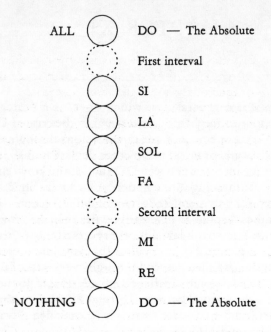

Fig. 39

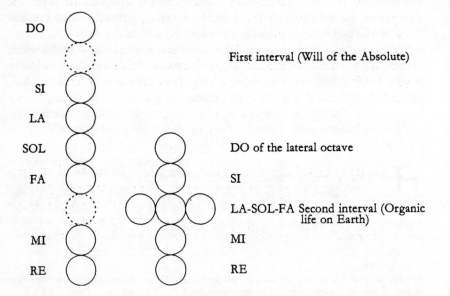

Fig. 40

(2)

Before going any further, it is appropriate to comment on the sense and purpose of the *lateral octave*, in its ensemble, and then to establish the proper significance of each of the notes that compose it.

Glancing at the diagram which represents the *Cosmic Octave*, we can constate that no intermediary body between the Absolute and the Sun is substantially different in its nature. In fact the notes SI–All Worlds—and LA–The Milky Way — our World — are composed of bodies at various stages of their existence, (formation, maturity, senility or death), but wholly similar or at least analogous to our sun. As we shall see later, the Sun, as well as all the stars of the astronomical Universe — each the sun of its own system—represent an ensemble. Between the Absolute and this ensemble, considered by the Tradition to be the body of the cosmic Christ,[4] there does not exist any intermediate body that is different in its nature. We find nothing but various groupings of bodies that all have the same solar nature. This is why the Spirit of this integral solar body has been considered to be the consubstantial Being of the Absolute, *begotten not created*, the Son of God,[5] the cosmic Christ as we said. His manifestation in our *Ray of Creation* appears precisely because the SOL of the *Great Octave* resounds as the DO of the *Lateral octave*, which is indissolubly joined to this *Ray of Creation*. The *lateral octave* is the conductor of life in the Universe, in all its different forms. Spirit of the Sun, Christ *lives*;[6] He comprises within Himself the fullness of solar, planetary and satellite lives in all their forms, present, vanished or to come.

This gives us a general sense of the *lateral octave*. Let us now see how this source of life, issuing from the Sun, manifests itself through the notes SOL FA, MI and RE of the *Great Octave*, as well as through the notes SI, LA, SOL, FA, MI and RE of its own octave.

(3)

Here let us guard ourselves against being too astronomical or astrophysical in our view of the Universe. We only partially perceive cosmic phenomena, to the measure of our limited perception. As we are *exterior* men, the mental element in the life of the Universe escapes us; to be more precise, we have no objective notion about it. Lacking the

---

4. Ed. 'Christ Pantokrator' in Orthodox terminology.

5. Cf. the *Credo*.

6. John xiv: 19.

knowledge,[7] we are reduced in this domain to beliefs: positive, that is to say emotional or religious; negative, and either rationalistic or atheistic.

In fact, we know very few things about our Sun, about its many functions, or about the influences by which it governs the three remaining notes of the *Great Octave*, especially MI, the note of our planet.

(4)

To better understand the action of the gamut in general, let us take an example from everyday life. We shall see from this that man always instinctively seeks to surmount these intervals, at the moment of origination, as well as in the course of realizing his projects.

We know that, to act with some chance of success, we should follow a plan carefully worked out in advance. What is the esoteric meaning of this principle? It is twofold: the first (sense) is known to all; it responds to the requirements of the *Law of Three*, which governs all creation; the second aims at materialization of the project — its implementation. The latter necessarily follows the *Law of Seven*.

Let us take an example in a field which is strange to no one, that of government. We know that a law is normally accompanied by one or more decrees of application, which are directly linked to it. These play the role of neutralizing force between the DO of the law, an active force, and a passive force, SI, where the execution of the measures implied in the law begins.

As a general rule, execution depends not on the (legislative) authority which sanctioned the law, but on a subordinate authority, as with the Son in the *Great Octave*. It is precisely this 'authority of second instance' which is charged with realizing the affair to the end, starting from the note SOL, which has behind it the notes SI and LA, representing the accumulation of mental and biological resources, and before it the note FA; material means of all kinds which are put at its disposal.

In the normal development of administrative action, the note MI shows the first results. In the note RE, the success is stabilized to permit the reaping of the final fruit. The fruit appears as the DO of the following octave, then fully engendered and capable from now on of independent life and development.

Theoretically, this is evolution in accordance with the *principal Octave*. However, the well conceived law, the happy choice of executive authority, the opportune accumulation of the necessary mental, biological and material support, cannot make creation advance beyond the note FA. It is only by means of the *lateral octave* that the action can, in practice, be taken

---

7. Fr. 'savoir'.

98

on to an objective result which, as we have seen, is only attained at the note DO of the octave which terminates the *secondary octave*.

The *lateral octave* starts with the note DO, which issues from the note SOL of the *principal octave*. This signifies that the 'authority of second instance', the SOL of the *principal octave*, takes the initiative of executing the planned law within the limitations of the legislation. This authority does not have total freedom of action; it is limited to a plan and made exact by decree. But within the limits defined by these, we await its initiative. If we do not commit the error of interfering in its acts, the secondary authority will act within the fixed frame as absolute master: in its own domain the DO of the *lateral octave* is analogous to the DO of the *principal octave*.

After having established the plan on a correct basis and collected the necessary means to execute it, the talent of the supreme executive lies in the judicious choice of his collaborators. In return,[8] the collaborator must bring his talents to fruition in every aspect of his life, particularly that of esotericism.

We can now understand that Jesus had this aspect of the *Law of Seven* in mind when He pronounced these words, which look odd at first sight: '*For to him who hath shall be given; and whosoever hath not, from him shall be taken away even that which he has,*'[9] or more exactly: '*that which he thinks he has.*'[10]

Man acts in his life under the authority of the *Law of Seven*, of course without knowing it. It is only when, shocked by the difficulties which erupt into his path without visible cause, and only by accumulating experience through successive failures, that he searches empirically for the way to overcome these difficulties.

(5)

S trengthened by the preceding, someone who has studied esoteric science can and must better understand the *comedy of life*, in which pretentious blind men lead other more modest blind men towards an abyss which will engulf both.[11] Once he knows this then, within the limited independence left to him after the commitments he has undertaken, and which still bind him, he will have the possibility of warding off the harmful effects of the 'A' influences. In the net of 'A' influences of which our life is woven, it is among the 'B' influences that he will find the necessary impetus to fill the two intervals in each gamut he begins — or to which he falls

---

8. Fr. 'en revanche'.
9. Matthew xiii: 12; Mark iv: 25.
10. Luke viii: 18.
11. Matthew xv: 14; Luke vi: 39.

victim. The *object* of their play, he must become *subject* before he can make himself *master*.

What eludes most of us is that, after we have begun our esoteric studies, we still continue as before, living and acting in the same *comedy of life* — produced by the 'A' influences. It often seems to us that, merely by pursuing such studies, we are already liberated. This is a mistake! We can also go to the opposite extreme. We must beware of following the example of Don Quixote, who persisted in attacking these 'A' influences head-on in all their forms, particularly as windmills. The seeker must learn how to master these influences, especially those which become factors in the film of his personal life. He will achieve this by drawing a complement of energy from the source of the 'B' influences, which he must utilize in his 'life' in strict obedience to the demands of the *Law of Seven*. For that, he must make himself recognize all the gamuts[12] — at least all the principal ones — of which he is either agent or victim, and in the midst of which he finds himself at every moment. This is the first part of his work, which corresponds in principle to *knowledge*.[13] The second part, no less important, corresponds in principle to *savoir-faire*. Having objectively recognized his place in the gamuts he meets at any given moment, he will next proceed to relate this data to the practical means at his disposal, in ways consistent *with a chosen or perceived aim within the esoteric plan*. Then the *savoir-faire* will gain force, allowing the seeker to act in two ways. He must first draw on the necessary energies at the source of the 'B' influences, to apply them later to the gamuts of 'A' influences of which he forms a part. This is done in a strictly realistic spirit, free from all hypocritical tendencies, all mechanisms of self justification, and, above all, free from all lying about himself. This last condition is indispensable to success. In every case which is subject to the *Law of Seven*, the period of application will bring conscious efforts into play by introducing *lateral octaves*, in a way analogous to that by which the *lateral octave* introduces itself into the *cosmic Octave*.

We must say immediately that, even if these conditions are strictly observed, only rarely does one reach the desired result without making many mistakes of appreciation or application. We must be one of the *just*[14] by nature not to make mistakes, nor persevere in errors. The unjust, the proud[15] — and this is the general case — fall again into their mistakes, because they think they alone are just, so consequently that they are right while others, as well as circumstances, are wrong. In their pretentious

---

12. Fr. 'gammes'.

13. Fr. 'savoir'.

14. Ed. In Orthodox monastic thought represented by the Greek word 'dikaios'; just or righteous man.

15. Fr. 'les orgueilleux'.

blindness they even go so far as to distort the facts in a deliberate way. The adage 'so much the worse for the facts' (or in an English version: 'my mind's made up, don't confuse me with the facts') has become famous.

He who studies esoteric science must watch, and take care not to return once again to the crowd, nor, 'like everyone else', to follow that broad way which leads to the abyss.

(6)

Let us return to the study of the first *lateral octave*, which is linked to the cosmic *Great Octave*.

We shall first repeat that its DO, issuing from the SOL of the *Great Octave*, appears here as the Absolute. It is, as we have said, the *Christos*, the *Anointed* of the Absolute I, the *Second Logos*, *Spirit of the Sun*, shining by his own light,[16] begotten not created, and consubstantial with the Father.

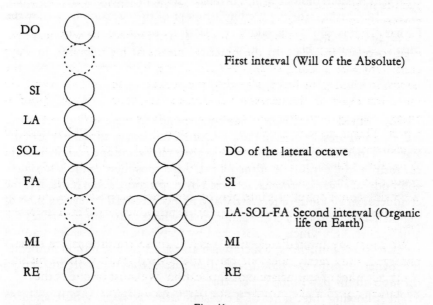

Fig. 41

The DO of the *lateral octave* represents the Absolute of organic life on Earth, the livening principle of the Sun. In other words, all the elements of organic life on Earth in their manifested or latent state—up to their limit of

---

16. Matthew xvii: 2.
Ed. 'As a lighted lamp needs no other light to make it visible, so the Self, being consciousness itself, needs no other source of consciousness to illuminate it.' Shankaracharya, *Atma Bhoda*.

possible development, and without a single exception — depend on the Sun. The interval between DO and SI of the *lateral octave* is filled by the creative will of the Absolute II, analogous to that of the Absolute 'I' of the *Great Octave*, which is Love.

Issuing from the Absolute II, this creative and conscious force intervenes as neutralizing force between the active force DO and the passive force SI, belonging to the ensemble of the Planetary World. As a result of the converging action of these three forces, the necessary condition for the existence and development of organic life on the surface of planets appears. It occurs on Earth as the atmosphere.

The three notes: LA, SOL and FA, represent the three forms of organic life: man, fauna and flora. The notes MI and RE of the *lateral octave* represent the livening influence of the Absolute II, penetrating the planet Earth and its satellite respectively, through the *station of transmission* LA–SOL–FA.

We have already said that the notes of the *Great Octave* SI, LA and FA represent mental, biological and material elements respectively, put at the disposal of the Son for the accomplishment of the Creation begun by the Father. That is why Jesus said that: '*All things whatsoever the Father hath are Mine*',[17] because — He said elsewhere — '*I and my Father are one.*'[18]

(7)

The note SI of the *lateral octave* corresponds to the creation, organization and preservation of the atmosphere of planets, as in the case of the Earth. With time, the atmosphere changes its structure and composition to conform to the evolution of the planet. An atmosphere is the *sine qua non* condition of organic life, characterized by respiration. Even more, it is the conductor of all kinds of terrestrial and extra-terrestrial influences including planetary, solar and cosmic influences whose radiation penetrates the atmosphere, and which are absorbed by respiration. Man is ignorant of many of these influences, which when absorbed by respiration immediately penetrate into the blood, and then pass through his organs and so through all his psychological centres.

The following three notes of the cosmic *lateral octave*, LA, SOL and FA, in their ensemble, make up *organic life on Earth*. FA corresponds to vegetable life, SOL to animal life, and LA to human life. Yoked together, these three notes constitute an organ of the planet, a kind of highly sensitive membrane, a *station of transmission* for the creative energy which issues from the Absolute I, which reaches it by the mediation of the Absolute II. It is by

17. John xvi: 15.
18. John x: 30.

means of carnal love—the note SOL of the *lateral octave*—and by perpetual rebirth, that this organ is maintained, evolves, and assures the transmission of the creative energy from the Absolute I across the interval between FA and MI of the *Great Octave*. The notes MI and RE of the *lateral octave* merge with those of the *Great Octave*, and are represented by the body of the Earth and that of the Moon respectively. The action of the two notes, MI and RE of the *lateral octave*, manifests as development of these two bodies.

In broad outline, this is the meaning and role of the cosmic *lateral octave*.

(8)

We were perhaps able to notice that, while filling the interval between FA and MI of the *Great Octave* by its action, the *lateral octave* itself was equally compelled to undergo a slowing down or deviation in the interval between its own two notes, FA and MI. How is this filled? When we have acquired certain background information which will enable us to approach the problem more effectively, we shall come back to this important question.

(9)

This brief analysis of the functioning of the *lateral octave* allows us to comprehend certain major problems in a new light; problems which occupy all minds, such as the overpopulation of the earth, the problem of food supply considered on a global scale, the general organization of human society, the cosmic significance of the wars of the past, and their role in the future, and even problems such as interplanetary and interstellar navigation.

CHAPTER XII

(1)

We have studied the structure of the Universe in the form of the *Ray of Creation*, its constitution according to the *Law of Three*, and its functioning in accordance with the *Law of Seven*. Already, this first study of the *Cosmos* allows us to understand all the depth of this term, to which the Ancients rightly attributed meanings of Order and Beauty. In previous chapters we have pictured the Universe in terms of the order underlying its creation and functioning. We have seen that this order applies in a strictly uniform manner. A vehicle of the will of the Absolute, it rules the Universe as much in its ensemble as in its smallest parts. This confirms the ancient esoteric formula: *'As above, so below.'* Now we are going to begin studying the Universe from the point of view of the *life* which animates it, given that its structure as we studied it, in some way constitutes the mobile framework[1] of the Universe. This will permit us to understand better, if still only partially, the ineffable beauty of the Cosmos.

Let us not forget that our capacity for representation is limited. Even the richest of the images we strive so hard to form are flat and colourless. In the environment in which we live, we cannot — without calculation and without special training — fully comprehend the measure of these continual changes, since our perceptions tend to register stereotypes of the objects surrounding us. We are thus normally transported to a static world of two dimensions, although in truth we belong to a three-dimensional world, evolving in Time, and including still higher dimensions — hidden from us so that we have no direct[2] perception of them. The representation of the Universe and its life which we can form for ourselves — penetrated, from the infinitely large to the infinitely small, by the perpetual vibration of Love — that representation will always be flat, banal, and will never reflect its ineffable beauty except from afar and in a purely conventionalized way. It is only by means of progressive evolution, after attaining the level of *being* of man 4, and then crossing the threshold to become man 5, that direct contemplation of the Cosmos becomes accessible to us in its twin aspects of Order and Beauty.

Yet the efforts of *exterior* man to grasp this order and beauty are not in vain. They are even indispensable. It is the same as in studying positive science; one must *learn* first to *understand* later.

It is in this spirit that we should approach the present chapter.

---

1. Fr. 'charpente'.
2. Fr. 'spontanée

(2)

How can we visualize the Universe to ourselves, while taking these factual reservations into account? The *Tree* is one image. Jesus used it, speaking of himself as the stem of a vine, with his disciples as the branches.[3] We can visualize for ourselves the 'tout ensemble' of the *Rays of Creation*, forming the branching crown of a tree... a triple root from which trunk and branches spring. This skeletal figure is covered with buds which give rise to leaves, flowers, and finally fruit. The tree is alive, and carries throughout its branches the varied manifestations of that life: manifestations that are interdependent, useful, even indispensable to one another since they ensure the existence, growth and development of the ensemble. Even though this image is far from being perfect, it is convenient, and we shall refer to it more than once. Its imperfection is that the different parts — at their different levels of the *Tree* — do not exactly resemble each other. If the branches resemble the trunk, and the twigs resemble the branches, the flowers, leaves and stalks have a totally different appearance from the 'wood'.[4] The life of the cosmos also has many levels, with seven principal ones; all seven levels of its manifestation are conceived in the image of the first,[5] in the heart of which the six others live. All in all, there are seven cosmoses, or more exactly, seven orders of cosmoses — of which the triple root is one — existing and living one within another following the branching of the *Rays of Creation*.

With time, this ancient teaching, which linked each *Ray of Creation* to a musical scale[6] of seven cosmoses, was partially forgotten or intentionally distorted. The enciphering of esoteric science has always been practised; the *Pentateuch* and the *Gospel* bear witness to that. But while hiding the exact meaning of the Doctrine, the ancients took care to impart to the profane — in one form or another — part of the truth that appeared to be a complete and systematic explanation. Thus through centuries and even millennia, through bygone and extinct civilizations, they gave the would-be-seekers of the future sufficient indications to incite them to deeper investigation.

(3)

An abridged version of the ancient teaching concerning the *Seven Cosmoses* has been given to us, notably in the Cabbala of Rabbi-Ben-Akiba, who speaks of two cosmoses: the small cosmos symbolizing

---

3. John xv: 5.
4. Fr. 'charpente'.
5. Genesis i: 26–27
6. Fr. 'échelle'.

man, and the large cosmos, symbolizing the Universe. The complete analogy between the *Microcosmos* and the *Macrocosmos* — to use the Greek terminology — reflected the whole paradigm of Genesis quoted above: '*man created in the image of God and after His likeness,*'[7] a thesis which clearly admitted the principle of the unity of the World. At the same time, this teaching was limited to describing two cosmoses, while the complete doctrine, as said, considers not just two cosmoses, but seven cosmoses which together form a complete cycle of life in perpetual rebirth.

It should be noted that the system of *Seven Cosmoses* contains within itself all that exists, that is to say, the integral Being which we conceive — much too astronomically — as the Great Universe. On the other hand this system comprises everything that touches the life of this Being, all his organization, and all his manifestations. This is important to remember, as it is from this fact that *Knowledge*, in the full esoteric sense of the term, necessarily starts: by the study of this system — with the obligatory condition that the study of the parts is always done in relation to the ensemble.

(4)

The form of the system of *Seven Cosmoses* is shown again with the *Macrocosmos* forming their ensemble:

Fig. 42

Here are the primary data for this doctrine.

Each cosmos is a living being. Each is three-dimensional like the *Microcosmos* — that is to say man — and, like him, lives in Time. Each cosmos is limited[8] by the two neighbouring cosmoses, and this triad of

---

7. Genesis i: 26–27; v: 1–2; ix: 6.
8. Fr. 'déterminé'.

106

successive cosmoses forms a complete unity. This does not, however, create watertight barriers between the triads since — and this is important to remember — the central cosmos of a given triad forms both an inferior element of the triad above, and a higher element of the triad below.

Concerning the *Ray of Creation*, we have already said — and this applies to the integral ensemble of the *Macrocosmos* — that the different cosmoses inside it are ruled by identical laws. But their application to each, although analogous, is not absolutely identical. Let us note in passing that action may be taken in a particular cosmos according to the laws of another cosmos. The classical example of such an action is, on the one hand, diseases of bacterial or viral origin, and on the other the active fight against these diseases by means of vaccination, serotherapy etc. This is the mixing of two cosmoses in each other's domain, that of man, and that of micro-organisms. The mixing of the laws of the higher cosmos in human life is rarer, or seems to us to be so. This involves phenomena which we call *miracles* in our current language.

(5)

L et us now proceed to a comparative examination of *the notion of Cosmoses* and of the *Ray of Creation*.

If the *Rays of Creation* are picturesquely defined as the boughs of the Great Tree which is the Universe, a tree of which the triple root is the manifested Absolute, then the *System of Cosmoses* appears as the life on these same boughs.

This life issues from the same triple root, the Absolute I, on Whom it is entirely dependent.

It is there, at the start, that the *Rays of Creation* and the *System of Cosmoses* join. This permits us to identify the Absolute I with the *Protocosmos* or *First Cosmos*.

We see that our *Ray of Creation* shows only a single bough, along the length of which the life of different elements of the *System of Cosmoses* emerges.

(6)

H ere we have to stop for a few instants to prevent an error of conception which might be inspired by this image of the *Tree*. By analogy, certain aspects of this image can help us grasp our object better, but it does not represent all the agreements[9] between the *Ray of Creation* and *The System of Cosmoses* at all levels. Our mental laziness, and a permanent tendency to drowsiness — the *inertia of matter* which is

---

9. Fr. 'l'ensemble des rapports'.

to new concepts — impels us to hasty conclusions and unfounded generalizations. Let us not forget that analogy is not similarity; even less is it identity. We must use all symbols with circumspection, and warn ourselves not to exceed the limits of agreement between the diagram and the object studied.

We have judged it opportune to give this warning, as with the study of the *System of Cosmoses*, we enter more and more the domain of new notions. On the other hand, the novel character of these notions, whether learned or conceived, requires conscious effort from anyone. In a certain way, this is a creative effort. It is the relatively heavy matter of our brains which always resists this effort. One can symbolically say that each new conception leaves a trace on the surface of the brain. The more the thought which forms this conception is new and striking, the deeper the groove it imprints on the brain. To fix this groove requires concentration of attention and thought. The thought must become fine and sharp, like the point of a needle. Then it will trace grooves deep enough that they do not fill up immediately, so that it is possible for the cerebral matter to do its work of fixation.

Meanwhile, this process runs up against two obstacles. First is mental fatigue, resulting in exhaustion of the reserves of forces necessary for the concentration desired. We shall see later that in *exterior* man this reserve is minimal. He generally lives at the limit of his nervous forces. Absorption of energy is almost immediately balanced by expenditure of the same magnitude. This semi-permanent exhaustion of the necessary energies drives man to abandon the path which leads him to the new and the unknown, and his thoughts slide back into paths they have taken before, a process which requires neither conscious effort nor concentration. The second obstacle arises from the fact that the cerebral matter itself resists this sharpened thought which, like the point of a needle, wounds it.

Hasty conclusions, easy generalizations, and slogans are the common techniques by which the dull and inert side of human nature continually tries to make the seeker abandon research into the domain of the new and the unknown ... which requires, as we have said, *conscious and creative* effort.

To fight against this double obstacle, which creates different difficulties for different people, but which we must all face, a practical method is recommended — whose object is also double. On one hand, it provides exercises which help us to accumulate force, and so build up reserves of energy. On the other hand, it provides exercises whose aim is to refine the working of the cerebral cells. These cells — endowed with the greatest permanence within the limits of the life of the body — can be educated. Their sensitivity can attain an almost miraculous acuteness. A noble nature is distinguished by the degree of refinement of its cells. Therefore, evolution is in principle possible for all; the door is wide open. But to make this leap requires persistent, conscious and creative effort, without which the refinement of the cells stops. In general it stops when the formation of the individual is achieved. Life then begins to exploit this formation, leading all too often to a sort of mental sclerosis, a 'hardening' of the brain, which makes man lose more and more of his capacity for adaptation and that—the strongest reason for acuity — in the domain of the unknown.

Without mentioning other causes, to which we have already referred, and to which we shall return later, the ideas and facts exposed in this passage explain why esoteric studies are the birthright only of the minority who are preoccupied by things of the spirit and are capable, like the knights of the Grail,[10] of *conquering knowledge*.[11]

(7)

W e have constated that, at root, the *Ray of Creation* and the *System of Cosmoses* are one and the same. Immediately after (this beginning), differences begin. The relationship between the steps[12] in the first and that between those in the second are different. In the *Ray of Creation*, these relationships vary, following the variations in the gamut;[13] in the *System of Cosmoses*, they are constant.

The relationships between neighbouring cosmoses are the same as those between an infinitesimal quantity and an infinitely large one. Because of the *Law of Seven*, this relationship never attains its limit, that is, *Zero* to *Infinity*, which would necessarily result in the rupture of the chain, and the breakdown of the system.[14]

Let us now try to understand the meaning of the names attributed to the different echelons of the *System of Cosmoses*.

We have already talked about the *Protocosmos*, and about the Absolute. The next two degrees, the *Aghiocosmos* and the *Megalocosmos*, are attached respectively to the notes SI and LA of the *Great Octave*, meaning, to All the Worlds, and the Milky Way of the *Ray of Creation*. These two steps[12] represent the psychological and physiological life of the *Macrocosmos*, the Great Universe, viewed as a living Being. As we are, we certainly cannot conceive a notion of this, or picture exactly to ourselves what we have just said. This kind of knowledge[15] and comprehension cannot

---

10. The *Holy Grail* or 'Sangreal'; from *sang-real* = *sang royal* (Fr. 'sang' – blood) the cup from which Jesus drank at the last Supper when he said: '*This is my blood, the blood of the Covenant which is poured out for many for the remission of Sins*' (Matthew xxvi: 28; Mark xiv: 24). The legend says that Joseph of Arimathea kept that cup and later took it to Brittany. (Ed. Or to Britain, according to British legend.)

11. Fr. 'savoir'.

12. Fr. 'échelons'.

13. Fr. 'gamme'.

14. Cf. P. D. Ouspensky, *Fragments*, p. 206 [p. 292], where one finds this notion.

15. Fr. 'connaissance'.

come except after esoteric evolution, so for the moment they have only theoretical value. At our level[16] of *being*, the practical significance of the system begins only with the *Deuterocosmos*.

But why *Deuterocosmos*, that is, second cosmos, when it is in fact the fourth stage[17] of the system? The answer to this question could be given by the reader himself. It is because, (cf. Chapter XI, p. 97) between the Absolute I and the Absolute II, the Sun, there is no intermediary of a substantially different nature. At the level of the note SI of the *Great Octave*, which corresponds to the *Aghiocosmos*, we find the nebulae. These emit immense energies, from which the galaxies of sun-stars are born by a process of condensation of atoms. Thus, while the Absolute I, DO of the *Great Octave*, corresponds to the *Protocosmos*, the Absolute II, DO of the cosmic *lateral octave*, comes second and is analogous to the first. For the moment let us leave the *Mesocosmos* to one side as a question to come back to much later. We shall only mention, in passing, that the life of this degree of the System is sometimes represented in the Tradition by the image of the *inferior Heaven*, ruled by the *Princes of the Air* or pneumatic Archons. We have mentioned this to locate the *Mesocosmos* in relation to the FA of the *Great Octave*, and to the note SI of the *lateral octave*.

Let us now begin investigating the problem of the *Tritocosmos* and the *Tessaracosmos*. We shall start with the latter. The Tradition gives no indication on the subject of the *Tessaracosmos*, and the Doctrine even less. We meet no more than a few allusions in the texts concerning this problem, which the progress of positive science and technology has put as the order of the day.

If the *Tritocosmos* is life on Earth — and the life of the Earth, in as much as it is a living Being — the notion of the *Tessaracosmos* is related in an analogous way to our satellite. This means that the Moon, from the point of view of the *System of Cosmoses*, is only a *fœtus*, approaching the end of the period of *pregnancy*: *the Tessaracosmos has not yet been born*. It must absorb the energies and elements made necessary by its incomplete growth. In fact, a massive supply of these elements is becoming accessible to it from the progress of technology, with the accelerated multiplication and new organization of human society, the growth of livestock breeding, and the rationalization of agriculture. These elements promise a rapid increase in growth in the next century. And like the fœtus in the mother's womb, the *Tessaracosmos* exercises an enormous influence on the *Tritocosmos*, and so on man, who is an integral part of organic life on earth and so contributes to the growth of the Moon, the cosmic fœtus.

This is all that can be said for now about the *Tessaracosmos*.

---

16. Fr. 'niveau'.
17. Fr. 'degré'.

110

Let us return to the *Tritocosmos*. It carries the name of the third, although the *Mesocosmos* comes between it and the *Deuterocosmos*, the second cosmos; but the same reasons which made us consider the *Deuterocosmos* as second are still valid, although there exist, between it and the *Protocosmos*, two other cosmoses.

The *Tritocosmos* is the Earth viewed as a living being. Within the limited measure of our possibilities of perception, the *Tritocosmos* is organic life on Earth. Let us try to determine its position in relation to the two neighbouring cosmoses. Let us consider the *Deuterocosmos* — the Sun, with the ensemble of its system — as a unity. We can easily constate that in effect the relation between these two cosmoses is comparable to that between an infinitely large quantity and an infinitesimal quantity — if only from the astrophysical aspect. To put it a different way, the *Deuterocosmos* is the next higher cosmos to the *Tritocosmos*.

Which then is the next cosmos below the *Tritocosmos*?

This can only be the organism which, although of infinitesimal size relative to the ensemble, is yet the most representative of organic life on Earth. Since the latter is assimilated to the *Tritocosmos*, man is undoubtedly its most representative organism.

Man is thus the *Microcosmos*, conceived—like every other cosmos—in the image and likeness of God.

One curious thing should be noted here: it is easy for us to represent the *Deuterocosmos* to ourselves as Christ in his cosmic aspect, or even have an individualized solar representation in the traditional anthropomorphic image, which probably corresponds to the objective reality. But it is difficult for us to represent the *Tritocosmos* — or even the *Mesocosmos* — in the same anthropomorphic form. Yet concerning the latter, in speaking of the *Celestial Hierarchy* or of the *Princes of the Air*, the Tradition has always turned to images of this kind, sometimes adding zoomorphic figures to them.

(8)

What is the place of the *Microcosmos*, conceived in this way, in the scale of the *System of Cosmoses*? It is given in figure 43 overleaf.

We must not continue to think that the *Microcosmos* is the final level[18] of organic life on Earth. We know at least that the physiological life of man rests upon that of the micro-organic world or worlds, starting with the transmitters of life, carriers of the principles of species, the spermatozoa and ova. Then there is a whole scale[19] of cells, large and small; protozoa,

---

18. Fr. 'échelon'.
19. Fr. 'échelle'.

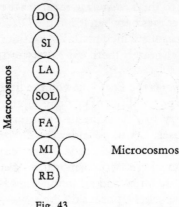

Fig. 43

bacteria, and viruses, which shape this world for us, but which are invisible without the help of instruments. Returning to the principle of grouping cosmoses in threes, we can conclude from the preceding that the life of man, as *Microcosmos*, is bound on one hand by organic life on Earth — the *Tritocosmos* — of which it represents an infinitesimal part and, on the other hand, by the life of the world of micro-organisms which evolve within him, and of which each unit is equally infinitesimal in relation to him. The following figure displays these relations:

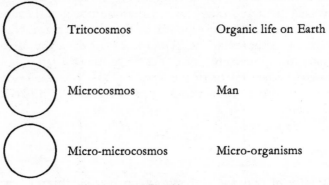

Fig. 44

This figure will help us understand the cosmic *lateral octave* which, viewed in terms of the active aspect, is that of the *Deuterocosmos* (Fig. 45).

We are thus led to the constatation that if, on the one hand, the development of the Universe has not yet been completed along our *Ray of Creation* — since the *Tessaracosmos* has not yet been born — then on the other hand, and at the other extremity of the gamut,[20] the evolution of man as an

---

20. Fr. 'gamme'.

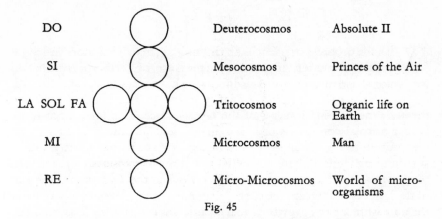

DO	Deuterocosmos	Absolute II
SI	Mesocosmos	Princes of the Air
LA SOL FA	Tritocosmos	Organic life on Earth
MI	Microcosmos	Man
RE	Micro-Microcosmos	World of micro-organisms

Fig. 45

individual is also almost at a standstill, marking time at the level of the three lower centres, that is to say, at the level of these three dissociated forces in *exterior* man. It is necessary for him to realize their unity, and this is the practical aim of esoteric study and work. The tasks to be carried out to achieve development of the *Macrocosmos* and *Microcosmos* are shown in the following figure:

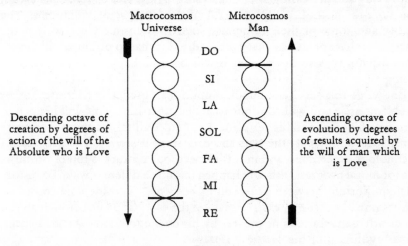

Macrocosmos
Universe

Microcosmos
Man

Descending octave of creation by degrees of action of the will of the Absolute who is Love

DO
SI
LA
SOL
FA
MI
RE

Ascending octave of evolution by degrees of results acquired by the will of man which is Love

Fig. 46

The ideas and the facts explained in this chapter allow the reader to perceive the role assigned to man in the ensemble of the *System of Cosmoses*, and the responsibility which this places upon him.

With the progress of science and technology, man takes more and more control of matter and, to a certain measure, of Earth's organic life on the biological plane. This organic life, as we have seen, serves as a *station of transmission* for the life giving energy going to Earth and the Moon, through the FA–MI interval of the *Great Octave*. This task is crushing. Under normal conditions of peace, insufficient quantities of energy are transmitted to the Moon as a result of the work of human society and its surrounding fauna and flora. This necessitates interventions on the part of the *Deuterocosmos*, which provoke convulsions in the *Tritocosmos*. The aim of the latter is to increase the energy expended at this level, so as to ensure the nourishment and growth of that cosmic fœtus that is the *Tessaracosmos*. This is, for example, the cosmic origin of wars and revolutions, of epidemics, and of all the other large-scale catastrophes that plague humanity. It was remarked, a long time ago, that a massive appearance of sunspots results in magnetic storms on earth, and in a psychological state which leads to conflict on the social, international and racial planes.

The more mankind multiplies in number, and the more man succeeds in improving and increasing livestock, enlarging the area of arable lands etc., the more the notes LA, SOL and FA of the *lateral octave* will increase the purity and force of their resonance following cosmic laws, so that the particular share of energy that every individual has to produce will diminish in quantity, and life on Earth will become happier and more easy-going.

But while this servitude imposed upon man gradually decreases, other problems arise and will continue to arise before him. This will happen to him on a different and higher plane, but before all this happens, humanity must successfully pass the tests and ordeals of maturity. The progress of technology accelerates, and in this respect, our century is full of promise. As for moral progress, this will happen in quite a different way. To restore the equilibrium between *Science* and *Conscience*,[21] considerable conscious efforts must be made by *exterior* man on the esoteric plane before man can efficiently contribute as he must — by his own evolution — to the harmonious evolution of the *System of Cosmoses*.

---

21. Fr. 'Conscience'.

CHAPTER XIII

(1)

We will remember that Time is the second great principle in the Creation and Manifestation of the Universe. The Universe — with all that it contains — exists in Time as in Space. It is ruled by the two fundamental laws, the *Law of Three* and the *Law of Seven*, whose purpose is to enclose the destructive action of Time within large and small cycles, and so allow creation to endure.

Our notion of time is inseparable from that of movement. To put it another way, we conceptualize[1] time in terms of movement, which in its turn is subject to the *Law of Seven*. Let us now try to penetrate the true nature of Time, so far as this is possible for us. The fact that we — with all our conceptions — are immersed in Time, makes this invest-igation difficult, and obviously limits its scope.

The study of Time brings us up against the *principle of Relativity*. This principle embraces all the many manifestations of the phenomenon of Time and makes them appear like a Magic Lantern show of fleeting forms in continual fluctuation. All that exists exists in Time, until the day when the *Seventh Trumpet* will sound to announce that the work undertaken by the Absolute has been achieved. Then the Kingdom of the World will become that of God and of His Christ, the Alpha and Omega of manife-station. In the vision of St John on the isle of Patmos, the angel swore that *there would be Time no longer*.[2]

(2)

In studying Time, we must never lose sight of the subjectivity of our senses. We cannot reach the *objective* except through the medium of the *subjective*. This is the underlying reason for esoteric studies: they allow the *exterior* man to give *objective validity* to his subjective mentality. He can achieve this by a technique analogous to one we apply to precision instru-ments: before putting them to work, we determine the *reading error* of each. By taking the 'subjectivity' of instruments into account in this way, we obtain correct readings from them, in spite of their flaws. To observe the phenomena of our internal world and those of the external world with precision, we must have recognized and determined the *reading error* of our

---

1. Fr. 'concevons'.
2. Revelations x: 6; xi: 15.

115

mental instrument for observation, one of the main tools[3] of the Personality. All esoteric teaching is oriented towards this goal, which is reached with the second Birth—when man attains a new form of consciousness and existence which is quite different, objective—and which *exterior* man can only represent to himself in a vague and obscure way.

As long as our nature remains subjective and therefore relative, it is only indirectly, with help of the *principle of Relativity*, that we can study Time.

(3)

Our perception of time varies. This is true in two ways: it varies from one person to another and, for each person, it varies with his physical or mental condition. The influence of age, health and emotional state are well enough known. Beside these general examples, there exist particular cases where the disappearance of time is complete: for example, during dreamless sleep, a brief loss of consciousness, or under general anaesthesia. The loss of the notion of time in such cases is due to physiological causes. But time can also be made to disappear by voluntary, conscious effort, especially an effort of *concentration*. By practising the latter assiduously, we observe this phenomenon from the very first exercises. As we intensify our concentration more and more, we perceive time less and less. If, by methodical and sustained effort, we manage to eliminate everything from our field of observation apart from the physical or moral object on which we concentrate, and if, in addition, we are able to hold this fixed attention on a single point — which gives birth to contemplation — time entirely[4] disappears. Conversely, the more man's attention is dispersed, the more time drags for him.

This phenomenon is objective in itself. It is a law. Its reason for being— as well as the mechanism by which it works—will be explained later, in the *Doctrine of the Present*.

It is interesting to point out another phenomenon: our ability to modify the rate of our own perception of time. This happens many times every day. We pay no attention to it, because this phenomenon occurs mechanically on a small scale. But it can also be produced voluntarily on a much larger scale.

A tennis champion told us that when he retrieved a particularly difficult ball during a match, he suddenly saw it coming towards him in slow motion. So slowly that he had unlimited time to judge the situation, take a correct decision, and finally return the ball by a masterly shot which aroused the admiration of the experts.

---

3. Fr. 'agents'.
4. Fr. 'intégralement'.

Cases in which time is *dilated* are the results of a considerable acceleration in the vibrations of centres, particularly the motor centre, which governs our perception of phenomena both in the exterior world and the interior world.

In general, the more the individual's rate of perception increases, the more an observed movement will appear to him in slow motion. Conversely, the weaker the perception, the faster the movement or flow of time will appear to him.

(4)

S ubjectively, we can distinguish four categories of movement by their relation to the rate of perception:

— Movements of such a low speed that the moving object appears to be immobile. Examples: general phenomena of growth; the movement of the hour and minute hands of a watch;

— Movements whose speed is perceptible, but where our perception of the form of the moving object remains unchanged—the great majority of movements in everyday life. Examples: walking, dancing, horse-drawn vehicles, cars, planes, ships, the second hands in watches, etc.;

— Movements faster still, so that our perception of the moving object is deformed in such a way that we can only grasp the trail of its movement. Examples: rapid gestures, especially if repeated; vibratory movements such as the movement of the branches of a tuning fork, etc.;

— Movements so fast that the object in movement 'vanishes'. Examples: The trajectory of a bullet, etc.

These categories are subjective, in the sense that an identical speed for a given movement will be perceived differently by different people—especially if this movement approaches the limit between different categories. But for any given person, these categories are objective in relation to his own rate of perception. This is important to note. By modifying our perception of movements, we can judge the results of attempts to control the motor centre and the motor sectors of the two other centres.

Acquisition of the ability to voluntarily modify the speed of perception in both directions plays an important role in esoteric evolution, since it applies to all movements. As all mental activity is essentially movement, it is possible, with sufficient training applied to thought, firstly, to encompass more easily an ensemble of ideas which would otherwise escape us, and secondly, to penetrate their finest details with great acuity. At the same time, this faculty considerably increases our capacity for work. Applied to the feelings,[5] this training allows us to directly perceive the latent aspirations of great collectivities — nations, or even groups of nations — and to

---

5. Fr. 'sentiments'.

give them form.[6] On the individual plane, it opens up unsuspected depths of emotional life.

The great leaders of humanity whose achievements gave new directions to the history of peoples, such as Alexander the Great, Augustus, and Peter the Great, possessed this faculty in highly developed form. This explains the secret of their extraordinary ability to use time, something that otherwise remains inexplicable.

Related to these considerations, we must mention one of the aphorisms of the Tradition, which says: '*Punctuality saves time.*'[7]

(5)

Taking the *principle of Relativity* into account, let us try now to determine some *units of time*. We shall see that these are natural but that their value — in essence absolute — is measured differently when applied to different steps[8] of the Cosmos.

Breath characterizes organic life. Is it not said that man was formed of the dust of the earth: '*God breathed into his nostrils the breath of life so that he became a living soul.*'[9] Did not King David raise his voice to cry: '*Let all that breathes praise the Eternal.*'[10]

If, as we have just said, respiration is the essential characteristic of organic life, the *primum mobile* which communicates movement to the ensemble of organs, and regularizes their working, it would be logical to take the period of respiration of the species as the base unit of time.

Organic life on Earth is subordinate to that of the human species,[11] and follows its evolution. With the accelerated march of progress, man takes more and more control over the evolution of the animal and vegetable world. He transforms the soil, alters the course of water, explores and exploits the earth's interior, and disintegrates atoms. We can predict that in the quite near future the intensification and rationalization of organic life will reach their limits. Without being conscious of it, man therefore contributes effectively to the development of our *Ray of Creation*, and so to the evolution of our planet and its satellite.

Looked at in another way, man contains within himself all the elements of Nature. It is therefore normal to take the duration of an adult man's

6. Fr. 'les incarner'.
7. Fr. 'la ponctualité est la réserve du temps'.
8. Fr. 'échelons'.
9. Genesis ii: 7; vii: 22; Acts xvii: 25.
10. Psalms cl: 6
11. cf. Genesis i: *passim*.

respiration as the base unit of time for the *Tritocosmos*, which is organic life on Earth.

We know that for an adult man the duration of each respiration is about 3 seconds. This is the first base-unit of Time.

A second unit for all organic life is a whole day. For man and for animal life, one whole day includes the cycle of a waking period followed by sleep; activity alternated with rest. Lastly, the greatest natural unit of time for man is the length of his life. We generally consider this to be eighty years.

Comparing these three units together, we will notice between them a ratio of approximately 1 to 30,000. In fact, each 24 hours contains 28,800 breaths of 3 seconds, while 80 years contain 29,200 days in all. If we now divide the 3 seconds, the duration of a breath, by the same coefficient of 30,000, we will get one ten thousandth of a second. This is the duration of lightning, which is our briefest visual impression.

On the other hand, if the duration of each breath for man is 3 seconds, that of Nature — specifically, the vegetable world — is much slower. The inhalation-exhalation cycle for plants takes 24 hours; inhalation takes place by day, and exhalation by night. As a member of organic life on Earth, man also participates in the respiratory rhythm of nature, whose cycle, as just mentioned, equals 24 hours. During sleep, man's breathing actually changes in its rhythm, as well as in its chemical content.

From the above remarks, we can conclude that the coefficient of 30,000 remains constant in the scale[12] of the units of time for the *Microcosmos*, as well as in the relationship between its respiratory cycle and that of the next higher cosmos, organic life on Earth. These considerations allow us to establish the following table:

	MAN	ORGANIC LIFE ON EARTH
Impression...	0.0001 second	—
Respiratory cycle	3 seconds	24 hours
Waking and sleeping time	24 hours	?
Normal duration of life............................	80 years	?

By analogy it would be tempting to apply the same coefficient of 30,000 to organic life as an ensemble. This, however, would be an error. We will quickly see why. Organic life on our planet would then be limited to 80 x 30,000 = 2,400,000 years, which is obviously insufficient.

---

12. Fr. 'échelle'.

Anthropology, using modern methods of determining the age of
prehistoric human and animal skeletons, has established a table of
periodicity in accordance with the evolution of the human species since its
separation from higher animal species. This data is only approximate, but
shows the orders of magnitude involved.

In order to better understand the basic role of man and his evolution in
the ensemble of the general evolution of organic life, and from this, to
comprehend the importance of his mission in the evolution of our *Ray of
Creation*, including the *Tessaracosmos* — it is instructive to take a quick
glance at the results obtained by anthropology using the methods of
positive science alone:[13]

	GEOLOGICAL PERIODS	PROBABLE DATES (years before our time)	STAGES OF DEVELOPMENT OF PHYSICAL TYPES OF MAN AND HIS ANCESTORS	ARCHEO-LOGICAL ERAS	EVOLUTIONARY STAGES OF PRIMITIVE HUMAN SOCIETY
QUATERNARY PERIOD (anthropogenic) — PLEISTOCENE	Holocene or contemporary era	14,000 years	Physical type of modern man *Homo sapiens recens*	Iron Age Bronze age Neolithic	Tribal organisation
	Most recent Ice Age	40,000 years	Physical type of modern man *Homo sapiens fossilis*	Late Paleolithic	Primitive commune, matriarchal tribe
	Middle Ice Age	100,000 years	Neanderthal Man	Early Paleolithic	Primitive horde
	Early Ice Age	800,000 years	Heidelberg Man Atlanthropus Sinanthropus Pithecanthropus		
TERTIARY PERIOD	Pliocene Miocene Oligocene Eocene	60,000,000 years	Australopithecus Ramapithecus Briopithecus	—	—

The antiquity of man, as judged by this table, should not surprise us. In
fact, some additional data allows us to form a general idea of the slowness
of the evolution of the human species:

---

13. *Earliest stages in the development of primitive man.* Chronological table after P. I. Boriskovsky,
The Earliest Past of humanity, Moscow, Editions of the Academy of Sciences, 1957, p. 212
(translated from the Russian).

1. The maximum volume of the brain of anthropoid apes is never greater than.. 600–800

2. That of *pithecanthropus* (height 165–170 cm)................... 850–950
   This kind of man already used rudimentary words, and walked upright.

3. Among *sinanthropus*, the first true human type, the brains of women had a capacity of 1050
   that of the men was.. 1100–1200
   The use of the right arm in preference to the left arm — the indicator that distinguishes man — is first clearly observed in *sinanthropus*, although among *pithecanthropus* it is barely perceptible. This dominance of the right arm is accompanied by a slight asymmetry of the brain.
   Sinanthropus made use of words. One sees the marks of this in relief in traces on the cranium of the posterior-inferior part of the lower frontal gyrus...

4. The volume of the skull of modern man varies between 1400–1500

It is as a function of his capacity for work, and because he has the ability to emit an extensive gamut[14] of sounds — allowing him to elaborate language — that primitive man has entered the long path[15] of material progress (*op. cit.*)

(7)

We can see clearly from the above that — at least in the present state of science — we would not, as some authors have suggested,[16] be able to apply the same coefficient of 30,000 to comparable units of time in neighbouring cosmoses. On the other hand, the data given in the preceding tables lead us to observe the following: This same coefficient of 30,000 expresses the relation between man's respiration and that of organic life: it is thus logical to apply it to the scale[17] of man's evolution, and not to that of the cosmos. If the table of units of time established above applies to *exterior* man — including man 4 — it would no longer be the same for men who have attained higher levels of consciousness, *interior* men 5, 6 and 7. Based on this principle, we would arrange the *units of time* as shown in the following table of the different stages of man's esoteric evolution. We should note that the first column is assigned to men 1, 2, 3 and 4, the latter still representing *exterior* man, but equilibrated.

---

14. Fr. 'gamme'.
15. Fr. 'chemin'.
16. Cf. P. D. Ouspensky, *Fragments*, pp. 329 ff [pp. 459 ff].
17. Fr. 'échelle'.

We should remember that types 1, 2, 3 and 4 of terrestrial man are those whose physical bodies are fully developed. With the integral development of the Personality, and the second Birth which follows — man acquires an astral body. Having become man 5, he not only belongs to the *Tritocosmos*, but at the same time to the *Mesocosmos*, which corresponds to the note FA of the *Great Octave*. We say of him that he is now endowed with *planetary life*. Having become man 6, with the mental body developed and born, he will also participate in the life of the *Deuterocosmos*. Having consolidated the results obtained there, he will become man 7. With that, he will come to the end of the evolution possible for man living on earth. Endowed with the body of grace, (or mental body), he will be admitted to that *Superior Brotherhood* about which the apostle St Paul said that in it the Son will be: *'First among many brethren'*.[18]

Here is a tabulated summary:

STAGES OF EVOLUTION ➤ UNITS OF TIME ↓	MAN 1, 2, 3 AND 4 PHYSICAL BODY	MAN 5 ASTRAL BODY	MAN 6 AND 7 MENTAL BODY CONSOLIDATED BY THE BODY OF GRACE
Impression	0.0001 second	3 seconds	24 hours
Respiration.............	3 seconds	24 hours	80 years
Complete day	24 hours	80 years	2,400,000 years
Life......................	80 years	2,400,000 years	72,000 million years

(8)

The *principle of Relativity* was known from the earliest times. The apostle Paul said: *'One day before the Lord is as a thousand years'*.[19] In the prayer of Moses we read: *'For in Thy sight a thousand years are like yesterday... like a watch in the night'*.[20] With the Gnostics we find a similar indication, drawn, as it seems, from the same source: *'A day of light is a thousand years of the world'*.[21]

---

18. Romans viii: 29.
19. II Peter iii: 8.
20. Psalm lxxxix: 4.
21. Pistis Sophia.

We do not know exactly what is meant in these texts by the words 'day', 'watch in the night', and 'day of light'. However we can see a clearly established principle. It is only by research into ancient sources that it would be possible to make all the interpretations fit harmoniously together.[22]

(9)

Here are the indications — necessarily summarized — that we can draw from a quick examination of the table of equivalence of Time.

Man 5, having reached the second Birth, and so endowed with an astral body, forms part of the *Mesocosmos* while still living on earth.

This would give him the ability to contemplate the next higher cosmos, which is the *Deuterocosmos*, the cosmos of the Son. This is why we find, in a hymn of the Easter cycle, the following exclamation which would otherwise seem bizarre: '*I see Your palace Lord.*'

A *planetary life* of more than two million years is certainly a rich reward for the work demanded from its students by esoteric science. Without talking of *solar life*, the prerogative of men 6 and 7, that of man 5 already looks — to the relative and limited consciousness of our Personality — like the Salvation and the everlasting Life which are the objects of prayer in the Christian liturgy. But because each cosmos is, in itself, three-dimensional and analogous to the others, perception of time in the various cosmoses is also analogous. This is because time itself is different in different cosmoses. It follows from the above that if the life of the physical body is normally limited to 80 terrestrial years, that of the astral body — in its turn — is found to be limited to 80 astral years or years of the *Mesocosmos*, and so on. It is by climbing the scale of cosmoses — in a life limited, except in exceptional circumstances, to the 80 years proper to his level[23] of Relativity — that human *Individuality* will reach the threshold of the *Protocosmos*, to be greeted there as the prodigal son in the bosom of the Absolute I.

---

22. The many trials made to establish such an equivalence with Hindu sources, though yielding much closer results, have failed to establish perfect agreement between the two traditions. Hindu sources use units of the same order such as 'Brahma's breath', or 'day and night of Brahma'. They arrived at the mahamanvantara — the great manifestation — 3.10^{14} years, while if we were to add one more column on the right to the preceding table we would reach — as far as the duration of manifestation is concerned — otherwise called eternity, 2.10^{15} terrestrial years (cf. Ch. X, p. 85). These numbers should be considered with great reservation, as the least error at the start, multiplied in these proportions, will *in fine* result in enormous differences.

23. Fr. 'échelon'.

We have established the characteristics of time for the *Microcosmos*, domain of the physical body, for the *Mesocosmos*, domain of the subtle body, and for the *Deuterocosmos*, domain of the mental body consolidated by the body of grace. That which is beyond the *Deuterocosmos* is closed to man as long as he retains[24] his physical body. This is equivalent to saying that the column of the *Deuterocosmos* in the previous table forms the upper limit of temporal relativity for terrestrial man. But in order that this table be complete, we must add another column, in this case to the left of that of the *Microcosmos*. It would be allocated to the *Micro-microcosmos*, that is, to the world of microscopic organisms, the basis and foundation of the human body. By applying the same coefficient of 30,000, but in the reverse direction, we obtain 24 hours for the life of an ordinary cell of the human body, and 3 seconds for its entire day. To be correct, a complete analysis of the equivalence between the *Microcosmos* of man and the *Micro-microcosmos* would necessitate a study of man himself as composed of an ensemble of seven cosmoses. For the moment, it will be sufficient to remind ourselves that, according to the *principle of Relativity*, the life of the *Micro-Microcosmos*, although corresponding to 24 hours of man's life, is felt and experienced by it as lasting 80 years, while its day, which lasts 3 seconds of man's life, looks to it exactly like man's day of 24 hours. This explains the otherwise as yet inexplicable phenomenon of the speed of the physiological reactions necessary to complete a whole series of complex operations in our organisms. The *principle of Relativity* makes us understand that, in fact, the cells have all the time they need to complete these operations. If, after taking a glass of alcohol, a man feels its effects almost immediately, it is because one or two seconds represent eight and sixteen hours for the *Micro-Microcosmos* — and this is ample time for it to complete all its operations, which will produce their effect in the various points of the organism.

(11)

To complete our brief study of Time, we must also touch on the question of *dimensions*.

We talk of a world having three dimensions, or of a three dimensional world. These terms, as we know, are conventional. In fact, if we do not give one single instant of existence in time to an object already in full possession of its three dimensions, it immediately disappears. Thus, all that exists in Space also exists in Time, so that the latter can

---

24. Fr. 'conserve'.

be said to form a fourth perpendicular; a fourth co-ordinate added to Descartes' co-ordinates.

Our perception of time makes this appear as a *line*. The characteristic notions of time: *Future* and *Past*, together with the point of the *Present*, where future events are mysteriously transformed into past events, are analogous to those which characterize the geometrical line, where everything is situated either *in front of* or *behind* a given point.

We shall return further on to an examination of this important problem, when we explain the *Doctrine of the Present*. For the moment, it will be sufficient to say that Time possesses not one but three dimensions, and that these dimensions are strictly analogous to those of Space. We have already made some allusions to these higher dimensions. We shall, for the moment, limit ourselves to saying that we know that the waking consciousness, that of the '*I*' of our Personality, is extremely relative and is able neither to grasp nor directly observe these two higher dimensions of Time, nor their effects. It confuses them, with the fourth dimension, in a single perception of the ensemble which is the *Line of Time*.

The fifth dimension represents the geometrical locus of all the possibilities of a given moment, of which only one is realized in Time — while all the others remain unrealized. It is a kind of *plane*. The *Line of Time* pierces it at the spot where the one possibility is located which — as a consequence — becomes realized. As for the sixth dimension, this is the Time of the Universe; due to its volume it not only contains the possible, but the accomplishment of all the possibilities of each moment — a complete cycle of all the *lines of Time*.

Lastly, there exists a seventh dimension which is a dot; a dot situated at the same time in both Space and Time.

Line of Time; Eternity and *All;* these are the terms of our current language which correspond to the fourth, fifth and sixth dimensions. The term *Zero* corresponds to the seventh and last dimension, which should perhaps be considered as the pre-initial dimension.

The notion of *Zero* plays a large role in esoteric philosophy. It is not the void.[25] It is the seed and the end, the *Alpha* and *Omega* of all that exists.

---

25. Fr. 'néant'.

CHAPTER XIV

(1)

After Space and Time, the third great principle of manifestation is Equilibrium.

The Universe is equilibrated as an ensemble, right down to its smallest parts. But one must not assume that this means a uniform, stable equilibrium at every scale[1] of Creation. It is only stable at the start. That is how the DO of the *Cosmic Octave* and the *Protocosmos* are but one. But the coincidence between the *Ray of Creation* and the *System of Cosmoses* ends there. This coincidence—or to be more exact, this unity—is assured by the nature of the Trinity itself, which is one and indivisible. Already in the note SI, which corresponds to the *Aghiocosmos*, the three consubstantial forces, which until then were a unity,[2] become manifest as separate[3] forces. It is these which will form the first triad and give birth to the first world which can be properly spoken of as begotten. This phenomenon is particularly worth noting for its simplicity — as well as for the depth of conception. Just beginning to become disunited, the first three forces converge towards the same point of application. However, because this creative convergence was preceded by disunion, the stability of the First Equilibrium — which was assured by the consubstantial nature of the Trinity—is broken. This is the cause of the divergence between the note SI of the *Great Octave* and the *Aghiocosmos*. This divergence becomes progressively accentuated along the *Ray of Creation* and the *System of Cosmoses*, down to their limits.

(2)

The notions and knowledge we have now acquired about the structure of the Universe will allow us to grasp the raison d'être and significance of the numerous groups of rectifying laws which multiply from 1 to 96 and act all along the *Ray of Creation* (Figure 30). Their object is to compensate fully for the progressive loss by the Equilibrium of its stability. The further we go from the *DO-Protocosmos*, the more this stability is compromised, and the more the effort to restore it gains in complexity while losing its intensity. In other words, unshakable stability of Equilibrium only belongs to the Universe in its ensemble. As for the six cosmoses which come

---

1. Fr. 'échelle'.
2. Fr. 'bloc'.
3. Fr. 'désunies'.

after the *Protocosmos* and which live in the bosom of that ensemble, they are in a permanent state of unstable equilibrium. The instability of this equilibrium is more and more accentuated in force as it recedes from the *Protocosmos*.

Due to its nature, the unstable equilibrium in which the world lives is broken at every moment, to be re-established immediately by the action of the corresponding groups of rectifying laws.

This is a mechanical aspect of the phenomenon. The essence does not lie in this, but in its biological significance. In fact, the use of unstable Equilibrium, with the mastery of the harmful[4] effects of Time provided by the *Law of Seven*, are the two basic conditions for the appearance of Life. The nature of these conditions remains the same all along the universal scale,[5] although life takes on a particular aspect at the level[6] of each cosmos.

If we were to imagine a perfect World based on a principle of perfect and stable equilibrium, it would be a petrified image—that of Death. Above all else, Life is movement; movement in the form of a flowing current. But a current is always the effect of a difference of potential. In turn, these different potentials appear in all domains as the effect of broken equilibrium.

Like a perfectly stable equilibrium, a straight line of Time would exclude the phenomenon of Life, as well as any idea or possibility of evolution. We must break the equilibrium to create movement. It is by introducing the *Principle of Imperfection* into the conception of Creation that Life was made to germinate on every step[7] of the *Macrocosmos*.

Man — the *Microcosmos* — was created in His image and likeness.[8] His higher centres, perfect, perfectly equilibrated and stable, form his own *Protocosmos* within him. But that equilibrium is found to be broken at the next step,[9] which consists of three mental[10] centres, their step analogous to that of the *Aghiocosmos*... and again thereafter.

(3)

To summarize, we can say that Life is the effect of a vibratory play at every step of the Universe, a play which in every case takes the form of a perturbation of equilibrium, followed by its restoration.

4. Fr: 'nocif'.
5. Fr: 'au long de l'échelle universelle'.
6. Fr. 'niveau'.
7. Fr. 'a tous les échelons'.
8. Genesis i: 26.
9. Fr. 'échelon'.
10. Fr. 'psychique'.

These perturbations are possible because all that exists in the Universe, though equilibrated, is in unstable equilibrium.

The *principle of Equilibrium* finds its practical application in compensating for perturbations. Yet rare are the cases where this compensatory action succeeds in re-establishing exactly the *ante actum* situation. In general this would not be desirable. As a result of the *principle of Imperfection*, all that exists is in a state of movement. Especially in organic life, the vibratory play—perturbation-compensation—often takes the form of an open cycle —a spiral. Here we can again constate the perfect logic of the system. We know, in fact, that a translational movement — such as evolution — is always difficult. The spiral slows the rate of progress, yet makes it easier. In case of a fall, it brakes the regression.[11]

(4)

Time, Space and Equilibrium, the three preliminary conditions of the Manifestation and Creation of the Universe, have given birth to three forces in the created Universe: *active, passive and neutralizing*, as already mentioned. The *principle of Equilibrium* takes dynamic form in the third category, as a reactive force with the task of compensating perturbations to restore the balance. Its manifestation always has the character of a unilateral reaction. Applied to the whole of the Universe, the *principle of Equilibrium* acts mechanically and is initiated automatically. As a result, all action, in every place, in every cosmos, is necessarily counterbalanced.

The above considerations allow us to understand and grasp the meaning of certain phenomena which remain unexplained by positive science. To begin with, the great problem of death. As life is born from perturbation, so death is necessary because of the *principle of Equilibrium*. In every case, without exception, the perturbation has to be compensated, and equilibrium re-established. It is by death that compensation is made. Birth, on all planes, is the work[12] of a revolutionary and perturbing act which is Love. Love itself is born before Creation, with the appearance — in the consciousness of the Absolute—of the idea of *You*, which necessarily arises from that of 'I'. This was the first perturbation of the stable pre-eternal equilibrium. That is why we have good reason, even if only instinctively, to contrast Death with Love, and not with Life. It is with equally good reason —against all evidence of the thinking mind—that the human heart feels that Love is the superior force which is able to overcome Death.

---

11. Fr. 'rétrogradation'.
12. Fr. 'le fait'.

To Overcome Death, that is the watchword of esoteric science. But let us clearly come to a common understanding of the true sense of this expression.

As they propagate themselves, the three forces act throughout[13] the Universe. They manifest in the following manner in the *System of Cosmoses* and the *Rays of Creation*: Love appears as the active perturbing force, death as the passive stabilizing force, and life as the neutralizing force, which measures out existence between limits defined by the first two. From the preceding, death is an indispensable condition of existence —and therefore of life—the fruit of which, in a later triad, is posterity. The question is whether the fight against death to win eternal life—humanity's highest hope, as preached by all religions — can in reality be undertaken with reasonable chances of success. The question is complex. To resolve it, one must examine it from many points of view. Religions treat this on the plane[14] of belief, and make an article of faith out of it. But now that we are on the threshold of a new Era, that of the Cycle of the Holy Spirit, such a position is no longer entirely satisfying to enlightened minds. They now want to grasp and understand something that yesterday was still considered as an article of *Belief*.

It is certainly easier to ask true believers to *trust* on this question, rather than attempt to explain something so difficult to explain. But esoteric science proposes an answer to the question.

The face of the world changes. The Cycle of the Son, as happened before with that of the Father, is coming to its end. With Christ, the Law received long ago by Moses, came to an end[15] and was replaced by the rule of Faith, Hope and Love.[16] At the present time, with the wars and revolutions of this century, and with the extraordinary progress of positive science, we have entered a period of transition whose purpose is to give us entry to the Cycle of the Holy Spirit. During this period, Faith will be progressively replaced by Knowledge, and Hope will end[17] in Accomplishment. This will be the final triumph of Love; '*For Love will never perish; even though prophecies will end, tongues will be no more, and knowledge will be abolished.*'[18]

---

13. Fr. 'dans l'ensemble de'.
14. Fr. 'plan'.
15. Romans x: 4.
16. I Corinthians xiii: 13.
17. Fr. 'l'Espérance sera abolie'.
18. I Corinthians xiii: 8, from the Slavonic text.

(5)

In the Tradition, we mean by victory over Death the victory of our perfected Personalities over Death. This is the meaning of Salvation, object of prayers and aim of the religious practices of Christianity. We have already quoted the words of St Paul: '*Behold, I tell you a mystery: we shall not all die but we shall all be changed.*'[19]

The underlying meaning of the word 'changed' in this sentence lies in the fact that all *exterior men*, as well as those who have reached the levels 5, 6 or 7, will sooner or later be called to leave their physical bodies. The difference is that the latter will do it as one abandons an old suit to take another, while the death of the physical body for men 1, 2 or 3 will result in the decomposition of their fœtal-Personalities. Death is an astral abortion. Salvation comes with the second Birth, when the entirely developed and born Personality is indissolubly joined to the real '*I*' to form an *Individuality*. Once born, this *Individuality* no longer depends on the physical body, in the same way that the child who has been born does not die, even if his birth has been at the cost of his mother's life. It is this to which the apostle alluded, saying, *we shall not all die*.

(6)

We have just seen that Time is different in different cosmoses. If we calculate a life in a higher cosmos in terms of terrestrial units, we obtain very high figures. Yet all this is relative. We have said that, if we admit the normal duration of life of terrestrial man to be about 80 terrestrial years, the life of an astral body, belonging to the *Mesocosmos*, corresponds to 2,400,000 of our years. That does not constitute, as we may believe, a true eternity; this figure only represents the same 80 years, but in astral years. In this way, once physical death is beaten, we will be faced with the problem of defeating astral Death, then mental Death, having at our disposition for the latter, once again, a life of about 80 mental years. It is only with the crystallization of the body of grace, in the bosom of the Absolute, that Death will be finally overcome. The being will then find himself in a state of primordial Being, in the bosom of the stable Equilibrium. That will not be provisional Salvation, but *final Salvation*.

This state of beatitude can no longer be characterized as life in accordance with the definition of life given previously. Life, as an act of voluntary imperfection, naturally ceases at the moment of return to the Absolute in the *Protocosmos*, where the *principle of Imperfection* is not admitted.

---

19. I Corinthians xv: 51.

Some people think that this state is one of total Non-Being, that is, Nothingness, absolute Zero. It is certain that it is not a life in Time as we know it, delimited by life and death. Such an existence, if we can still use this term, is located beyond Space and Time. As we are, we certainly cannot picture for ourselves a valid representation of such a state. But contrary to the frigid images — or those which appear to be so — that we often associate with *Nirvana*, the Orthodox Tradition calls upon the only notion known to human language which reflects the divine condition: Love. *God is Love*, says St John the Apostle.[20] He who achieves a triple victory over physical, astral and mental death, will be received in the bosom of the absolute-Love who is without beginning and consequently without end. This is the *Pleroma* of the Orthodox Tradition.

(7)

This absolute-Love is accessible to the human soul even here. However, neither man nor woman can reach it separately. It is only accessible to a couple, and on the condition of a conscious and total integration of both into a *single* Being by a synthesis of the real 'I' and 'You' who have had the strength to break the crust of their respective Personalities.[21] In practice, this can only happen when the two Personalities are already very advanced, and both rich with the experience that each has separately acquired in *exterior* life.

What is the meaning of that long path of regeneration which, starting from the fall of Adam, has as its final goal a perfection that touches on divinity? Orthodox Tradition gives no definite answer to this question. It simply indicates that the ways of God are unfathomable,[22] and that: '*All is in Him, by Him and for Him.*'[23] As for the description of the state of Beatitude which circulated in the early Churches, this was withdrawn by the Fathers of the First Council, lest it constitute a scandal because of its character, which seems to have been erotic. But we find this indication in the Doctrine: that human earthly love is nothing but the debris of celestial Love. We have already indicated this.

If it is certain that the state of Beatitude cannot be properly described in human language, yet the Tradition insists on the fact that in spite of its immense difficulties, it is possible to attain it. With this goal in mind, esoteric science has elaborated a complete science[24] of exercises.

---

20. I John iv: 8.
21. Matthew xi: 12; Luke xvi: 16.
22. Romans xi: 33.
23. Romans xi: 36.
24. Fr. 'technique'.

(8)

We have established that death is one of the manifestations of the *principle of Equilibrium*, which automatically reacts to the perturbing action of carnal love in the created world. The latter, although imperfect, then gives birth to life. Human love is imperfect because it is instinctive and impulsive. As long as man automatically follows his impulses, his love will serve only the cosmic goals of the ensemble. The pleasure he always gains from this is as much an equilibrating element as a reward. As it is, it will not serve his esoteric evolution in any way. Yet Love is the surest and most powerful means of achieving this evolution. This is because Love is the one objective element in our lives. That objectivity remains true in all Love's many aspects, and through all the variety of its manifestations.

Love can, in effect, serve man in his esoteric evolution. However, to achieve this aim, man must apply *conscious* efforts to this love, not allow himself be led on by impulses. In this way he will neutralize the perturbing action of Love on him, which will inhibit — and render powerless — the intervention of the *principle of Equilibrium*, with its lethal reaction. In this case, the contribution of energy which Love provides will not be spent immediately to serve general aims, but will remain in man's possession. It can then be used to accelerate the growth of his Personality and its progress towards the second Birth, the first tangible result of esoteric practices.

This is the theory of monastic work, and it essentially applies to the sexual centre. We strive to master its impulses by exercises. Without detailed examination of the advantages and inconveniences of this method we must say that, in the new Era, esoteric work is to come out of the crypts and the monasteries. From now on, it must instead be pursued inside life, in the field of everyday activity of human society. This task is certainly more difficult, for we are neither protected within life, as in a monastery, nor sheltered from the greatest part of 'A' influences. On the other hand, life offers more effective means, and leads to less fragile results; esoteric practice inside life also allows simple control of the sexual centre, permitting cultivation of the manifestations of love by means of the emotional and intellectual centres, making the creative spirit spring up in all its different forms. This higher order of culture will have as its aim to focus all creative efforts towards one and the same point of application, the integral development of the Personality: the second Birth; the crystallization of the astral body, and its junction with the real 'I' to form an *Individuality*.

This work, done by man and woman working together, can develop with extraordinary power and give rapid results... on condition that from

132

the esoteric point of view the two beings entirely[25] suit each other, and also on condition that they are a *perfect couple*, that is, that their combination[26] — with reservations concerning the peculiarities of their human type — reflects the relation between the absolute '*I*' and the '*You*' before the Creation of the Universe. This is the case of those beings known in esoteric science as *polar beings*.

We shall return further on to this important question, which becomes a real question with the beginning of the new Era. In centres of culture in the cycle of the Holy Spirit, the love-romance — a feature of the previous Cycle — will give place to the unique love-romance of polar beings, those who will be called upon to shape the society of tomorrow.

The *principle of Equilibrium*, by virtue of which all perturbations and all free movements — particularly in organic life, and especially in its human sector — demand and receive compensation, appears as a severe yet impartial guardian. With the *Law of Seven*, it assures the duration of all existence according to law. Human wisdom has been conscious of this fact from time immemorial. It is the principle of *Karma*, the Nemesis of the Greeks, the Archangel[27] Uriel of the Christian celestial hierarchy — according to the Tradition one of the seven *Spirits of God*, who — alone in the Universe — never change. He supervises the restoration of broken equilibrium at every degree of the cosmic scale,[28] including the *Micro-Microcosmos*.

Karmic action is initiated automatically. We should always remember this automatic response, and take it into account at least in our premeditated actions. This is not easy, for we are rarely conscious of the perturbations and effects that our acts produce. That is why karmic action so often surpasses the limits of the predictable. We must however repeat that *Karma* loses its threatening aspect for the *just;* it only brings them joy. This is because their acts never create perturbations that transgress general and local cosmic laws. *The just do not fall into error*, while ordinary men, even acting in good faith and believing they are acting correctly, do commit errors. They start with errors of conception,[29] which are the actual source of sin. Sin does not hold in itself any element of a so called mystic nature. In the sense that it is error, sin can be liquidated by adequate compensation. The Tradition points to the preceding statement when it says: '*There is no unforgivable sin except sin without repentance.*'[30] We can easily understand the true meaning of this maxim. Repentance is above all an act

---

25. Fr. 'intégralement'.
26. Fr. 'ensemble'.
27. Fr. 'Archistratège'.
28. Fr. 'échelle'.
29. See Appendix.
30. *Philokalia*, St Isaac the Syrian, 2nd/30th sermons.

of consciousness, resulting naturally in benevolent and effective compensation for the error that has been made. This is the theory. In practice it is not so simple; it requires the minutest study of each case. It is obviously easier to commit no sin, rather than finding them and making compensation afterwards. If repentance, in the exact sense attributed to that word here, does not come in time, the equilibrating karmic action automatically acts strongly. Once this has started, we are obliged to submit to it passively.

Once karmic action is launched automatically and acts mechanically, it compensates for each perturbation on its own plane. Compensation is made for each account individually, as in a ledger, and not between totals of good and bad results.

(9)

We shall now examine the influence that the *principle of Equilibrium* exerts over the *Law of Seven*. Because of this last law, the cyclic character which affects any prolonged movement gives birth to a rotation — either slow or rapid — which in either case goes only in one direction. This necessarily has a perturbing effect. Consequently, it will need compensation. This compensation will also take cyclic form, rotating in the opposite direction. Thus each gamut of work — that is, each descending gamut—will immediately give birth to another gamut which is its exact compensation but ascending; the product of the original work. If the work has developed well, the gamut of results will bring to the worker corresponding positive results, and *vice versa*.

We should know that each descending gamut of action, beginning with the cosmic *Great Octave*, will automatically give birth to another gamut — this one parallel to it, at the same scale,[31] but ascending—a gamut which is the result of the initial action. This is a general law, one of the effects of the *principle of Equilibrium*. In nature, these two kinds of gamut are so conceived that they help one another. Studies of the application of this law to phenomena—physical, chemical, or biological—present a wonderful and magnificent spectacle through which one can perceive the Intelligence that rules them. In certain cases this study also allows us to find answers to problems which — given our *linear* way of thinking — would otherwise appear insoluble. This is true, for example, of the question of the nutrition of the Universe in its ensemble.

The nutrition of plants, animals and human creatures is conceived according to various cyclic arrangements. Man and animals absorb oxygen and give out carbonic acid; plants absorb carbonic acid, and give out

---

31. Fr. 'échelle'.

oxygen. Man and animals eat plants; on the other hand, their excretions serve as food for the plants. In all these cases, and in many others less easily observed, we find ourselves in the presence of an action that combines ascending and descending gamuts, action whose ensemble is perfectly equilibrated. Nutrition, as we know, can be concisely described as the absorption of solar energy by a complex process of metabolism, which science does not yet fully know; parallel to this, the substance of these foods, after supplying the organism with the materials and energies it needs as it passes through the digestive tract, leaves a remnant which will feed the vegetable world. Its products will later return to the table in the form of food. Here, the ascending gamut of metabolic products is balanced by the descending gamut that transforms meals into excreta. We can find an infinity of other examples of the balanced interplay of gamuts in different domains and on different planes: physical, mental[32] or moral. Naturally, movements produced according to these balanced and compensated schematic plans do not provoke any karmic reaction.

If we now move on from the particular cases to the general case, and if we examine the problem of nutrition in the whole of the Universe, in so far as it is a living being, we would still be obliged to admit that it will not find food outside itself, because nothing exists outside it. The Tradition, however, insists on the fact that the great Universe, the *Macrocosmos*, is a living being,[33] as are all the other cosmoses of the *System*. Composed in actual fact of living elements, the whole ensemble can only be a living being. As a living being, it needs food. But since, as we said, the *Macrocosmos* cannot find food outside itself, this leads us to conclude that it finds it within itself. This is our first constatation. Thereafter we can say that, if the Universe in its ensemble remains in a perfect state of equilibrium, its nutrition too can only be conceived in the form of a cyclic system of coupled gamuts.

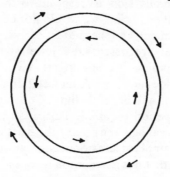

Fig. 47

32. Fr. 'psychique'.
33. E.g. Origen, *'Principles'*, *passim*.

We have already perceived how this mechanism functions in the form of a current and counter-current[34] of energies all along the *Ray of Creation*. We shall return to it in a more detailed manner in the second volume.

(10)

We must quickly examine another manifestation of the *principle of Equilibrium*. This concerns the organic relations between *form* and *content*. This problem is as vast as it is complicated; the outline of the present chapter does not allow for detailed analysis. But it would perhaps be useful to give an example which has been quoted many times since the beginning of this century. This concerns a law that governs relations between the form and content of political regimes.

This law can be easily discovered by reflecting on the subject, but unfortunately, the political leaders of any regime give the problem little thought, and that rather instinctively than by rigorous reasoning. The law is exact: with time, growing elements develop and, after reaching the peak of this development, they start to decline, degenerating and sliding towards total decay.

All political regimes, 'classical' or 'new', are found to be governed by this law. Circumstances change, especially political ones. They change in response to modifications that affect the life of human society, which can be said to progress in certain aspects while others regress. The *principle of Equilibrium* manifests itself on the interior political plane of States, to maintain a certain equivalence between the form of government and the political content of the existing system. These two factors must be equilibrated, yet in reality, they hardly ever are. For varying reasons, governments are generally slow to respond to the sequence of events. In the face of historical evolution, we would not be able to conserve both the form of the government, and the content of the regime, beyond certain limits. When these limits are passed, a revolution starts. The latter starts on new bases, and impels politics in a new direction which in principle is aimed at progress. But time does not stop. After a certain period, the revolutionary government in turn will be left behind. The more violent the revolution, the shorter the period required. This was the case for the French revolution in 1789. It was also the case of the Russian revolution in 1917.

England offers an example of an astonishing traditional stability. But one often loses from sight that it is a *stability in movement*, the only possible one in a Universe where existence and life are based on a perpetually broken unstable equilibrium. The British Government conserves its traditional form through the centuries because the statesmen of this country know

---

34. Fr. 'flux et reflux'.

how to modify its content with an extraordinary political suppleness—and in time.

The government of the emperor Nicholas II—obstinately and against all the evidence — persisted in its desire to preserve the imperial form and autocratic content of its rule. The result is well known.

(11)

Sometimes the disequilibrium between form and content can reach unmanageable proportions at a scale[35] larger than that of States. It is undeniable that the crisis in which humanity is struggling since the beginning of this century contains the greatest dangers. Apart from the direct cataclysm that the chain reaction of atomic explosion can provoke, there exists another danger of a totally different order, the accumulation of what we could call *karmic decay*. When such a case occurs, equilibrium is re-established either by a catastrophe such as the Flood or, if the weight of *Karma* is considerable, by intervention from the higher cosmoses. This was the underlying reason for the incarnation of Christ and His mission on earth, His torture and sacrifice. Quite obviously, the karmic danger which was accumulated just before His advent was real and great. The apostle John says that God sent His Son *'that the world should be saved by Him'*.[36] We must believe that the preaching of Christ, followed by His sacrifice, counterbalancing the excess of karmic decay at that moment, re-established the equilibrium of the planet and so saved the world, and the whole of humanity with it.

---

35. Fr. 'échelle'.
36. John iii: 17.

THIRD PART
THE WAY

CHAPTER XV

(1)

The *Way* is the ensemble of practices which, carried out properly according to the principles of esoteric science, will allow man to evolve. The earlier study of the fundamental factors concerning man and the Universe, the subject of the first two parts of this book, allowed us to acquire the minimum knowledge necessary to begin studying the *Way*.

Esoteric science starts beyond the area explored by positive science. Between these two branches of knowledge is a *void*, a zone of illusion, created intentionally to form an obstacle. This *void*, which can only be crossed at the cost of considerable effort or even of *superefforts*, operates selectively. The character and the quantity of effort necessary differs for each person, depending upon the nature and degree of deformation of the mind[1] of each *exterior* man; an individual factor. To cross this *void* requires theoretical study, accompanied by a planned program of practical work.

We can now begin to study the question of the *Way*. This can be done from many angles, but it is most convenient to reveal the philosophical and esoteric meaning of the *Way*, starting from considerations developed in chapter VIII. There, man was compared to a cell of organic life on Earth. Because he belongs to this organism, man is subject to the *General Law*, and it is only when he has escaped it that he is elevated to the *Law of Exception*.

We are not aware of how much we are bound by the action of the *General Law*.[2] Acting on us as it does on our cells, this law immobilizes us or constantly tends to bring us back to our place. Its strength leaves us little freedom of action outside the limits of its direction and scope. It acts in various ways. One can say that if man lives 'like everyone else', if he does not venture off the beaten track, he will never perceive the existence of this force, or rather this force will ignore him. But if his enterprises are out of the ordinary, no matter what field they are in, but especially in esotericism, this force begins to act, and stirs up all sorts of obstacles in order to bring him back to the point where — according to the *General Law* — he must reside. Even without knowing this force, we have an intuition of its existence and of the many forms which clothe it. The Holy Scriptures speak of it more than once, especially where esoteric work is concerned. On this subject Jesus says that: *'a man's enemies are those of his own house'*,[3] and more directly, that: *'a prophet is without honour only in his own country, among his*

---

1. Fr. 'esprit'.
2. cf. Chapter VIII.
3. Matthew x: 36.

parents and in his own home.'[4] Thus, if this conservative force, which is the servant of the *General Law*, does not succeed in 'calming' man by acting directly upon him, it tries to reach him indirectly through the people of his household, either through the feelings they invoke or the coolness and contempt they openly show him. The classical example of this indirect action is the seduction of Adam by Eve, his *alter ego*, after she herself had been seduced by the Serpent by means of the fruit of the *Tree of knowledge of Good and Evil*. This myth is full of significance. To start with, why the *Serpent, the most cunning beast of the field?*[5] The Serpent personifies Illusion, more exactly the power of illusion implanted in the human organism, and the strength at its disposal. We should note that this power, as well as bringing danger, has nett positive results, notably creative imagination.

The force of illusion itself can be mastered and directed *integrally* in a constructive direction; but this reversal of its effects cannot be obtained except at the price of work pursued, with tenacity, towards and on the esoteric *Way*. In *exterior* man, this power leads to negative consequences as a result of the series of illusions it generates.

In the Tradition, we call this force the *little serpent*. The reason for this name is that when we awaken it and direct it in a constructive direction, its action in the organism gives the impression of undulatory movement. This is the reason for the choice of the serpent as personification in the myth of the fall of Adam. The fruit of the *Tree of knowledge of Good and Evil* is knowledge accessible to the intellectual faculty: the pure or practical reason (*ratio*), which cannot transcend the limits of the zone of 'A' influences. In the end, when exhaustively analyzed, this is revealed to be illusory. It is in fact no more than a knowledge of the elements of the phenomenal world, that is, the 'A' elements, whose algebraic sum, in their ensemble, equals *zero*: the *revolving magic lantern show*.

The cunning *Serpent* approached Eve by hypnotizing her with the sparkling play of the *lantern*. Mistaking the unreal for the real, Eve drew Adam into her fall. Since then this seduction manœuvre, enriched by numberless variations, has become habitual in human relations.

It is by entering the esoteric *Way* that man can swim against the current to redeem this original sin; this error of our common ancestor, an error which we repeat every instant. As long as it is not mastered, the force of illusion keeps each one of us in his place, obliging him most often to mistake the false for the true. Submerged in unreality, instead of advancing, man marks time; one step forward and two steps backwards; two steps forward and one step backwards, and so on. The draining exhaustion which results leads to death.

---

4. Matthew xiii: 57; Mark vi: 4; Luke iv: 24; John iv: 44.
5. Genesis iii: 1–7.

In this factitious life, ruled by Illusion, yet strewn with 'B' influences, we must reaffirm our values almost every day if we are not to fall into another trap. We generally agree to recognize the existence of the danger of Illusion, but rather theoretically; most often, we see its action on those round about us, but not on ourselves. We continue to live day by day in the same old way, so that the power we know as the *Devil* still triumphs. Whatever name we give it, it remains ever-present. We live in an artificial, illusory world. It is interesting in this context to quote the words of a Buddhist monk. Asked: '*How do you describe the creation of the world?*', he answered: '*The world is created anew for each newborn person.*' This is exact. The power of illusion which chains us exerts its action individually on each one of us, as well as collectively. Each mind is falsified[6] in a way peculiar to it. What can be the outcome of such a situation? If we keep quietly to our place, human careers open to us ... just as long as we stay far away from the *void*. We may have a happy or unhappy life; a family life; a life of loves; we may make discoveries, travel, write. Then comes the end.

Our reasoning starts to become more realistic if our attention is concentrated on this end. Everything can happen to us in life; or nothing. Our aspirations can be fulfilled or unfulfilled, but there is a *sure end*, which is death. In our studies we must start from this fact.

The next question has been asked as long as mankind has existed: is Death absolutely inevitable? Is there no other alternative? Can we accept that we have been born, trained and educated purely and simply to be *annihilated?* Can our heart and head manage to accept this fate without revulsion?

The fact is that we do not think about it, or do so very rarely, to the great satisfaction of this force of illusion, known by the Tradition as the *Devil*. However, man today is more aware of the vanity of the things of this world, especially after the events of this century: world wars, revolutions, civil wars, cold wars, political and social tensions, the disintegration of empires and the lightning growth of population.[7] We shall return to all these events later, as their reason for being is cosmic in nature.

Faced with this spectacle, a feeling of the absurd arises within us. Instead of reassuring us, the headlong progress of technology inspires a fear and uncertainty which saps the previously unshakeable force of Illusion. We start to experience increasing interest in the problem of death, which only yesterday remained hidden behind the scenes of waking consciousness.

---

6. Fr. 'faussé'.
7. Fr. 'démographie'.

(2)

We have already quoted the text of St Paul's saying: '*I am telling you a mystery: we shall not all die but we shall all be changed.*'[8]

Let us comment on this again from a different angle.

What is meant by: '...we shall all be changed'?

Sooner or later, each one of us will abandon his physical body, and we shall all in fact be *changed*.

Then what is meant by: 'We shall not all die'? For *exterior* man, the destruction of the physical body, which serves as a womb for this astral fœtus which is the Personality, necessarily[9] brings on the decomposition of the latter. In the language of the Tradition we call the decomposition of the Personality, with that of the personal '*I*', the second Death. By the second Birth, when the astral body is born, with its fusion complete, and it is integrated with the Real '*I*' to form an *Individuality*, we attain to *planetary life* and so escape the second Death.[10] The latter will still occur, not forty days after the death of the physical body, but after 80 astral years, meaning 2,400,000 terrestrial years. For man 4, when he has crossed the threshold of the inner circle of esotericism, the death of the physical body will be equivalent to abandoning an outdated or tattered piece of clothing. He will take another if he needs it. This will no longer be a catastrophe. This is the meaning of St Paul's words.

This text sheds light on the initial data for the problem. According to the Apostle, it is the ensemble of the conditions to be fulfilled so as to reach that goal which is known in esoteric science as the *Way*. These are: the pursuit of certain studies; the observance of principles;[11] respecting certain rules, and carrying out practical work; all this must be done with the spirit of precision and discipline which prevails in the world of positive science. Even more than in the latter, one must exercise, develop and sharpen his critical spirit. This is necessary because precise limits do not always exist in our inner world. Though logic tends to formulate clear definitions on the intellectual plane, it remains no less true that the working of intelligence is controlled by Illusion, which distorts our judgment in many situations. On the emotional plane, the situation is even more muddled, as it is very difficult to orient ourselves and in a clear cut way — to differentiate — that which is born from ourselves from that which is the result of exterior impressions; in other words, it is difficult to know what is and what is not *me*. The easy differentiation between object and subject in the physical

---

8. I Corinthians xv: 51.

9. Fr. 'obligatoirement'.

10. Revelations ii: 11.

11. Fr. 'préceptes'.

world, already less easy in the intellectual world, is particularly difficult in the emotional world, but the emotional life is the primary object of esoteric work. That is why we attach so much importance in esoteric teaching to the development of a critical spirit directed towards ourselves, that is to say, towards the phenomena of our inner life.

(3)

As a cell of organic life on Earth, man plays a part in the development of the *Ray of Creation*. The vivification of the Moon, that cosmic fœtus, is one aspect of this development. This requires considerable quantities of energy, which is produced in particular by the human part of organic life. Illusion, which plays such an important role in the waking consciousness of man, was introduced into that state so that he would accept this aspect of the cosmic work, participating in it without rebellion.

If we become conscious of this situation and desire to escape it, we must conceive and create a screen which will protect us against this devouring influence of the Moon. We must meanwhile guard against falling into Illusion again by erecting a false screen; the result would be an aggravated waste of these forces instead of an economy of force. The quantity of force necessary to genuinely oppose the influence of the Moon is already considerable. The first imperative, then, is to stop wasting these forces, to turn off the taps which let the energy escape uselessly: sterile emotions, in particular negative emotions; fantasies from uncontrolled imagination; uncoordinated mental gymnastics, gossiping and chattering. We must thus act like a wise minister of finance and carefully economize our energies, yet without all the time sterilizing either our activity or our intelligence. On the contrary, we must store and as far as possible augment these forces to build up our reserves. These are the two main aspects of the first objective we have to attain.

(4)

In the pictorial language of the Tradition, the *void* of which we spoke at the beginning of this chapter is given the name either of *moat*[12] or *threshold*. Further on, we shall use the last name rather more, but here we shall use the first in relation to a symbolic fragment. Esoteric teaching has always presented its disciples with symbols; either diagrams or literary fragments in symbolic form. These fragments must be learnt by heart, then represented by an appropriate figure. The exercise is also practised starting from the diagram, in which case a literary fragment must be written.

12. Fr. 'fosse'.

(5)

Here is one of these fragments:

Lost in a forest full of wild beasts, moved by confused but deep feelings, a bewildered man searches for the way. Exhausted after running the gauntlet of a thousand dangers, he emerges at the edge.

Spread out before him is a view which fills him with admiration mixed with fear: a great castle of primitive beauty is on the other side of a large moat filled with clear and living water. Behind the castle a happy valley opens out, lit by the last rays of the sun. To the left, a dark reddish horizon warns of a coming storm.

Marvelling, and seized by a passionate desire to reach the castle, he forgets the dangers and fatigue to which he has been exposed.

— 'How do I get there?' He asks himself.

Suddenly he hears a Voice speaking to him from his inmost heart.

'The moat', it says, 'can only be crossed by swimming... the current is strong and the water icy.'

In spite of this, the man feels a surge of new strength mounting within him. Committed, he throws himself into the moat. The cold paralyses his breathing, but by an extreme effort of will he reaches the other side in a few strokes and jumps onto the first step of the stairs, where he gets a foothold. Three more immense granite steps tower above him. They lead to a large stage in the form of a semicircle, defended by two towers. Two closed doors give access to them.

A roaring sound comes to his ears. The man turns. At the place where he stood only instants before, a pack of wolves paw at the ground.

The day is coming to an end. In the dusk he can still distinguish the blazing eyes of the hungry beasts.

Again he hears the Voice telling him:

— 'All in all, the risk was not that great. If you had refused, you would have been torn to shreds by the wolves.'

Terrified by his escape from that danger, the man estimates the difficulties that will accompany his climb.

He had hardly started to climb the second step when a deluge of rain falls, making the stones slippery and obstructing his movement — yet he ends by getting a foothold. The storm passes and the rain diminishes. His face and clothes drip heavily onto the stone.

— 'Little does it matter,' says the Voice, 'you had already got wet crossing the moat'

The man regains his breath again and starts climbing. Night falls, and the crescent of the new moon appears pale and golden on his right, towards the setting sun.

— 'A good sign,' he hears within himself.

The man smiles. Now he clings to a tiny ledge, reaching for the third step. He reaches it, hands and legs stained with blood. No sooner had he stood up than a gust of glacial wind almost throws him off again. Clinging to the ground, he climbs up to the wall forming the fourth step, and finds shelter there.

— 'That is not all,' says the Voice. Do not waste time taking shelter. The step can split, and then the earth will swallow you up.'

His resistance to the storm, instead of exhausting him, redoubles his strength. Now he climbs the fourth step with little difficulty, although it is as high as the preceding ones.

Standing, he hears an alarm trumpet like thunder. Suddenly, a scorching wind strikes him in the face. He lifts his eyes. In the obscurity of the night, a shining figure stands to attention before him: It is the Guardian, clad in armour and shining helmet, arms outstretched, a blazing sword in his hand and pointed towards the man.

— 'Who are you, pilgrim?' he asks. 'To what end and in whose name have you passed these obstacles and climbed the steps of paradise?'

Overcome by a surge of ineffable joy, the man repeats in a loud voice the words he has just heard in the depth of his heart. He feels as if they are now his, and answers the Guardian with courage.

— 'I am the *Soul* in search of divine happiness; a particle aspiring to unite with the Creative Principle!'

— 'Your answer is correct', replies the Guardian.

The door to the tower on the right opens. The sword returns to its sheath. The Guardian takes the man by the hand and leads him across the threshold of the open door...

Dawn gilds the eastern sky. Precursor of the Sun, the morning Star shines above the happy Valley.

(6)

Here is another of these fragments, taken from classical literature: a passage from Turgenev.[13]

I see a great building, one enormous mass. In the front wall is a narrow arch with open doors; behind them, dark mists. In front of the high threshold there is a young girl... a pretty Russian girl.

A breeze comes from the dark and icy mists, a current of freezing air, bringing with it from the depths of the building the sound of a slow and muffled voice.

— 'You who aspire to cross this threshold, do you know what awaits you here?'

— 'I know,' answers the young girl.

— 'Cold, hunger, hate, mockery, scorn, injustice, prison, illness and even death?'

— 'I know it.'

— 'Do you expect to be shunned by everyone? Do you expect to be totally alone?'

— 'I am ready. I know it. I shall bear all the suffering and all the blows'.

— 'Even if they do not come from enemies, but from parents, from friends?'

— 'Yes... even from those...'

— 'Good. Do you accept the sacrifice?'

— 'Yes'.

— 'An anonymous sacrifice? You will perish and nobody... but nobody will even know whose memory to honour?'

— 'I have no use for recognition and pity. I have no use for a name.'

— 'Are you ready for crime?'

The young girl bowed her head.

— 'Even for crime.'

The voice which was questioning her did not continue right away. At last it started again:

---

13. I. S. Turgenev, *Poems en prose*, Editions Le Seuil. First complete edition published in the order of the original manuscript with notes, translated by Charles Salamon, Gap, Imprimerie Louis Jean, 1931. The poem was censored and forbidden in its time. (See bibliography)

— 'Do you know that one day you will believe no more in what you believe in now, and come to think that you have been a dupe and that it was for nothing that you have lost your young life?'

— 'That too I know. Well though I know it, I wish to enter.'

The young girl crossed the threshold. A heavy curtain fell.

Gritting his teeth, someone uttered behind her:

— 'A foolish girl!'

At which, from another place, a voice replied:

— 'A saint!'

(7)

These two fragments, both of esoteric origin, give some idea of the access to the *Way*. The further our studies progress, the better we will decipher their meaning, as everything they say is significant. For now, we draw the attention of the reader particularly to the first clue, the most important for him: *the way is a one-way street*. Meaning that whoever begins to walk it is forbidden to turn back. This is not because of some kind of external imperative, but due to the fact that each step forward on the *Way* irrevocably modifies the content of whoever has started walking it. It follows that he will become more and more of a stranger to his surroundings; that he will lose more and more interest in *exterior* life, in which only yesterday he participated fully. The appearance of things, and especially of beings, undergoes a deep change in his eyes. He will one day be surprised to constate that certain faces which only yesterday he found very beautiful now reveal to him marks of bestiality behind their features: not all, but many of them!

— 'What do you see? ' said Nicholas Gogol in a moment of clear perception.

— 'Fog... and the snouts of pigs...'

The more man progresses on the *Way*, the more his feeling of being a stranger is intensified. Soon he will become boring: later still he will become unbearable, and finally, odious. That is why *'the prophet is despised in his country, among his close relations and in his own house.'*[14] That indication is precise and leaves no room for doubt. He who wants to start esoteric studies is invited to think it over twice, and weigh it all, before he rushes to cross the *moat-threshold*. We repeat that it will not be possible for him to return to *exterior* life and to find his place, his pleasures and his satisfaction there as in the past. However, as well as the difficulties which are the first results of his evolution, such a man will receive comforting impressions, especially in his human relations. He will be surprised to perceive one day that certain faces which only yesterday appeared to him ordinary, today shine in his eyes with a bright beauty. It is because his sight, sharpened by

14. Matthew xiii: 57; Mark vi: 4.

148

esoteric work, has acquired the faculty of penetrating beyond the external crust. It is amongst these brighter beings that he will find his new friends. Their society will welcome him as one of their own. He will be understood among them, and their community of common aims and interests will be a stimulus and a help for all.

We give below a diagram from Abba Dorotheus, a figure which is presented in the Orthodox Tradition when we begin facing the problem of the *Way*. It indicates that those who walk towards the Truth come progressively nearer to one another.

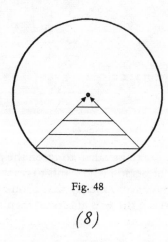

Fig. 48

(8)

We have spoken of the *Way* as if it were already open to us, and as if it were at our door, so that we must take only one step to enter it. In fact, this is not so at all.

We must first be penetrated by the idea that *exterior* life is a true *wilderness*, where 'A' influences reign; but that there exists, in fact, a *Way* marked out by 'B' influences. We must also understand that the *Way* is unique: that there is no way outside the *Way*. Then we must realize that as we are, we do not and cannot possibly find ourselves on the *Way*. To attain it, we must first find, then follow a *path of Access*. Serious and objective reflection will lead us to the logical conclusion that we not only find ourselves off the *Way* but, equally off the *path of Access*. We are, in fact, in the midst of the *Wilderness*, with only one trump card in hand: our desire to reach the *Way*.

If this desire is sincere and strong enough, we will with very little difficulty, find a *track* leading to a *path of Access* by which we will finally reach the *Way*. The diagram overleaf represents this situation in which man finds himself:

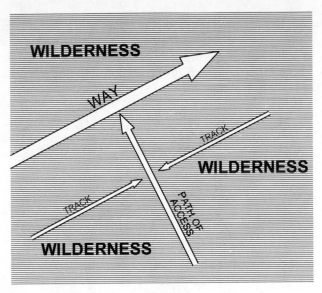

Fig. 49

We see that the direction to be taken to reach the *path of Access* depends on the whereabouts of the person who wants to reach it. No general answer can be given. We can say, symbolically that if one person has to go in a northerly direction to reach the *path of Access*, then another who is on the other side of the route he seeks will need to walk towards the south. It is the same for the *Way*.

Prudence and caution are necessary when facing decisions that have to be taken, as well as in appreciating one's own movements and of those of others.[15]

---

15. Tr. Sri Aurobindo, the great Indian philosopher and sage, devoted much of his work to detailed explanations of the higher stages of the supra-Mental. He predicted that this was to be the goal of future humanity. St Paul preached this when he indicated, as a final aim to his more advanced disciples, that they should approach the Intelligence of Jesus Christ.

CHAPTER XVI

(1)

When man goes in search of the *Way*, it generally signifies that something within him has collapsed. Apart from exceptional cases, this collapse is preceded by a re-assessment of moral values, which in the searcher's eyes lose the value he had previously given to them. This re-assessment itself has been provoked by the accumulation of more or less violent shocks which have given birth to negative emotions.

To be inclined towards esoteric work by positive emotions and success, one should be *just*, naturally pure, and not having been soiled by life. For most men success and joy, instead of awakening them, plunge them into mental sleep. Success, they say, turns the head. From the esoteric point of view, disagreeable shocks are a better base for work than happy accidents. The humility demanded by the Tradition is necessary as a screen against the noxious influences to which the least exterior or interior success exposes man. However, here as elsewhere one must avoid extremes. *Everything*, says St Isaac the Syrian, *is adorned by measure. Even beauty, out of measure, looks deformed.*[1]

Interior collapse leads to certain consequences. Man starts to see things in a different light. Two diametrically opposed effects can result. If man is sufficiently strong and impartial, he will not lower his eyes before implacable reality. He will have the courage to face things directly, and to accept the constatations which are imposed on him, no matter how disagreeable they are. This signifies that he has firmly started on the *track* which leads to the *path of Access* to the *Way*. On the other hand, if the man is weak, this experience will weaken him even more. The law is explicit: '*To whosoever hath, to him shall be given. But whosoever hath not, from him shall be taken away even that which he hath.*'[2] If man does not accept his situation and, in particular, his inner state as it appears to him, thanks to brief illuminations from the consciousness of the real 'I'—if he is obstinate against all evidence, justifying his Personality by protecting himself behind logic, legitimacy and justice, he will then turn his back on the *path of Access*, and thrust himself further into the *wilderness*.

We repeat: unless he is one of the *just* or *righteous*, nobody can reach the *path of Access* to the *Way*, without first passing through an interior bankruptcy; a moral collapse. That alternative is rather rare.

---

1. *Philokalia*, St Isaac the Syrian, 1st/1st sermon.
2. Matthew xiii: 12; xxv: 29; Mark iv: 25; Luke viii:18; xix: 26.

(2)

This is, or should be, the attitude of man towards himself when he starts to look for the *Way*. We shall now examine what his attitude will be towards the milieu in which he lives, as well as its attitude towards him. The question is important: an incorrect attitude at the start will create added difficulties and obstacles, which can be avoided. Economy of energies too is a must, as the walk to and on the *Way* demands their total mobilization. Any unjustified expenditure can lead in the end to failure.

We must always keep this in mind.[3] In general, the reaction of those around towards someone who begins to search for the *Way* is negative. This negative attitude is the result of the action of the *General Law*, which, as we know, tends to keep man in his place. Not being able to do this directly by the action of Illusion, the *General Law*, when it loses its dominion over the man who 'moves', acts indirectly by the mediation of those around him. It is a classic situation. From his side, after having passed through moral bankruptcy, he who seeks the *Way* becomes different from men who continue to live within the limits permitted by the *General Law*, and thus take mirages for reality. Due to this, he will feel himself more and more isolated. The centre of gravity of his interest will progressively turn to esoteric work, which will end by absorbing him completely. But it is entirely in his interest not to show the new attitude which he has taken towards *exterior* life. The 'World' will be hostile to him, because its own purposes are different; it is not in his interest to provoke this tendency, and even less to keep it alive. The day will come — if he remains in the same milieu — where, apart from rare exceptions he will be openly or secretly hated. Jesus said:

'*If the world hates you, ye know that it has hated me before you. If ye were of the world, the world would love its own: but because ye are not of the world... therefore the world hates you.*'[4]

And then:

'*In the world ye have tribulation; but be of good cheer; I have overcome the world.*'[5]

If we ponder this in depth, we shall understand that psychologically this hostile attitude of the 'World' towards someone who carries on esoteric work is not only a normal phenomenon but is so to speak, a necessary one. If he who lives in the *wilderness* — and is satisfied to be there, were to approve of the attitude of one who walks on the *track*, it would be equivalent to recognizing his own bankruptcy. That is why the 'World' considers the latter as a failure. The more he progresses with his work, the

---

3. Fr. 'esprit'.
4. John xv: 18–19.
5. John xvi: 33.

more he becomes an object of hate. That is why it is said that: *'no prophet is acceptable in his own country'*[6] and also: *'A prophet is not without honour, save in his own country, among his own kin and in his own house.'*[7]

(3)

Long before reaching the *Way*, he who has entered the *track* must know that it is a voyage with no return. We generally translate that by saying that the *Way* has a single direction. That is correct, for somebody who throws himself into the adventure which is the seeking of the *Way*, cannot return to the state he was in before his departure. The Word of Truth is a living word, and works within anyone who has tasted it, even if he does not think of it at all. Knowing this, one must think well before taking the *track* which leads to the *Way*. But for him who has already started this journey, all hesitation must be banished. Firmness is then indispensable. To someone who wanted to follow Jesus, but asked his permission to go first and take leave from those of his house, Christ said: *'whoever has put his hand to the plough and then looks back is not fit for the kingdom of God.'*[8]

We repeat, the *Way* is a one way road. For him who walks it, salvation is found ahead of him, never behind him.

(4)

One must not think, however, that if man has resolutely started on the *track*, everything will immediately change for him, and that his life will marvellously begin anew. It is true that his esoteric researches are a new element in his life, but that does not mean that the old elements, which only yesterday entirely filled his existence, have disappeared. They are still there. Most often, they form an impediment to esoteric work. In taking to the *track*, man places himself under the aegis of the *Law of Exception;* for this, it is evident that he must escape the hold of the *General Law*. This escape always takes on the character of a fight — sometimes a fight to the death: a fight, as we have already said, against the 'World'; against the ensemble of influences of those around him, which, in principle, will be negative and hostile. To defeat the 'World', this is the watchword for everyone who aspires to real Life.

Once the problem is recognized, it acts to define the means which will permit us to solve it. To attack the 'A' influences frontally would be to repeat the experience of Don Quixote — charging the windmills.

---

6. Luke iv: 24.

7. Mark vi: 4; Matthew xiii: 57; John iv: 44.

8. Luke ix: 62.

Thousands and thousands of well intentioned people have perished without profit by making this error of conception, inspired by the *Devil*: believing in the possibility of the impossible. The 'World' is incomparably stronger than the isolated individual, as long as he remains an *exterior* man.

Anyone who wants to benefit from the *Law of Exception* must first achieve a victory over himself, over his own interior world, before he will be able to overcome the 'World' and — by doing so — escape from the *General Law*.

The principle of this method is simple. One must remember Plato's proposition by which like can only be perceived and understood by like. Extending this, we say that exterior influences cannot act on the individual, except by the mediation of similar elements which form part of his interior world: the interior world of the individual is also subject to 'A' and 'B' influences. The accumulation of the latter within him forms the *magnetic centre*, which in some way forms a new centre of consciousness. As gradually the centre of gravity of the interest we take in life is displaced towards the *magnetic centre*, finally installing itself inside it in a permanent manner, the pressure of the *General Law* is increasingly intensified. Also, the spirit of the ensemble of 'A' influences, who watches over the application of this Law from the outside, seeks to act on man by its agents; by the 'A' influences of his interior world. We can easily understand that mastering the latter closes the door to exterior 'A' influences, and this ends their power.

In the picturesque language of the Tradition, it is said that the beast must be tamed, and the wolf transformed into a trustworthy guard dog. The *General Law* will then have no more power over the individual, who will come entirely under the aegis of the *Law of Exception*.

We shall now better understand the words of Jesus: '*The prince of this world cometh and hath nothing in me.*'[9] The man who goes in search of the *Way* should aspire to this state. We repeat: by mastering the 'A' influences within his interior world, he will escape the action of these same influences coming from the exterior world, which means he will escape from the clutches of the *General Law*.

That is the theory. Its application poses a multitude of problems. The infinite variation between individual cases leads to the difficulty that these problems cannot be classified or gathered into one general category; equally, it is not possible at this point to classify them in groups which would allow us to describe standardized methods to resolve them. That is why the method to be followed can only be individual. Some indications can how-

---

9. John xiv: 30–31. The so called St Jerome edition gives a shortened version of this text: '... *He has no power whatsoever upon me*'. That version, as we see, does not alter the narrative meaning, but it loses the esoteric meaning which can be clearly shown when we put this text together with that quoted above: '*I have overcome the world*'.

ever be given which, if they will not always resolve the problem or problems that arise in each separate case, can at least allow us to view them correctly. That is important, for problems incorrectly viewed lead *ipso facto* to erroneous solutions, distorted by Illusion. These, instead of simplifying the situation, complicate it even more.

This observation contains the first indication of a general nature: '*A correct, that is objective, statement of a problem results, at least in part, in a simplification and clarification of the situation.*' Conversely, if as a result of measures taken to resolve one or more problems the situation becomes even more complicated, this provides an *objective* indication that there is an error of conception at the start.

A second general indication is that the sum total of the 'A' influences is much stronger than the resistance of an individual who has not yet undergone esoteric training. As we have already said, frontal attacks only make us repeat the experience of Don Quixote attacking the windmills. The latter are effectively the giants they appeared to him to be; on this point the ingenious Hidalgo had seen correctly. But their power is imaginary; it is effective only to the measure that man takes it as real, especially when it acts in the inner life. To master the 'A' influences in his inner world, man must modify his attitude towards them. Man as he is, 1, 2 or 3, has no power over the *facts*, even though he often thinks that he has, in spite of the evidence. But even if the facts themselves are outside his control, the attitude he takes towards them depends entirely upon him. In a somnolent waking state, this attitude can arise according to the principle: *trust in God*. This is the general case, but man can also make conscious efforts to examine the facts. The absolute necessity recurs here that someone who searches for the *Way* must move on to re-assess the moral values of his life; to a re-evaluation of his situation within his surroundings; a deeper examination of his ties and relations with those around him. This re-assessment of values demands time, since man's judgement has not, and cannot suddenly acquire the necessary objectivity. The development of judgement towards acquiring objectivity corresponds to the progress made by a man in esoteric work. From the above we deduce that this process of re-evaluation goes on inside him continually. In serious and complicated cases, as well as in simpler cases, he will return time and time again to his problems, which he will view each time under new and more objective illumination, and in consequence in a more disinterested manner. The day will come when, having ceased to dramatize the facts and justify himself, each problem will appear to him as it is, unhidden and unembellished. It is at this moment that the objective and just solution will appear possible and desirable to him, even though it involves some painful process ... because in this solution he will have found the road to the Truth which sets him free.

The result of this brief analysis is that the precept of not lying to oneself, when applied to actual situations, demands a repeated and unceasing revision of the moral values of our life which, most often born of our arbitrary nature, are soiled with all the errors which this carries with it.

(5)

We have said that the ensemble of the 'A' influences, which rules man at the moment when he decides to search for the *Way*, is much stronger than his power of resistance. This constatation leads us to elaborate a psychological policy, in relation to ourselves and to the exterior world, which will allow us to compensate for our lack of strength and available reserves by an appropriate strategy. We must not forget that, strong as he is or appears to be in *exterior* life, from the esoteric or objective point of view, man 1, 2 or 3 is weak. Everything within him is limited, beginning with his nervous resistance. The rule which can be deduced from this is that *he must as much as possible work silently so as not to draw increased attention and pressure upon himself.* Otherwise he will be lost, as the reaction of the 'World' against him will be extreme. What he must do is to consciously master the 'A' influences of his interior world, by dividing them in such a way as to accumulate force and put it in reserve. When the *prince of this world* has nothing in him, then he will be able to wave him good-bye.

We repeat, however, that this is only possible if man works silently, without drawing himself to the attention of the guardian spirit[10] of the *General Law*, and of the forces of life which are systematically hostile to anyone who persistently searches for the Truth.

To do that, two means can be used. The first is to shelter oneself physically from the harmful influence of the 'World'. This is the reason for the existence of hermetic and monastic life. For those who undertake esoteric work in the world, the shelter must be built in his inner world — by the seeker himself, not outside him but within. The picturesque language of the Tradition says that man must build a *cage*[11] in himself. This must be provided with all means of connection with and direction of the centres. It must also be solid enough to effectively resist all rebellions of the little 'I's', singly or 'federated'. This construction takes time. To play its role as an organ of direction, it must be continually enlarged, improved and perfected.

In this picture the reader will easily recognize the *magnetic centre,* the new centre of consciousness which, as it gradually grows, takes the three lower

---

10. Fr. 'l'esprit conservateur'.

11. *kljet'* in Russian , a somewhat archaic term which means a *room, a little apartment,* and also means *cage.* We have chosen the latter as it is also used by the Tradition to designate the big space which contains and encloses the whole of the Universe.

156

centres under its control, and establishes an absolute authority over them — in their ensemble, on each one taken separately, and on all the possible functional combinations which they can form between them and between their various sectors. That clearly demands time, work, a great deal of patience, and perseverance. He who takes up esoteric work, says the Tradition, will greatly ease his task if he proves capable of thinking about it non-stop, *like a lover who thinks of his loved one*. He must do his best at the same time permanently to establish his abode in the *cage*. Meaning that he must not only put himself continually in a state of *presence*, but also in a state of *presence in himself*, which is not the same thing. This subtle distinction is important. *Presence* corresponds to the consciousness of the '*I*', while *presence in oneself* corresponds to the consciousness of *I AM*.

When man is *confluent*, and consequently forgets himself, he is simply carried away by one of the mental[12] currents which pass through him—but he is not conscious of it; he thinks he *acts*, when in reality he is carried away, all the while plunged in mental sleep. When he practises the '*tresvenic*',[13] that is, whenever he is *present*, and as long as this state lasts, he will realize that he is being carried away. But that is all. He still continues to be carried away. Nevertheless, this is great progress, as it will permit him to concentrate on the idea: *I AM*. By doing this he will make the first effort to attach himself to the permanent by detaching himself from the temporal. With the formula *I AM*, man for the first time can make an effort to resist the many mental[12] currents which carry him away, and for which he is otherwise like a plaything. It is by this sort of conscious effort that he will start to build his *cage* — his future command post.

(6)

Having reached this point, man must watch carefully that the 'A' influences do not penetrate into his *cage*. The latter must be a sacred corner within him, where only 'B'–'C'–'D'–'E' influences may be admitted. If this condition is not fulfilled rigorously, all his esoteric efforts will be doomed to failure in advance. However, in his inner world the 'A' influences will for a long time rage outside his *cage*, in obedience to external influences. He will continue to live and act among the 'A' influences. Yet man will henceforth have a refuge within him, and he will do the impossible to consolidate it, to make of it, as has been said, a true command

---

12. Fr. 'psychique'.

13. *Trezviet'* or *protrezviet'* means in everyday Russian: the return to a normal state after drunkenness. By this, the Tradition indicates that the ordinary *waking consciousness* is a state of drunkenness, of mental alienation from which one must *return* to the true normal state, that is, to that state which corresponds to the higher level of consciousness, the consciousness of the *real 'I'*.

post. This will only be possible at the express condition of not admitting any 'A' influences into his *cage*, right from the start of esoteric work.

It is evident that to reach this stage man has to know how to discern these influences. This is easy in certain cases. It is altogether different when the action of the *General Law* manifests itself in the form of *temptations*, of *prelest*.[14] In this form, 'A' influences offer a whole gamut of variations starting with seduction in its classical manifestations: *money, women, ambition*. If we resist these successfully, then *prelest* takes more and more refined forms, parallel to the 'B' influences, one might say. These forms vary infinitely, because they are related to personal cases. Among the most refined nuances on the emotional plane we can find considerations full of nobility, charity and compassion.[15] On the intellectual plane, we find considerations relating to the 'well understood' benefit of esoteric work. These influences, which are parallel to the 'B' influences, but of an 'A' nature, must be uncovered by subtle attentiveness, and a firm, unambiguous attitude must be taken towards them.

(7)

We have just constated that even though we persevere in searching for the *Way*, we continue to live among 'A' influences, which will continue to form the *circumstances* of our lives. From now on, however, our attitude towards them begins to change. Previously we sought to master one group of these influences in ourselves by identifying with another group. Now, lodged in a *cage* exclusively filled with 'B' influences, strengthened by our weapon, the formula *I AM*, our attitude towards the 'A' influences takes a new aspect. They certainly remain our field of action; but we no longer enter the arena to hurl ourselves head down into the tournament; from now on we act as agents for the 'B' influences, working on their account, following their goals in accordance with the words of King David: '*not unto us, Eternal, not unto us, but unto Thy Name give glory.*'[16]

This passing from one state to another cannot be done without conscious effort, without work and without struggle. The man who decides today to enter the *track* in search of the *Way* has, in principle, become another man; but in fact he remains as he was yesterday: weak, drowsy and pitiful. In this state, how can he overcome the resistance of the *General Law*

---

14. Otherwise said in Russian, *prelestchenic: charm, attraction*. In the Tradition, the Doctrine of Temptation is developed in detail. It is divided into two parts: *Temptations of God's friends*, which are good, and *Temptations of God's enemies*, which are wicked. We find in this practical and particularly suggestive clues.

15. Cf. Dostoevsky, *The Brothers Karamazov*: the conversation with the devil.

16. Psalms cxv: 1 (French translation of the Bible by Louis Segond).

and so finally reach the *Way*? It is impossible. To attain this aim, he must first accumulate strength. That is why we insist on the necessity of silent progress in esoteric work, so as not to provoke greater pressure from the *General Law*. This would quickly drain the new reserves of strength, which had been accumulated at the price of sustained efforts in the fight against this same law. One must therefore gain time and as much as possible delay the reaction of the *General Law*.

This is easier in a monastery. There the action of the 'A' influences is practically reduced to zero. There is no struggle for existence; we can benefit from the permanent help of the superior, who is presumed to have attained a high degree of evolution. Esoteric work carried out in life in the world does not naturally offer these advantages. The presence of a guide, without whom this work is not possible, does not exclude the influences of life, to which we remain fully exposed. Neither is the construction of a *cage* nor the discovery of a guide enough. For the seeker will infallibly *have tribulations in the world*.[17] He must find the forces needed to face these, by making the efforts necessary to accumulate them.

He will achieve this by adopting an adequate *esoteric policy*. This policy, or if we want to say so, these tactics, consist of the following: man must continue to live in the same circumstances as he did yesterday; but instead of *confluence* with factitious life, which he mistakes for reality, he must if possible live in a state freed from *confluence*, and freed from *inner considering*, while frequently using *outer considering*.

Inner considering and *confluence* are the direct consequences of man's constant drowsiness, a drowsiness which results in this strange phenomenon of almost permanent forgetfulness of oneself. This drowsiness, which is an effect of original sin, has made an object out of Adamic man—when he was previously by divine right a subject. With the animal and plant world, he has fallen under the dominion of the *General Law*. This is what has allowed the 'A' influences of the external world—from which he now wants to free himself—to penetrate so deeply into his interior world and so dominate him.

As for *outer considering*, we insist on this point; that it demands conscious efforts of discernment, of judgement, and of sustained attention that are beyond the forces of man whose reactions are mechanical in character. This consideration for others does not become possible except by the effort to be present in oneself. By practising the latter conscientiously, by developing it, someone who seeks the *Way* receives a double advantage. On the one hand, the effort for a state of *presence in oneself* accelerates the march towards the *Way* by the following cycle: *presence in oneself — outer considering — presence in oneself*, which thus tends to be self sustaining. On the other hand, this exercise tends to build the screen—of which we have spoken above—

17. John xvi: 33.

159

against the influence of the *General Law*, whose role could be compared here to that of gravity.

This is the way this exercise must be oriented in order to attain the desired result. *Outer consideration* must take the form of a *game*. The man who walks towards the *Way* must understand that he can never again participate enthusiastically in life — this permanent wave[18] — and that he must acquire prudence and circumspection if he does not want to be crushed by the blind forces of 'A' influences, forces which can be unleashed by conscious movements too weak to master them, but which move too far beyond the range of habitual mechanicalness to pass unnoticed. Man therefore must no longer live his life as before, *but must play it, through conscious efforts of outer considering.*

He must play his *role* in life. Each man is born to play a predetermined role, but rare are those who play it correctly, although conscience is always ready to inspire us. Man gives more weight to his reasoning and his judgements, always deformed by a life of lies, than to this inner voice. He thus falsifies his role, which no longer coincides with those around him, or with the circumstances and times in which he is called on to live and act. Not only does he forget his role in deforming it, but he also forgets that the scene in which he plays is not real life.

This complex subject is treated further on, in the chapter dedicated to the *film of life*, in which we shall examine the authentic contents of this *film*, its deformations, how it crosses the *films* of persons who, one way or another, enter our lives, etc. For now, without going that far, we must say that, from his first steps on the *track*, man must apply the principle: *'feed the crocodile so that we are not devoured.'* The same idea can be expressed in equally figurative form by saying that our approach must be that of a player who is engaged in a game where the usual rules are reversed, meaning that whoever wins loses; a game of: 'whoever loses wins'. This analogy is, in fact, almost exact.

(8)

At the same time, man must cultivate calm, while reacting externally as if he were in his accustomed state of *confluence*. For a long time, for reasons already explained, his aim will be to appear like everyone else: only to *appear*—not to *be*. Entrenched behind the walls of his *cage*, purified of all traces of 'A' influences, he will soon understand — and he will be able to measure — how great a distance there is between these two notions, although only yesterday they were confused within him.

---

18. Fr. 'houppée permanente'.

While playing his role in life in this way, man will sometimes find playing this role so attractive that he will enter into *confluence* with it anew, again as before mistaking the scene for real life. These will be *falls*. These falls, these returns to the mirage, are practically inevitable, and will repeat themselves for a long time, at intervals that are sometimes closer, sometimes further apart. They must not frighten him, and even less must they obsess him. Returning to himself after having constated his fall, man must simply resume his role, his new attitude and, as if nothing reprehensible had happened, must without slackening continue this *invisible struggle* which will lead him to the *Way*.

However, we must watch here that we do not fall into a trap. The principles of the *game*, and *forgetfulness of the past*, make it very easy for us to justify to ourselves our weaknesses and our falls. This not only acts in falls undergone while in full *invisible struggle*,[19] but those which result when we compromise with ourselves for the satisfaction of carnal, sexual or other desires, for our ambitions, or for the acquisition of some advantage. '*This is stronger than I*' is no excuse for him who aspires to the *Way*.

(9)

We shall now better understand the attitude of the Tradition to lying. If man wants to reach the *Way*, it is imperative that he stops lying to himself from his first steps on the *track*. If not, he will not be able to build his *cage* or, if he is able to start building it, the walls will tumble as soon as he intentionally seeks to cheat himself. He must no longer try to justify himself when a fall occurs, while he knows in his inmost heart that the reasons he is giving himself are not valid. A sincere error is forgivable, but an 'arranged' error ruins everything. We have here one of the aspects of blasphemy against the Holy Spirit, that hypocrisy towards oneself that will not be forgiven now, or in the time to come.[20] This concerns the famous *leaven of the pharisees*, which in spite of all its dangers, always finds human hearts in which to settle.

Next to the interdiction of lying to oneself, there is another less rigid rule which, put into practice, yields great advantage to anyone who observes it: that is not to lie uselessly. If lying to oneself excludes from the start the possibility of esoteric work, the useless lie is a nonsense, and a harmful nonsense, as any sort of lie results in the loss of fine energies which are most precious to us.

When man lies because he can do nothing else, or because he is pushed to it by his emotions or by positive considerations, this attitude can be justi-

---

19. Fr. 'combat invisible'.
20. Matthew xii: 32; Mark iii: 29.

fied within certain limits: in such cases one can say in effect that 'the end justifies the means'; but to lie for lying's sake is a proof that we have fallen to the lowest degree of degeneracy.

(10)

We are living in an extraordinary time. In the traditional language, we are entering the era under the sign of the *mystery of Accomplishment*. This *mystery of Accomplishment* is being realized in various degrees on all planes of the *lateral octave* of our *Ray of Creation*. It applies integrally to organic life on Earth, and therefore to humanity, whose centre of gravity is situated in the Christian world.

The whole of humanity will be saved anew, and the menace of the *Fire* predicted by the apostle Peter will be averted[21] if a new governing elite, composed of men who have attained at least levels 4 and 5, is formed in the near future. If this is not the case, then there are enough indications today to attest to the clairvoyance that inspired the words of the apostle: '*the day of the Lord will come as a thief in the night; in that day the heavens shall pass away with a great noise; the elements, set on fire, shall be dissolved, the earth and the works that are therein shall be burned up.*'[22] It will mean that *the experiment would have proved unfruitful* and, after having erased all traces of the past, the divine Will will begin a new experiment, once more starting from zero.

Even in the worst eventuality — and there is nothing to prove it will happen fatally — no effort expended in search of the *Way* which leads to Truth will ever be lost. The will of the Absolute to create a *Unity*, starting from *Zero*, remains constant on all planes, including the individual plane. *Interior* men are necessary for the accomplishment of this aim. It is they who plough the field of the Lord. Thus; '*He that ploweth must plow in hope.*'[23]

---

21. II Peter iii: 10.
22. *Ibid.*
23. I Corinthians ix: 10.

CHAPTER XVII

(1)

We live in a world ruled by lies. Lying and stealing are the dominant elements of human character whatever the race, creed or caste. Whoever says that this is not true simply tells another lie. Man lies because in a world ruled by lies it is not possible for him to do otherwise. To all that has already been said, one must add the following peculiarity which at first looks paradoxical; that the progress of this civilization, which is the fruit of an intellectual culture, considerably increases the need for lying.

Jesus told the Jews: *'your father is the devil and it is your will to do the lusts of your father ... He standeth not in the truth because there is no truth in him. When he uttereth a lie, he speaketh of his own: for he is a liar and the father of lies.'*[1]

It is evident that this sentence does not only apply to the Jews and to biblical times, but applies to man, whatever era and whatever race he belongs to, as soon as he identifies himself with his Personality, which is under obedience to the *General Law*. Talleyrand used to say that language was given to man to conceal his thoughts.

Yet man feels that he should not lie. In his inmost heart lives a vague memory of the pure, unperverted consciousness he had before the fall of Adam. Every normal and sane human being experiences, more than once, nostalgia for an uncorrupted life, and bitter regret that they are snared in the meshes of cheating, both moral and material.

Man, however, lets himself be bound more and more in life: his faculty for lying gives him the marvellous impression of being able to arrange things for the best in difficult situations, but he forgets that lies, once uttered, put him under obligation. Imaginary facts created in these acts demand a context which, if not completely identical,[2] must at least support[3] the circumstances within which we live and act. As long as we deal with insignificant facts, lying does not often result in serious consequences; conversely, in the *absence of an adequate context*, a serious lie unfailingly leads to a catastrophe commensurate with the importance of the problem. We remain unaware of this link between statement and context, which is the underlying reason why this law applies with the harsh rigidity to which Jesus drew our attention by saying: *'There is nothing covered*

---

1. John viii: 44.
2. Fr. 'coïncider'.
3. Fr. 'concord avec'.

that shall not be revealed; nor hid that shall not be known and exposed to the light of day.[4] In talking about this to his disciples, Jesus added: '*Before anything else, beware ye of the leaven of the Pharisees which is hypocrisy*,'[5] the form of lie which is most pernicious, as we saw in the previous chapter.

(2)

If we refer to the different aspects of this subject, an analysis of lying permits us to distinguish the following modes:
— Lying to others;
— Lying to oneself;
— Useful lies;
— Useless lies.
To these classic cases of lying, one must add two particular cases:
— *Hypocrisy*: the pretence of virtue, of praiseworthy sentiments, with the intent to deceive persons of good faith;
— *The integral lie*: this characterizes that person who, from a habit of lying and cheating on every occasion, ends by believing his own lies and thus loses all sense of truth.

These two last cases are the hardest to cure: hypocrisy, in fact, must be deeply rooted in the Personality of the human being to become an element of his behaviour. To overcome this tendency within oneself requires considerable and painful efforts. No fruitful esoteric work can be undertaken by anyone who has not first rid himself of this vice. It is dangerous for a hypocrite even to start searching for the *Way*, as he is condemned to fall in advance. It is the same for him who has become a prey to integral lying. Nevertheless, if these lies are not soiled with hypocrisy, meaning that if the intentional mythomaniac element is entirely lacking, this case is easier to cure than the preceding one.

It is anyway rather rare for persons suffering from these defects to become interested in esoteric teaching. Oriented towards the *true*, this teaching exercises a strong repulsion on those who suffer from these mental[6] anomalies. Thus we can now concentrate our attention on the more widespread cases, which are related to the four modes listed above.

One can say in general that all men lie in these four ways, and those who approach esoteric work do not escape from this rule. It is only the intensity which differs from one person to another. Setting aside cases who lie for the sake of lying, at the root of lying we can distinguish a whole series of motives; they can spring from the baseness of our natures or be inspired by

---

4. Matthew x: 26; Mark iv: 22; Luke viii: 17; xii: 2.
5. Luke xii: 1.
6. Fr. 'psychique'.

the noblest sentiments. For example, we do not tell the truth to persons who suffer from a malady which is hopeless. We lie sometimes to attenuate the brutal effect of bad news. On the other hand, there exist cases where we try to ameliorate the effects of facts by lies not out of hypocrisy but, if we can say so, out of a taste for the marvellous and for the miraculous. Such cases deserve our attention because they are out of the ordinary. We may remember the text of the liturgical prayer by which, Jesus addressing Himself to the Father, said: '*Thy word is Truth*'.[7] This creative force of the Word, of the logos, which is the Son's very nature, lies within us in our inmost heart.

We must note that we currently attribute to the subconscious world phenomena and messages which really come from higher levels of Consciousness. Moved by vague recollections, the man of good faith and a generous heart sometimes feels the need of bringing consolation, a note of optimism, and so distorts the facts by presenting them in a favourable light. It is doubtless a praiseworthy attempt, but it is ineffective because of the insufficient means available. For our word is not yet a word of Truth. If they had had the power of the word of Jesus our lies, taking miraculous power, would actually have improved the facts. The facts, however, remain in the same context as they were, before the man of good faith attempted to improve them. This sort of lie could be defined as an attempt to perform a miracle with insufficient means.

(3)

Lies gravely affect our mind; they distort the undeveloped organs of the Personality, upon which depends the effort that must lead us to the second Birth. In an *exterior* man who starts esoteric work, these organs, which are in an embryonic stage, are more tender and more delicate than those of the physical fœtus in his mother's womb. Each lie attacks and distorts them. Time and conscious efforts are needed to correct the effect of these true traumas and revert back to the previous state. Even more, lying makes the man who aspires to evolution go backwards. It bars his path to esoteric growth, by accentuating the imbalance between his three lower centres. These are the organs which, in spite of their incomplete character, permit man to receive 'B' influences, and feel drawn towards them. The growth of these, if it happens in a normal way and in favourable conditions, assures the formation and development of *magnetic centre* in man.

When we live in a world where lying rules, it is certainly difficult if not impossible to exclude lying from the start. This is the reason why religious law does not categorically forbid us to lie. Among the Ten Command-

---

7. John xvii: 17.

ments, given in negative form such as: '*Do not kill, do not steal, do not commit adultery,*' etc., we do not find the imperative: '*do not lie.*' Not that lying is permitted, but it is recognized that it is impossible to suppress it completely while man lives in an environment of illusion; the anaesthetic by which the *General Law* keeps man in the meshes of a net with hardly any margin for *free movement*. The Decalogue therefore envisages only a very narrow sector of human relations where lying is forbidden: this concerns giving false testimony against friends; and while frankness, *thirst for justice,*[8] and a *pure heart*[9] are praised in the New Testament, we still do not find an explicit interdiction against lying.

We can see from this that the Cycle of the Son, like that of the Father, belongs to the *Mixtus Orbis,* not yet transfigured; a mixed world where the Light shines in the Darkness and where Darkness has not yet abandoned its efforts to possess it. To live in the true, with all lies excluded, is the prerogative of the Cycle of the Holy Spirit; Light without Shadow.

While we wait for the coming of this era, an interdiction against lying nevertheless applies to certain *Individualities*: we speak here about certain men who have attained or who are about to attain the Second Birth, that is, *interior* men. We find only one indication on this subject in the New Testament, but the text of St Paul the Apostle leaves no room for any ambiguity:

'*Lie not one to another: seeing that ye have put off the old man with his doings and have put on the new man, that is being renewed unto the knowledge after the image of Him that created him: where there cannot be Greek and Jew, circumcised and uncircumcised, barbarian, Scythian, slave and freeman; but Christ is all and in all.*'[10]

This is only addressed to a small minority of *interior* men, in their relations between themselves, yet such a restriction applies fully as soon as a given degree of evolution is reached, since this governs our capability for truth.

Addressing himself to his disciples of Corinth, St Paul also wrote:

'*Aspire earnestly to the best gifts. And I will show you a way that is perfect above all.*'[11 & 12]

That way, a way of Love, was defined by the Apostle as follows:

'*Love,*' said he, '*is patient, it is full of kindness, Love is not envious; love vaunteth not itself is not puffed up with pride,*[13] *does nothing dishonest, does not seek its own interest, is not provoked to irritation, does not suspect evil, rejoices not in injustice but*

---

8. Matthew v: 6.
9. Matthew v: 8.
10. Colossians iii: 9–11.
11. I Corinthians xii: 31.
12. Fr. 'par excellence'.
13. Fr. 'orgeuil'.

166

rejoices in the truth; it forgives all things, it believes all things, hopes all things and endures all things.'

'Love will never perish even when prophecies come to an end, when tongues cease to be, when knowledge disappears.'[14]

He who reaches Love would not know how to lie. But to triumph over lies requires an esoteric culture, which is inaccessible to ordinary men.

(4)

The analysis we have just developed will allow the person who enters the *track*, in hope of reaching the *Way*, to see more clearly the facts of the important problem of lying. The struggle against lying is long and drawn out. It is first of all a struggle against ourselves, against our spontaneous tendencies, and against that mechanicalness that makes us revert constantly to lying.

In the preceding chapter we briefly examined the case of lying to oneself.

Useless lies to others are classed in a separate category. This is far less harmful than lying to oneself — and easier to master and heal; much easier than lying to oneself, which sometimes takes on extremely finely shaded forms that necessitate total and sustained attention, together with methodical and persistent efforts of *presence in oneself*. To eliminate useless lying to others does not demand continual effort: one must simply watch to see that it does not slip into conversation. At the moment when it is on our lips a simple effort of attention is sufficient to stop it. That is why in struggling for truth it is recommended to begin with this type of lie.

We must note a peculiarity which distinguishes work on these two categories of lying. We easily understand that lying to oneself, or the struggle against this kind of lie, is not perceptible from the exterior. Certainly, as soon as this struggle is undertaken, the inner attitude of man towards those around him, and more generally towards people with whom he comes into contact, can undergo certain changes. Nevertheless, these changes must not take on too obvious a character. One must let time make the necessary adjustments between interior evolution and the response from one's surroundings.

When we stop lying uselessly, this will also be unnoticed by those around us. One can say that in practice the struggle against these two categories of lies does not alter man's relations with other men in any way, although it is very effective for the person who undertakes it. We can therefore begin it without delay, as long as we do it discreetly so as not to draw attention to ourselves, and so do not provoke increasing pressure from the *General Law*.

---

14. I Corinthians xiii: 4–8. (Tr. from the French text in the original of Gnôsis.)

As in all the easier inner struggles, the only real difficulty in the struggle against useless lies comes from the fact that we do not pay attention to it, so that today, as yesterday, our tongue mechanically continues its deceitful talk. It is generally after prolonged chattering that we notice we have lost sight of our decision no longer to lie uselessly. We nevertheless gain a lot in turning off this 'tap': thus we conserve a considerable quantity of fine matters.

As for efforts at suppressing lies to oneself, they entail quite different and important consequences. Such lies grow deep roots. In this domain, para-doxical situations sometimes arise, some of them of such psychological subtlety that it is difficult to draw them out of the shade. It is enough to mention the question of marriages where one of the partners, having realized that this union is an error, persists in trying to convince himself of the contrary. If he is of an affectionate nature, he will redouble his amiability towards his partner as if truly toward his polar being. The absurdity of the situation reaches its limits if the other partner reacts by adopting a corresponding attitude — without truly feeling any sincere or spontaneous glow of tenderness. This true 'play of love' is evidently to the greatest profit of the *General Law*. The danger from the esoteric point of view is that, by mere force of habit, such a situation takes on for one of the partners, or even for both of them, the value of true love. This kind of lying to oneself can go on for dozens of years with people who are amiable and of good faith, and they entail tragic disillusions in the end.

The man who starts to struggle against lying to himself must be fore-warned of these difficulties, and of the possible collapse of some or all his greatest values. But it also happens that such inner collapses are produced in people who never approached esoteric work, but afterwards come to search for something more solid and permanent. All should know that true esoteric work only begins after the novice has passed through a *general bankruptcy*, and has had his gods helplessly thrown to the ground.

(5)

We have indicated the absolute necessity for anyone who aspires to esoteric development to cure himself as soon as possible of this deep-rooted habit of lying to himself. We shall now look at this problem from another angle: that of the objective results which man obtains when he is able to stop lying.

Gradually in this work, which takes time, demands the courage to face disillusion, and needs self confidence and faith in the teaching he follows, the seeker as he advances feels a new sentiment. He will sometimes feel bitter regret as his beautiful dreams vanish, but at the same time he will feel himself more and more liberated. His growing sincerity towards himself will establish an atmosphere of truth in his inner life. The law proclaimed by Jesus: *'ye shall know the Truth and the truth shall make you free,'*[15] will apply to him in its fullness. It is not useless to concentrate for a moment on these words. Jesus lived and preached in a world ruled by a regime of slavery. The word *'free'* was chosen by Him to contrast to the state of slavery. After each operation of inner purification, painful as it may be, the seeker will feel more and more fully a profound gratitude for being freed from this absurd slavery, quite unintentional, which made of him, a *subject* by divine right, an *object* according to imagined human rights.

Having reached a certain stage in this internal liberation, man will understand the full value of the magical power expressed in the word *freedom*.

(6)

We must insist on the fact that the conquest of this inner freedom is the *sine qua non* condition of success in esoteric work. This alone makes it possible to observe the work of the lower centres objectively. This observation begins from the *magnetic centre*, this command post, this undivided domain of the 'B' influences whose existence permits impartial observation and judgement.

When our interior world is purified by the penetration of 'B' influences, the rays of the cosmic Sun; when the interior *cage* is built and organized as a command post; when we have ceased to lie to ourselves; what attitude must we then take to the world and to other people? As we have seen, this problem is far from easy to solve. Let us try to recognize it more clearly. By so doing, we will be brought nearer to the solution. For the latter to be correct, it is important that we do not hurry things. If it is written: *'the kingdom of heaven is forced, and it is the violent men who hold it,'*[16] then we must not forget to compare this text with the principle according to which the kingdom of God is within us and not outside us.[17] It is therefore proper to resort to force and violence above all towards ourselves. This method is always useful, and is sometimes necessary to eliminate the roots of Illusion within us, the mother of lies to ourselves. In our actions in the milieu in which we live, we must take care not to believe that those around us automatically follow our evolution stage by stage, and that they are at each moment at the level we have reached by following conscious and sustained efforts which they have not made. Such an idea would certainly be absurd; but does not man live in the absurd?

---

15. John viii: 32.

16. Matthew xi: 12. The Slavonic text says: 'the kingdom of heaven is forced, and men of violence will take hold of it.'

17. Luke xvii: 21.

The feeling of liberation, even though partial, and the joy felt after each victory over oneself, surpass the limited and weak understanding of *exterior* man; and he feels the need to express them. This need is in a certain way legitimate. We must nevertheless be prudent. The Tradition's rule on this subject is explicit; it prescribes: '*keep silent*.' But it would be an error to think that it requires a true vow of silence. To *keep silent*, in the esoteric sense, means *to talk*, but to talk within well defined limits: *man must say what must be said, when it must be said, and to whom it must be said*. This naturally excludes all gossip and loquacity.

Another prescription, which we must force ourselves to respect from our first step in esoteric work, is added to the rule which prescribes silence. If we observe people who participate in a conversation or general discussion, we will constate that, instead of listening *for themselves*, in order to learn, and speaking *for others*, each speaks for himself, and listens to others out of politeness to them. We do not escape this rule. Everybody wants to *insert* his ideas somewhere, and searches for the most suitable occasion to do this. While waiting for our chance, we listen with patience and more or less attend to what is being said. When a conversation is being led in such a way, it is of course a conversation of the deaf, where we can rarely learn, and where generally we learn nothing. When they separate, each participant takes back the luggage with which he came, with this difference, that this sort of conversation provokes a considerable loss of fine energies.

Lastly, it is firmly recommended to *remain earnest* in contacts with people like ourselves. This precept demands a comment. Being earnest, in this case, does not mean being morose, still less taciturn. Esoteric work requires a vigour of the mind. What we are asked to do is to maintain a positive emotional attitude within us, and to acquire inner serenity. Man must keep an attitude of benevolence towards all; he must rejoice with the happy, be charitable towards those who suffer, and indifferent to the wicked. He must not play the role of a clown. Much as this may be astonishing, such an attitude is much more harmful to him who is addicted to it than we may think. In reality, it tends to debase everything to the level of triviality and platitude. Clowning, derived from scepticism, is a true opponent to the enthusiasm indispensable for passing through those difficult moments which will never be wanting in esoteric work.

These rules must therefore be observed. That of *keeping silent* is imperative. Jesus attached great importance to it. So much so, that when expressing it to his disciples, He chose a form of striking brutality. This was to better anchor in their minds the need for preserving the tender and delicate germ of the new life, of real Life, when that germ is just starting to appear in man following his first conscious efforts. Jesus said: *'give not that which is holy unto dogs, neither cast your pearls before swine,'*[18] and he indicates the penalty: *'lest they trample them under their feet and turn and rend you.'*[19]

Nevertheless, people whose *magnetic centres* have made their appearance and are developing feel the need to talk about it. *'It is out of the abundance of the heart that the mouth speaks.'*[20] But let them only share their joys and experiences with those who, like them, have undertaken esoteric work. Besides, the rule of *keeping silent* is not obligatory, except at the beginning of esoteric training. Soon, by virtue of his conscious efforts, man starts to evolve and perceives the futility of most mundane relations. To mix the fruits of evolution with this life is always erroneous.

(8)

We return now to the general conditions made necessary by the very nature of the *Way*. Bishop Theophan the Recluse insists on this question. He says that divine grace will not act within us if we do not make efforts to obtain it, also, that human efforts alone cannot produce anything stable and permanent within us. *The result*, he says, *is to be obtained by a combination of effort and grace.*[21] What is above is in fact nothing more than an authorized commentary on the text of Revelation: *'Behold I stand at the door and knock: If any one hear my voice and open the door, I will come into him, and I will sup with him and he with Me.'*[22]

Divine grace in its substantial aspect exerts a constant pressure on us; but it is up to us to: *'hear the voice'* and to *'open the door'*, otherwise it will not act within us.[23]

Every man can *hear the voice*. If he hears it, the 'B' influences start to penetrate and to establish themselves within him. But he does not know yet how to *open the door*. For that, he must find a guide, a 'C' influence man. Bishop Theophan insists that such help is indispensable. Without it, he strongly assures us, *nobody* can reach the *Way*. The Tradition regards this as a strict rule.

---

18. Matthew vii: 6.

19. *Ibid.*

20. Matthew xii: 34.

21. Here it is not *grace* as an attitude that absolves, but *divine grace, blagodat* in Russian, which is not an attitude but a real force that becomes tangible, though in a very subtle manner, in the form of a substantial energy which, under certain conditions acts within us. Precise indications are given in the Tradition of different ways to receive, it or to evoke its action within us.

22. Revelation iii: 20

23. In the Hindu Tradition they make use of the following image: They say that *grace* — Sanskrit *daya*, the water of mystical renewal, a notion analogous to *blagodat* — can be compared to the water for irrigating fields already present in various canals, but hindered by small gates (Fr. 'écluse'). When the cultivator opens the gate, the water flows by itself, by virtue of the law of gravity (*Patanjali Sutra* IV: 3, commented by Swami Vivekananda).

The disciple freely chooses his master. But to attain the aim he has set for himself, he must strictly follow the indications given by this master. An evident truth, often neglected. St John Climacus said on this subject: '*If you see in your master some faults or some weaknesses because he is a man, do not dwell on them. Follow his instructions, otherwise you will achieve nothing.*'[24]

This is due to the fact that the esoteric teaching binds the one who teaches it: his instructions must remain strictly within boundaries fixed by doctrine, and must contribute to the attainment of the intended aim.

(9)

The conditions required to search for the *Way* are four in number:
— a passionate desire to reach it;
— discernment;
— a discipline of steel;
— initiative.

The first condition is, of course, indispensable. If this is not met, it is useless to continue. But once this passionate desire exists, one must then apply himself to develop the faculty of *discernment* by every means. Let us repeat that we live inside the *Mixtus Orbis*, where we find real and imaginary facts and phenomena inextricably intermixed. The difficulty in separating them is due to the fact that *the Imaginary resembles the Real* in the same way that the space beyond a mirror reflects what is actually present on the facing side. When surrounded by mirrors, we can easily lose all notion of what is real. Using mathematical language, we would write the equation:

$$I = R\sqrt{-1}$$

where I, the Imaginary, is equal to R, the real, multiplied by the imaginary number, the square root of minus one. To recognize $\sqrt{-1}$ wherever it exists, means acquiring discernment. Even though the Imaginary closely resembles the Real, as in the case of the mirror there is always a difference between them, because the image is inverted with regard to the object: this applies to all sorts of products of the unreal, and puts us on the way to detecting them.

The 'A' influences among which we live are by their nature imaginary; but they can result in or produce real effects. This is what constantly happens in life. Thus the fear of some imaginary danger pushes us to take concrete precautionary measures. International politics of every era form an obvious example.

---

24. *Philokalia*, St John Climacus, Sermon IV, 6.

Two practical methods are recommended by the Tradition to develop the faculty of discernment: each of them is adapted to one of the two types of *exterior* man most widespread in our civilization:

— The *negative method*, or method of exclusion, is recommended to man 3, that is, the intellectual type;
— The *positive method*, or method of integration, is recommended to man 2, the emotional type.

The value of each of these two methods is equal. The difference is, that if he follows the first the seeker will not see the light except at the peak of his efforts; if he follows the second, he will be encouraged by sparks from the consciousness of the real '*I*' which will accompany him all along the path.

In principle, man 3 is endowed with a tendency not to believe.[25] He is of a rather sceptical nature: he often and easily progresses to a critical analysis of the facts and problems that face him. The centre of gravity of his mental[26] life is in intellectual activity. The *negative method* takes these characteristics into account. In observing the movements of the inner life, it undertakes a critical analysis of the most scrupulous and impartial type possible. It observes the comings and goings of the little '*I*'*s* or groups of little '*I*'*s* and, recognizing them as being *Non-I's*, makes an effort not to be identified with them. Little by little, he thus discards that which does not indicate a real and permanent tendency in the currents of his mental[26] life.

When such constatations are repeated in a controlled way, over and over again, the observer will perceive that certain elements are permanent, and consequently cannot be subjected to the principle of exclusion with true objectivity: he will then find himself not far from the threshold of the real '*I*'. We can see that such a method asks neither for an ideal nor for faith. It nevertheless has its danger: it requires total impartiality in the observations and conclusions to be drawn from it. If such impartiality is not observed from the start, the man risks falling deeper into Illusion. His situation will then be worse than it was before. As a result of these exercises, a certain modification is produced in the structure of his Personality, so that the ties between the centres, of which we have spoken in chapter VII, atrophy and eventually fall. If, at that moment, the *magnetic centre* is not strong enough to establish its authority directly over the centres, the man will become amoral, and dangerous to himself, as well as to others.

This is one case where the powerful parable of Jesus applies, that tells of the *seven evil spirits* who make *the last condition of man worse than the first*.[27]

---

25. A sharp distinction should be made between the following notions: *to believe* and *to have faith*. To believe is nothing much: *demons believe and they tremble* (James ii: 19). Thus we can say that everybody believes in God or at least in something, in money for example. But that kind of belief does not have the strength which would be capable of moving mountains.

26. Fr. 'psychique'.

27. Matthew xii: 43–45; Luke xi: 24–26.

The second method is *positive*. It can only apply to man 2, the centre of gravity of whose mental life is found in the heart. This man may have an ideal and try to reach it. For this he will attempt to reassemble those elements of his Personality where the seeds of his ideal are scattered. This method is the reverse of the preceding since it tends not to the exclusion of unstable elements but to a synthesis, an affirmation. If such a man is called hot, it is because he has given free rein to his positive emotions: exactly the opposite of the cold method of critical analysis and exclusion. This is not without danger, but the danger is of a different nature. It comes from an initial error in the choice of an ideal, or rather from the attitude when the choice is made. The fact that this ideal has been approved by the master changes nothing. It is a question of lack of sincerity towards oneself. The profound divergence between admitted and unadmitted aims can cause an interior rupture which, when strongly emphasized, can go so far that it provokes division in the Personality.

A rapid analysis of these two methods of work reveals the role of impartiality — that form of objectivity of which man is capable — and later of sincerity. Not to make conscious use of these two qualities, especially towards ourselves, is the source of many errors in our lives which we will not know how to mend later on.

There is within us a dominant aptitude either for impartial judgement or for sincerity. This aptitude corresponds to our type, and determines in principle what method we should choose to follow. We must not forget, however, that our natures are mixtures as much from the fact of our birth as from our education and upbringing. This means that, while applying the method which best suits our dominant aptitude, we must not lose sight of the other method; both have their roles to play in our efforts towards evolution, but in different proportions for different people.

There is another source of confusion which in practice plays an important role. We often think that it is sufficient for us to gather theoretical esoteric knowledge, and that this will then produce its effect on us — like a healing medicine: that no other effort will be necessary on our part. This is a common error of conception. In reality, esoteric work requires continuous efforts of analysis and synthesis in order to create and consolidate each 'grain' of success[28] that we gather in our march towards and on the *Way*. The influences to which life — that great way — constantly exposes us, are mixed, and contain corruption. To choose between them, we possess certain resources, a certain liberty of action, and a force which makes it possible for us to accomplish this work of selection. This force is *attention*. Attention is the sole capital we possess. But we can use it in either a good or a bad way. Often, we cannot even say that we use it at all: we leave it to

---

28. Fr. 'chaque grain de succès'.

disperse. Yet attention is indispensable to us, especially for the control of *negative emotions*, which impoverish us and provoke in us losses, sometimes considerable, of forces we have accumulated at the price of sustained effort. In certain cases this can go so far as to provoke true collapse within us. A watchful attention allows us to stop these negative emotions the moment they are born. Afterwards, on ground which has been purified in this way, we will be able to let *positive emotions* flow freely, so as to enrich us and permit us to accumulate the force necessary to continue our esoteric work.

CHAPTER XVIII

(1)

The study of the *Way* as found and followed in ordinary life raises the question of the relation between man and woman, seen from the esoteric point of view. We have already spoken of this, and will return to it more than once, as it is one of the most important questions; more significant than we usually believe. The most important questions pass unnoticed, especially where they concern problems of an esoteric nature. The reason is that our level of *being* does not allow us to *contain* the relevant knowledge. For this reason, right down to the present day, the Gospel and the New Testament are little understood and assimilated. It would not be an exaggeration to say that only five to ten per cent of the true content of the Scriptures is used, even by specialists. This is because they are studied without taking into account the *keys* they contain. Without going too far, one is sometimes surprised by the lack of attention given to certain clearly given clues.

In what concerns the relations between man and woman, viewed from the esoteric angle, St Paul is quite definite. He says that the Apostles who, after Pentecost, were surely men at level 7 or at least 6, each had a sister-Wife[1] beside him. Generalizing, he says that: *'Nevertheless, neither is the woman without the man, nor the man without the woman in the Lord.'*[2] We rediscover here the idea expressed by Plato in the myth of the *Androgyne*.

We must say clearly that Esoteric evolution, by its nature, is evolution that involves *both* man and woman. The fall was not, as we say today, the fall of Adam, *but of Adam and Eve together*, each having fallen in their own way. In the same way, redemption is not the work of man alone, nor woman alone, but of both together, each pair of polar beings constituting one of the infinite variants of the first couple.

This being so, let us consider the role of each sex in esoteric work — oriented towards the great Redemption. It is on the whole comparable to that played on the occasion of the fall. Let us take a closer look at how to understand this postulate.

Firstly, man is capable of walking directly towards a goal. Woman is deprived of this capacity. If she wants to reach a specific goal, she must find

---

1. I Corinthians ix: 5.

2. *Ibid.* xi: 11. We must note how this text goes against certain practices, notably monastic practice. The explanation of this apparent contradiction is given elsewhere. Neither the Apostle Paul, nor Saint John the Baptist had a sister-Wife beside them. They belonged to that group of beings who had reached a high degree of evolution, who had a specific aim, and consciously participated in the *Mystery of Realization* under the guidance of Jesus-the-Messiah.

a man with the same aim, and pursue it with him. This can be her husband, her brother, a relative, a spiritual guide, a clergyman or priest, or even a master of esoteric work.

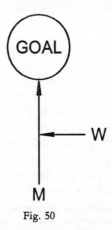

Fig. 50

We have just said that the role of a woman, on the ascent[3] to Redemption, must be comparable to the part played by woman in the Fall. This role was that of *inspirer*. Having conceived in her fertile and artistic imagination the notion of Illusion, the woman, after tasting its fruits, offered them to her husband, and both of them having fallen here below, then began the long path of study that is the fruit of the *Tree of knowledge of Good and of Evil*.

We return here to the precept of discernment, without which nothing tangible can be acquired on the esoteric path. The difficulty lies in the fact that it is not given to man to have an absolute concept of Good and Evil. Each light which shines in his eyes brings with it some shadow. This misleads even beings of good faith who are gifted with subtle intelligence. In all equity, even when we sincerely want to solve a problem, we always find an almost equal percentage of arguments for or against the proposed solution. So much is this so that we are unable to decide on anything; we are immobilized and wait *ad majorem diaboli gloriam*... A man whose psyche is not oriented by a ruling idea is generally stationary, until the moment comes where, often by fortuitous impulse, he takes decisions which will direct his life for scores of years.

For one who begins to search for the *Way*, all this changes. This search constitutes a *permanent goal*. Even without leaving relativity, such a man is now able in practice to define his notions of positive and negative: whatever guides him towards his proposed goal, helps him to attain it, or contributes to this attainment, is for him a *Good*; whatever turns him away, retards him, stops him, takes him backwards, and in general

---

3. Fr. 'courbe'.

anything that creates material or psychological obstacles on the path that leads him towards the goal he seeks, is for him an *Evil*.

This definition is general; but it particularly applies to the search for the *Way*.

(2)

The more progress is made on the path of Esotericism, the more inner sensations are intensified, at times immeasurably. Where interior shocks were previously overcome without great harm, they can now plunge the seeker into true crises of conscience.

Sometimes, lacking the necessary force of character to face this inner struggle between affirmation and negation, a struggle which monopolizes all his being and plunges him into terrible doubts, he abandons the work. In reality, this struggle is of the utmost necessity for him. It is that struggle which provokes an inner tension which grows until in most cases it appears to be physically unbearable. It is at this moment that the frictions between the various elements of the Personality become intense enough to make the flame burst out, which will light the heart. This *fire*, taking the proportions of an inner furnace, finally provokes in man the *fusion* of which we have already spoken and which, correctly implemented, constitutes the first important and tangible result of esoteric work.

If the work is done by a couple — and if the couple is polar — the role of the woman will be as important as that of the man. As his inspirer, she will uphold the man during the crises of inevitable discouragement in this kind of work which, done correctly, always follows the *Law of Seven*. The woman will also generate the complementary shocks that are necessary, at moments when the work would otherwise stop short in its progress, despite the efforts of the man. One can say that this kind of collaboration, if it succeeds from the start, provides evidence confirming the polarity of two beings.

We must add that now, at the threshold of the era of the Holy Spirit, where all that is wrong — however well-intentioned — must fall and break, the problem of the real polarity of couples becomes crucially important. Two beings, man and woman, who are supposed to be polar, cannot be absolutely certain of their polarity *until later on*, when they have reached the level of man 4, on the threshold of level 5. This is because, although polar in essence, each of them brings with them a past that covers their real 'I' with a dissimilar crust. Those who are polar *in essence* must take this fact into account. It is only when they gradually shed this crust that the qualities of their essence will progressively shine through, bringing at each discovery an abundance of ineffable joy. Thus their love will always grow;

they will love each other more each day, today more than yesterday but much less than tomorrow. It is the path of Triumph.

In this true Romance, the attitude of the Lady contributes much if not all to the victory of the Knight. Her refined and artistic intuition will understand the meaning of love: that is, to love with all the fibres of one's being, up to integral identification, in a glorious dash towards the same goal.

It is not sufficient for her to wait and see and, during this time, just allow herself to be loved. This observation is important.

(3)

Let us now examine the general indications that the eastern Orthodox Tradition gives concerning the *Way*.

It states, as already said, that the *Way* is one. But the *paths of Access* that lead to the Way are three in number, corresponding to the three fundamental types of *exterior* man. The *Way* is represented as a river, pouring its water into the Ocean through three arms. The river takes its water from a peaceful lake high in the mountains. This lake reflects the beauty of the heavens.

To reach the estuary and its arms, it is necessary to cross a bar, and to navigate between a great number of reefs and islets.

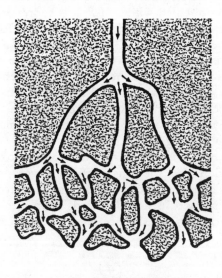

Fig. 51

The Ocean in which the river casts its waters is the *Ocean of Ignorance*. The three arms are the first three Gospels, the river is the fourth, the

Gospel according to St John. The Lake of Silence represents the Book of Revelation.

The three synoptic Gospels are conceived in such a manner that each of them applies to a particular type of *exterior* man: 1, 2 or 3. The Gospel according to St John addresses itself to man 4; Revelation to man 5. The latter is revealed in images and symbols appropriate to the perceptive modes of the higher emotional centre. Since the perceptions of the higher intellectual centre are of a transcendent order, the messages of this plane of Consciousness cannot be expressed in human language. The Revelation is the most transcendent message that can be expressed in words.

It is useless to try to understand the Revelation through the centres of the Personality. The seeker will read it profitably when, during his evolution, he moves on from the stage of man 4 to become man 5.

Each of the three *paths of Access*—the three arms of the river—that lead to the *Way* is conceived beforehand for one of the three fundamental human types: the first for man 1, the second for man 2, the third for man 3.

According to the esoteric Tradition, the three synoptic Gospels were conceived as guides to reaching and following the *paths of Access*. They have been given distinctive signs, which serve as the first *keys*:

— *Luke* is represented with a *Bull* beside him; it is addressed to man 1;
— *Mark* is represented with a *winged Lion*; it is addressed to man 2;
— *Matthew* is represented with a *Man*; it is addressed to man 3;
— *John* is represented with an *Eagle*; it is reserved for man 4.

According to the Tradition, the Gospel is a *Book sealed by seven seals*. This means that it must be studied in seven consecutive stages, each time studying the full text from the beginning to the end by means of a new *key*. The first *keys* are given in the form of the signs described above. By working correctly with the Gospel appropriate to his type, at each new reading in that Gospel, the seeker will find the *key* which will unlock the door to the following stage.

From what has been said we can see that evolution towards Consciousness is a progression from the zone of effects towards that of causes. In other words, it is an ascent up the ladder that goes from being a *product* towards being a *producer*: a step that leads from mechanical existence, which is Death, towards an existence ruled by the creative spirit, which is Life.[4]

(4)

The question of *aim* is closely involved with the subjects we have discussed. What is the aim of life? What could be its aim? Life is

---

4. John v: 24.

meaningless without an aim — in the esoteric sense of this word, and this point of view differentiates between the indirect and direct aims of human existence.

Indirect aims or goals govern the general case — that of the whole of humankind. Man follows life's flow. Without knowing that he does so, he serves the interests of Nature through the game of birth, love and death, and so contributes to the growth of *The Ray of Creation*.

The direct aim has been created for special cases. Here, man goes against life's general current. He climbs the ladder of the cosmos individually, after first neutralizing that influence within him which the Moon exerts on organic life for general ends. The direct aim cannot be grasped, formulated, and followed, by man except at the price of conscious effort.

These two possibilities open to man are represented by the following diagram:

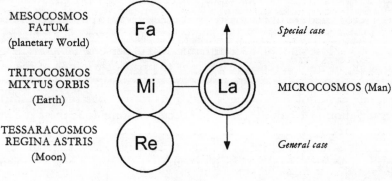

MESOCOSMOS
FATUM
(planetary World)

Fa

Special case

TRITOCOSMOS
MIXTUS ORBIS
(Earth)

Mi   La

MICROCOSMOS (Man)

TESSARACOSMOS
REGINA ASTRIS
(Moon)

Re

General case

Fig. 52

There is only one direct aim, but it is a long term objective which can only be achieved by stages. On this road, short or medium term direct aims must be formulated by the person who seeks to attain the *Way*. They must be approved by the master. One single aim must be followed at a time, and it must not be beyond the strength of the seeker. The analogy between this method and that now in use for the preparation of university theses is very close.

Here are some examples of possible direct aims:
— to become master of one's self;
— to acquire the creative spirit, the source of inspiration;
— to raise physiological processes to the level of waking consciousness;
— to acquire new faculties (the gifts of the Spirit of Saint Paul);
— to enter as an active member into some esoteric work;
— to totally[5] regenerate one's being etc.

---

5. Fr. 'intégralement'.

181

The further one goes in esoteric development, the further the aim formulated at the start must be adapted in its form and modified in its scope. The master must be consulted whenever changes in the disciple's consciousness call for such modifications.

(5)

While treating these individual aims or goals, one must give some indication of general conditions for access to esoteric work. Even if he finds a master who accepts him for guidance, the seeker will not progress very far if his efforts only tend to accommodate knowledge and *savoir-faire*. His case is quite comparable to that of a person who studies at a university. When his studies are completed, the student, armed with a degree, generally seeks to apply the acquired knowledge and aptitudes to life. It is the same in the esoteric field: the disciple, having been recognized apt by the master, must seek a way to put the accumulated knowledge into practice. Although he must always consult his master, he must never lose sight of the fourth rule, that of personal *initiative*: he must not wait, he must act in such a way as to participate in one of the many esoteric works being actually carried out in the world. In this, our present era, one can quote two. One is analogous to the construction and right organization of Noah's Ark, which occurred some four thousand years before our era. As in the distant past, this work consists in collecting, in a compact, schematized form, the sum of acquired knowledge and experience, preserving them, and then transmitting them to the new humanity.

Another esoteric work, which has been pursued in a more immediate and more intense way since the beginning of the century, even more since the first world war, aims at the formation of a new human type. The problem of the *new man* is placed before us by the logic of History. We shall try to elucidate the elements of this problem, whose proper solution will determine the fate of tomorrow's humanity.

This analysis draws its very great importance from the fact that, although we are not generally aware of it, definite plans must quickly now be taken to the point of preparation for the future. The rising generation, those who have entered life since the second world war, could and should in fact provide the first members of the elite who must assume responsibility from the beginning of the Cycle of the Holy Spirit, which must succeed the present cycle. The analysis we are now beginning should in particular allow us, after considering the position relating to this problem in its ensemble, to place the latter in its historical context. Then, by passing from the general to the particular, we should be better able to grasp the meaning of the esoteric work actually being pursued in the world to form that new elite. This should allow us to discover how those who are engaged in the search for the *Way* can contribute their mite.

(6)

The image of this world is transient. Everything changes. Before our eyes, these changes sap the foundations of the ancient order. Technical development marches on at an accelerated rhythm, and nobody knows how to slow or stop it. New sources of almost unlimited energy, and the automation of industrial production, modify or are just about to modify all aspects of life and of human society. Taking account of this fact, it is not too far fetched to say that in the not too distant future the *struggle for existence*, this great regulator of human life, will be no more than a matter of historical record. As soon as he is born, man will be provided with all he will need. What is luxury today will be given freely tomorrow.

Such a perspective can be joyful; it can also be terribly frightening. The necessity of earning his daily bread, which has occupied man until now, and has automatically restrained his ferocious instincts, will be abolished. What will he do then, free from the fatigue of his daily work? We can already constate that an increase of crime coincides with the general reduction in working hours. The yearly holidays are marked by an increased number of accidents, and by a loosening of morals. Such signs must encourage us to reflect. Can we better occupy 'freed' man by reorganizing his leisure time? Such men will soon be fed up with having four or even five Sundays a week, and with automation, one can foresee that four to six hours per day, two days a week, will be all that will be needed.

How will he be able to equilibrate his social life when this safety valve—the imperious necessity of earning one's bread—will be superseded?[6] One cannot say. No basic concept seems to exist on this subject, and no serious proposals to solve this problem have yet been formulated by the people responsible for industrial, social and political life. Yet it is clear that the constraint exerted on man by nature, meaning by the divine Will, cannot be replaced by some human constraint such as policing. We must search for the solution of the problem on a higher plane.

Let us condense the question. One of the first consequences of the widespread application of automation in production will be the proportional weakening of the political and social power of money. Why do people today still seek to win money? Money represents an equivalent of human labour; it permits the acquisition of the fruits of this labour without any effort. If we can obtain the same results by automation without, or almost without, the intervention of human work, money will

6. Fr. 'suprimée'.

progressively lose its buying power. The progress of technology will guarantee an easy life, and the almost unlimited satisfaction of his material needs, to every infant as soon as he is born.

Under these conditions, we can say that humanity is undoubtedly reaching the most important turning point in its history. If money loses its purchasing power, it will inevitably loose its political and social power as well. The real power is held in the world today by a minority who *possess* money — capitalism — or who *administer* money — communism. With automation, the rivalry between capitalism and communism will lose its meaning day by day. Deprived of its object, the great controversy of today will tomorrow be left behind without ever being solved. The question is: who will form the ruling elite of the new era? In other words, by what new force will the cruel power of money be replaced?

The last great turning point of the history of Christian civilization which can be compared to the present evolution, and in which all proportions are the same, is the passage from the Middle Ages to Modern Times. This passage from the XIVth to the XVIIth century, with the beginning of the XVIIIth century, opened the first page of contemporary history. It is instructive for our study to examine briefly the process by which the modern elite replaced the old medieval elite.

The elite man of the Middle Ages was the knight. Chivalry formed the nobility, the ruling class in that epoch where money did not yet hold the reins of public and private life. To be noble still meant to be disinterested. A nobleman of those times was characterized by his physical and muscular strength. He must be able to wear armour, and to handle heavy lances and swords. In his turn, deviations and abuses aside, the knight — whose vigour and strength of arms made him master of those around him — obeyed the orders of the Church. He was obliged to defend the weak and the oppressed, and to regulate public life, which was based on the work of the peasants and on craftsmanship.

From the intellectual point of view, the typical knight of the high Middle Ages did not shine. The great lords very often could neither read nor write. Their mental level hardly surpassed that of the boxing champions of our day. The tournaments of that time, which much resembled modern sporting matches, were an examination and test of the capacities of the elite. They actually took place in the courts of sovereigns before the eyes of the ladies. Common folk were not all that interested in this.

With the Renaissance, which secularized minds, the ideals of the medieval knights faded and then became the object of mockery by the rising elite. With *Don Quixote*, Miguel Cervantes gave the old concepts the coup de grace. Increasing intellectual power took the place of physical strength, establishing a new social hierarchy. Sure of himself, and of his superiority over the preceding mental[7] type, the man of the new epoch opened up new sectors for human activity: the exploration of Nature; calculations of all kinds; the appreciation of profit and gain — previously despised — and finally the new notion of a comfort and a luxury surpassing those of the Orient. All these became factors in the new criteria on which he based his scale of values. Unnoticed, money, whose manipulation had been forbidden to the knight in the name of religious principles, according to the precepts of St Thomas Aquinas, became the principal goal of the elite's activity. The new man applied himself to defend his own interests before defending the cause of the community, which had previously been the sacred duty of knighthood.

The existing regime collapsed. The physical strength of the knight, and the recognized authority of the Church in temporal matters, gave place to intellectual power. Rationalism was born. As intelligence is by its nature agnostic, Religion, which was once the supreme power, conceded its place to Science.

The victory of science was far from easy. In a contest which went on for centuries, Religion tried to defend the pre-eminence of its positions. The only thing, and that was fatal, was that it did so by using unacceptably outdated means, in other terms, by recourse to material force: it backed the sword of the knight — whose effectiveness had dwindled due to the appearance of firearms — by the fire of the Inquisition. In doing this, it was sapping the very force of its reason for being. This internal contradiction provoked the revolt of reason expressed by the Reformation. Rationalism prevailed in all fields. In the new society Voltaire, instead of being burnt, as was Giordano Bruno two centuries before (1600), was raised to the summit of honours. The Universities and Colleges created under the aegis of the Church became citadels of secular science and liberal thought.

It is above all by means of the new elite's capacity of calculating and appreciating material values that the victory of intellectualism over the ancient forces was assured: the new elite's world view,[8] written in the Encyclopædia, fatally pushed the concepts of the new world towards Revolution: the high bourgeoisie and the intellectuals took the place of the nobility. This was the consecration of the long process of formation of a new elite.

Having come to power, exploring and calculating man then directed the essentials of the West's activities towards the industrial Revolution, which called once more for modification of the face of the world. But science, which has produced marvels since then in the field of means, has never described practical procedures that would permit control of those means. It promises free luxury, but has neither established nor outlined the new

7. Fr. 'psychique'.
8. Fr. 'conceptions'.

organization of society, where men would be free from the servitude of winning their daily bread by the sweat of their brows.

The intellectual, the man of science, has created the machine, but today the machine is a force of which he is no longer master. Yesterday's governing class is being surpassed, and is incapable of taking the responsibility of power in the coming world. Thus the logic of history demands the formation of a new governing elite. We are still left with the necessity of precisely specifying the essential characteristics of the *new man*, and imagining the proper order of things in the new era, whose coming has been announced by lightning, as it was with the descent of the Law from Mount Sinai. This time the lightning of world war, the fire and flames of Hiroshima and Nagasaki, is in the hands of men.

Let us reason by analogy. We have said that the transformation of the ruling class from the high Middle Ages until the time of the Encyclopædia has depended on the emergence of a man of a new type: the intellectual, the man of science. In the same way, during Antiquity, Philosophy abandoned its predominant position in favour of Religion, and this in turn dwindled and faded away after the Middle Ages with the rise of Science.

Only four ways in all exist for the perception and study of man's exterior and interior worlds: *Philosophy, Religion, Science* and *Art*. We can see that civilizations succeed each other by displacement of the centre of gravity of the elite's activity from one field to another. That is how a periodicity is established in the history of civilizations.

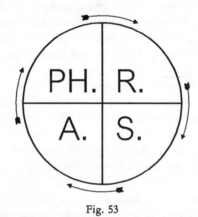

Fig. 53

We can note in their succession the alternating predominance of men of type 2 and 3. That is why the Platonic era clearly bears the intellectual mark, which can be constated in several works like the *Symposium*, where one would expect to find the mark of emotion in its pure state. Next comes the period where the Christian sentiment burns, which reaches its height in the Middle Ages and essentially expresses itself by type 2 men; the knight, the wandering bard, or the cathedral builder. This emotional intensity was quite evident from the foundation of Christianity, and manifests in the personality of the Apostles. We rediscover type 3 in the Renaissance; this expands into the rationalism and intellectualism of the XIXth century, of which Auguste Compte is undoubtedly one of the most notable representatives. Lastly the approach of the Cycle of the Holy Spirit brings us back to man 2, in other terms to emotional dominance, but this assertion is only partly true: in reality the new era has the character of a synthesis: it tends to go beyond the rotation of previous periods and bring to the fore men of type 4, who have established equilibrium between their mechanical, emotional and intellectual tendencies. This gives a clear clue to certain aspects of Revelations, especially those which refer to the period of one thousand years without war, during which Satan will be tied.[9]

It must also be observed that each of these periods expresses a dominant trend, not an absolute. Outside his laboratory, the scientist can express philosophical, artistic, or even religious tendencies. It is difficult to appreciate the exact measure with which these tendencies are reflected in his scientific work, whatever the desire for objectivity he brings to that work. If we look to the ensemble of scientific work in a particular period, it is practically impossible to decide what was the impact of prevalent philosophical concepts on scientific theories, or what were the reactions of individuals to such concepts. The same reasoning could be applied to periods where the dominance was religious or philosophical, which shows that no such period can be considered as manifesting a human tendency in its pure state, but that each period mixed certain tendencies in varying proportions, as a faithful expression of the character of our Cosmos, the *Mixtus Orbis*.

In the ancient world, under the general classification of Philosophy, Religion and Science were so to say 'philosophized', for the man of antiquity had above all a contemplative spirit. He did not think he was obliged to save time and money. The Middle Ages grouped Philosophy and Science under Religion. Finally, in modern times, it was the turn of Philosophy and Religion to be subordinate to Science. Art can be distinguished from the three preceding domains in that it contains them all without distorting them. It is in an epoch subordinated to art that the three previous human activities will be called on to develop their natural forms without any contraction or hypertrophy, completing each other in a harmonious ensemble. Art, which is currently degenerated and intellectualized, will in future play the dominant role which Science now plays. It will penetrate all categories of human consciousness; *Aesthetics* will absorb even *Ethics*. During the final advent of the new era, woman will play an

9. Revelation xx: 2.

187

essential role. But this accomplishment will require that tomorrow's elite be composed of supermen. We must not be frightened by such a word. In the eyes of a knight from the time of Pierre D'Amiens, the scientists and technicians of today, with the means of building and destruction, of transport and thought transmission which they create and command would, without any doubt, appear to be supermen. They have developed new faculties, *intellectual* faculties which existed only in a latent state in the knight. In the same way, in the ruling elements of our epoch which constitute the higher classes now destined to disappear, new faculties exist in a deep embryonic state. It is the full expansion of such new faculties which will let the *new man* come to light. The distance which will separate the latter from the technocrat, the financier, the diplomat, the general, or the professor of our times, will be no less than that which separates the contemporary intellectual from the knight of the Middle Ages.

Next to curiosity, the principal faculty whose development created the intellectual is the ability to calculate and combine. In the Cycle to come, the new characteristic of the elite man will be his ability to distinguish, spontaneously, without warrant or demonstrating proof, the true from the false. Such a man might also be endowed with the *spiritual gifts* of which St Paul speaks.[10] It is obvious that those who add faculties of this nature to existing culture will automatically reach the head of human society. Their commanding authority will be accepted, in the same way that the authority of the intellectual was accepted when he substituted himself for the knight, and for the same reason: an obvious superiority.

(7)

Technical progress confronts the world with a more and more clear alternative. If the already precarious equilibrium between the divergent tendencies of the past century is accentuated, life tomorrow will either be placed entirely under *diabolical* influence, to be annihilated in a cataclysm foreseen by the Apostle St Peter,[11] or will then be *sanctified* so that, in accordance with the Apostle's words, there will be established '*new heavens and a new earth wherein dwelleth truth.*'[12] The conditions which will realize the first part of this alternative and drag the world towards general catastrophe are already well established. It is far from being the same for the advent of sanctification. So that a *new earth* can be established, the ferocious instincts of man must be mastered at the time when the masses, having been liberated from labour, have a great deal of leisure. These new economic

10. I Corinthians xiv: 1.
11. II Peter iii: 13.
12. *Ibid.*

188

conditions, as already foreseen, must logically lead to a period of chaos, when the power of money and that of the governing class will collapse. The state of anarchy then will be the prelude to catastrophe.

The new elite who will be called to avert this mortal peril which threatens humanity will not be formed except by conscious efforts, which are indispensable for acquiring the new qualities of which we have spoken above. These efforts must be sufficient to satisfy the *principle of Equilibrium*, in accordance with which everything must be paid for at the right price. As for the ordinary man of the new era, he will continue to live outside the Truth, as he does today, as long as he can dissimulate his thoughts. The latter will however be easily read by any person who has attained a degree of culture which can be compared, all proportions maintained, to those who give University teaching today.

This new culture will, in fact, be based on the assimilation of millennia of human experience, in addition to the methodical development of new faculties. The latter, not yet cultivated, have not manifested until now except in a sporadic and partial way, so that they cannot yet find their practical application in the organization of human society. Tomorrow's elite will all be *twice born*, in accordance with the famous word of Jesus to Nicodemus.[13]

(8)

Esoteric Tradition teaches that any civilization is none other than a projection of the consciousness of the 'I's of elite man onto the exterior world. The 'I' of the intellectual already differs from that of a knight. In the coming civilization, characterized by Art inspired by the sacred, the elite man will possess an 'I' consciousness altogether different from the three preceding epochs. He will have, as has already been said, the consciousness of the real 'I', of a permanent and unshakable 'I', not that of the personal, unstable and composite 'I' which our times accept and glorify. Thus the edifice of the future civilization will not be built by the elite on *sand*, but on the *rock*[14] of the consciousness of the real 'I', the divine spark.

(9)

We must take account of the advantage which man 2 possesses in the transitional times in which we live. The formation and environmental conditions which, at least throughout the West, emphasize intellectual effort and sport, will permit him to equilibrate his mental[15] organism more easily. Certainly, in this excessively intellectualized world,

---

13. John iii: 3.
14. Matthew vii: 24-29; Luke vi: 48.
15. Fr. 'psychique'.

man 2 is constantly hurt, and is rarely one of those who reach the summit. Conversely, if he knows how to weaken the effect upon him of the 'A' influences — which are particularly powerful at the present time — by holding on to the 'B' influences more and more, his emotional nature will permit him to achieve equilibrium between his lower centres more easily and more quickly. For man 3 in a 'world 3', this is much more difficult. For his mental[16] constitution, reinforced by education, instruction, and the intellectual environment, ends by making a perfectly one-sided being of him. This is the underlying cause of the weakness of the governing class, which today is not able to stabilize and equilibrate the life of human society even though technical progress offers all the necessary material means to reach this end.

It is the same with the woman who, in this modern world, is endowed with refined emotions, and finds herself in conditions which permit her to realize rapid progress on the esoteric plane. In fact the tendency to develop the intellectual qualities in our civilization favours the equilibrium of her centres, on condition, however, that even if dazzled by science she does not lose her feminine emotionality and does not become too calculating. For her, this preservation of her femininity is an obstacle, a competitive test by which selection is automatically made. She must beware of acquiring a masculine mentality and identifying with this. A male mind in a woman's body excludes the possibility of esoteric development. This type of woman is unfortunately widespread in our days, as is that of the effeminate man, representing what the Tradition calls the *neutral sex*. Union between these people who have thus deviated from the normal represents the opposite pole to the *Androgyne*, the summit of deified human power. The Kingdom of God is closed for them.[17]

(10)

The evolution of the *Tritocosmos*, meaning of organic life, is in principle parallel to that of the *Microcosmos*, that of earthly man. The possible stages of the evolution of man have already been analyzed. It would be convenient now to examine the way in which humanity in its ensemble evolves, since it forms an essential element of organic life, and the planet's very fate depends today on the attitude of humanity in facing the problems which confront us. We have seen that the fate of humanity itself depends on the formation of a new elite, capable of solving the problems of our epoch. Whichever way we envisage things, we are always led in the final analysis to consider the problem of the *new man*.

---

16. Fr. 'psychique'.
17. I Corinthians vi: 9.

190

We have seen that the esoteric evolution of man starts with the formation of a *magnetic centre* within him; a new centre of consciousness, sometimes called the fourth centre. The symbolic reference to magnetism comes from the fact that, when it attains a certain degree of development, this centre magnetizes the 987 little 'I's who are generally dispersed. They are then led to revolve in its orbit, and so follow the orientation which he himself holds because of his resonance to the 'B' influences. The *magnetic centre* can develop normally: the stages of this development have already been described in Chapter VI. But it can also, in exceptional cases, be reabsorbed; even in these cases, it generally tends to reconstitute itself, as we shall soon see. The reabsorption has always the same cause. It comes from a duality of tendencies in the individual at the time of the constitution of this centre. Egoistic 'A' influences have already come to soil the new-born *magnetic centre*. This results in internal conflicts for the man, and in sufferings which cannot be appeased except by the reabsorption of the centre. The latter, when reconstituting itself takes account of the experience it has acquired, but in such cases the rebirth of the centre is preceded by a new moral bankruptcy which recurs, and recurs again if necessary, until 'B' influences appear as the only possible refuge, and assume the sole paternity of the centre. After having been on the brink of such an abyss, a man will only drink at the one source of salvation.

If we consider the ensemble of mankind as an entity, a process analogous to the formation of the *magnetic centre* is actually now manifesting itself in humanity. This formation is accompanied by struggles, suffering, anguish and all the symptoms of general bankruptcy. The idea of an international organization which would govern humanity in accordance with higher principles came into being a long time ago. The first concrete trial in this direction was the Holy Alliance, whose tendencies were far from purely idealistic so that it disappeared rapidly. Almost a century later, in 1898, Russia invited the great powers to participate in the conference of The Hague, and it put forward for the first time on the international level the problem of the limitation of armaments: this idea then appeared so revolutionary that the powers invited finally rejected it. As a result, the first conference of The Hague was reduced to a convention concerning work for women. After this, they fixed the date for the second conference, which took place in 1908 with no noticeable practical result. A third conference was planned, but did not take place because of the first world war. The horrors of that war impressed upon responsible men of State the idea that the presence of a permanent international organism endowed with certain powers was necessary. This was the League of Nations. This embryo of the *international magnetic centre* was afterwards reabsorbed by several crises which undermined its authority, which had been weak from its birth. It collapsed in 1939. It was after the second world war, which cost humanity some 50 million lives, that a new conference was convened in San Francisco in 1945, and adopted the Charter of the United Nations. The United Nations still does not constitute a proper world organization. Neither does the *magnetic centre* in man immediately take the three centres and their sectors under its control. Any growth demands time. But what is certain is that, in spite of the bitter criticisms of which the United Nations Organization is the object, nobody today wishes its liquidation. It is not that we are satisfied with the results obtained, not that we believe — except for some enthusiasts — that a brilliant future is reserved for this international political organism, but because all the world is perfectly aware that if the United Nations disappeared the international situation would be aggravated further, and the chances of a third world war would increase. A new world war would probably involve the whole planet, kindled by the fire and flames of atomic explosions.

The United Nations actually represents a centre analogous to that of the embryonic *magnetic centre* of a man who pursues esoteric work. This centre can neither be neglected nor liquidated, unless the governors of one camp or the other have become insane. Normally, the international Organization must emerge reinforced from the crises and dangers it must undergo. We already foresee the signs which make us feel that, with time, it can become a true world organization, capable of being transformed later into a superstate authority, guaranteeing just and durable order on this planet. It will then co-ordinate constructive efforts for the whole of humanity.

This task of international Organization will only be fully realized by ensuing generations, when the *new man* assumes the reins of power.

It would be useless, in the context of our present study, to pursue this examination any further; it is enough for now to draw the attention of the reader to the striking analogy between the formation of the *magnetic centre* in man and — in the form of an international organization — in the body of the whole of humanity.

(11)

These considerations show where the centre of gravity of esoteric work can actually be placed. It is in the accumulation of efforts which tend to form the new type of man. Yet this formation is inseparable from work on oneself: it is conditioned by this, and starts with it. This is the thread of Ariadne.

Conscious personal efforts, especially efforts *between two* polar beings, and the joint efforts of people who have already progressed in the search for the *Way*, mark out the route for those who want to serve, who wish to be useful to the task of redemption which esoteric work wants to accomplish today in the whole world.

CHAPTER XIX

(1)

There is an essential difference between esoteric Knowledge[1] and purely intellectual Knowledge. The latter is independent of the moral qualities of the student or scientist.[2] Being wicked or hypocritical does not in the least prevent anyone making a scientific discovery. This is why intellectual Knowledge neither rises above the plane[3] of information; nor pretends to. To assimilate it requires only intellectual efforts. The nature of esoteric Knowledge is different. For this kind of theory to be understood and correctly assimilated, not only is intellectual effort required, but participation of our *being* is also needed. This is particularly true concerning the practice which is an essential part of this work. Neither should we forget that traditional esoteric Knowledge — the fruit of Revelation — is a living Word. Once received, it works within us even when we do not think about it, whether we are awake or asleep, and impregnates us little by little.

Intellectual Knowledge is in its nature objective, in the sense that it does not depend on the Personality of the student or scientist: it is placed outside it. Esoteric Knowledge is necessarily subjective, since the object of its study is the student himself. It will not become objective until the Personality of the student has itself reached the objective level of *being* — through its union with the real 'I'. The Tradition calls this sort of Knowledge *living water*,[4] in contrast to knowledge which is purely intellectual; *dead water*. In fact, both orders of Knowledge are indispensable in esoteric work. Furthermore, by the discipline of thought it imposes, and the methods it teaches, academic training greatly assists this work. This is particularly true when esoteric teaching uses the psychological method, as in the present work. One must not conclude, however, that a purely rational, theoretical and thus intellectual study of esoteric doctrine can ever on its own lead to the way of evolution. Esoteric science goes beyond *knowing* and *understanding*,[5] objectives common to all the sciences. From its viewpoint attainment of these objectives has value only to the degree that it gives access to *savoir-faire*. Seen from this point of view, esoteric science has a nature similar to that of applied science. The great difference is always that the scientist and in general the technician seek to master the elements of the external world by external means, while the *inner* man arrives at

---

1. On this page, 'Knowledge' is 'connaissance' unless indicated.
2. Fr. 'savant'.
3. Fr. 'plan'.
4. John iv: 10.
5. Fr. '*savoir* et du *comprendre*'.

analogous or even greater results by his efforts to master the elements of his inner world. In both cases, the same principle is applied: pure theory must lead to practice, and in both cases it is only the result which counts.

(2)

While observing himself and others by the means available to him in a state of waking consciousness, *exterior* man often confuses the notions of *being* and *appearing to be*. Observed through the prism of the underdeveloped and therefore imperfect organism of the Personality, the Real appears to be relative. Discerning real from relative is particularly difficult for man 1, 2 or 3 who, finding no criteria for making such a distinction, says: '*all is relative*', an assertion which itself has only a relative value.

To be able to penetrate the deep significance of the difference between the notions of *being* and *appearing*, we must go back to the source, to the very origin of Creation. When Manifestation appears, in the form of the created Universe, the relation of *Infinity to Zero* gives place to the relation between an infinitely great quantity and an infinitesimal quantity: from the quantitative point of view, this approximation represents a very small variation, but from the qualitative point of view it is considerable. When these two relations are confused together instead of being clearly distinguished, this confusion is transmitted from step to step,[6] reaching a point where it is no longer possible to differentiate between *being* and *appearing to be*, both of which are distant reflections of the first two formulae. The relations between neighbouring cosmoses are not those of zero to infinity, as sometimes said, but of infinitesimal to infinitely great. In these relations, the infinitesimal is not a negligible quantity. For the *Microcosmos* who is man, the sperm—which is the *Micro-microcosmos*—is not zero. Man himself comes from it. In the same way, man would not be considered as zero in relation to the *Tritocosmos*, which is organic life on Earth. Man transforms it extensively, and even pretends to master it completely. The three consecutive cosmoses form an ensemble and, in certain respects, a closed cycle. Thus a galaxy, like our Milky Way, which is a *Megalocosmos*, forms a closed cycle both with the ensemble of the stars, that is to say, the many *Deuterocosmoses* of which it is composed, and the planetary system of each of them, that is, with their *Mesocosmos*. To put it a different way, a galaxy is one of the organs of the *Macrocosmos*, the Great Universe. The laws which rule this system of three consecutive cosmoses contained by the galaxy — the *Megalocosmos* — are, as we have seen (Chapter IX, p. 81), twice as many as the laws that rule relations between the different galaxies in the ensemble of the *Aghiocosmos*, embraced by the *Protocosmos*. While each galaxy is ruled by six groups of laws, the higher cosmos, the *Aghiocosmos*, is governed by only

6. Fr. 'échelon en échelon'.

three groups of laws. Some laws of Nature to which the lower cosmoses are subject have no effect on the higher cosmoses.[7] It must be noted that in the interior of groups of three cosmoses, the influence of one on the other is only exercised by one step on the neighbouring step.[8] Thus the *Micro-microcosmos* has no influence on the *Tritocosmos*.

(3)

In the ultimate abstraction, the relation between the Infinitesimal and the Infinitely Great, viewed in dynamic terms as a perpetual cyclic movement, underlies the fundamental schema of Creation and makes its *raison d'être* intelligible. The first condition of Creation is the action of the *principle of Imperfection*,[9] with the *principle of Asymmetry* which results from it: these, in turn, are the conditions necessary for the emergence and duration of Existence in Space and in Time.

The relation between the Infinite and perfect Zero is the formula for universal immobility, and expresses the *Absolute* in his unmanifest state:

$$\frac{\infty}{0} = \infty \qquad\qquad\qquad (I)$$

The meaning of Creation consists in the realization, relative to Zero,[10] *of a Unity resembling*[11] *Infinity*. The first concept of Manifestation is therefore expressed in the following equation, Unity being designated by α:

$$\frac{\alpha}{0} = \infty \qquad\qquad\qquad (II)$$

from which, by comparing (I) with (II) we deduce:

$$\frac{\infty}{0} = \frac{\alpha}{0} \qquad\qquad\qquad (III)$$

and also:

$$\infty = \alpha \qquad\qquad\qquad (IV)$$

---

7. This fact may explain the recent theory according to which Newton's law is not universal, but applies only in limited sectors of the Universe.

8. Fr. 'à l'échelon voisin'.

9. Cf. ch. XIV p. 127.

10. Fr. 'à partir du Zéro'.

11. Fr. 'semblable a l'infinie'.

This series of four equations designates, in mathematical language:

I. — the unmanifest Absolute;
II. — the idea of Creation;
III. — the formula of pre-Creation (in dogmatic terms: the *begotten not created* Being);
IV. — Creation having reached achievement. In other words, at this stage the *Universe*, being *accomplished*, would have crossed over the distance separating it from *God the Creator*. This is the meaning and goal of *Manifestation*.

The method[12] of Creation is that the initial Zero, which is general, voluntarily becomes imperfect and is divided into an infinite number of particular zeros. This is the *fall of Souls*. This fall has not been uniform. The Tradition tells us that its depth varied for different Souls. This fact conditions the infinite variety of the Universe, ordered by the *System of Cosmoses*.

We can understand that each of us has his source in one of the differentials of the general Zero which had been made imperfect: this differential is our Personality. The meaning and mission of our lives is to create a differential of *Unity*, starting from this differential of *Zero*. For the ensemble, the fourth equation will thus take the following form:

$$\alpha = \int_0^\infty d.\,\alpha \qquad\qquad (V)$$

or, for each particular case:

$$d.\,\alpha = d\,0.\,\infty \qquad\qquad (VI)$$

Let us note that the explanation which has just been given is the starting point for the study of an important branch of esoteric science, the *Doctrine of Numbers*.

(4)

The Personality is thus nothing but a differential of Zero, rendered imperfect. Due to this fundamental imperfection, it has only a *borrowed* existence. That is also why *appearance* has for it the value of *being*.

The point of evolution which the whole Universe has now reached — with all it contains, including each one of us — is situated between the third and the fourth stages, between *pre-Creation* and the *final, accomplished Creation*. Equation VI permits us to understand the creation, through esoteric work (∞) starting from our Personality (d. 0), of a new

---

12. Fr. 'technique'.

Individuality (d. α) to participate in the general evolution of the Universe. This creation contributes, in fact, by inserting infinitesimals appertaining to the Real (d. α), to complete the formula: $\int_0^\infty d.\, \alpha$ which, *in fine*, would be equal to:

$$\int_0^\infty d.\, \alpha = \alpha \qquad\qquad \text{(VII)}$$

The ideas just described will open our eyes to the depth and audacity of Creation. We may now perhaps joyfully feel the inestimable value of the divine loan bequeathed to us; this body, as depositary of the Personality, will allow us to become a real Unity. We can also doubtless experience a feeling of fear when we think of the casual way we use this loan. We let our lives slip away without giving a thought to the questions they pose, without a thought for the *term*, when this loan of life comes due. If we stop for a moment to ponder these ideas, we will understand in a new way the true meaning of the parable of the Talents.[13]

Let us try to understand, within the framework of our search for the *Way,* the practical means that can so marvellously allow us to transform the factitious into the real. This, as the parable says, is a practical way of winning five talents for five, or at least two for two.

(5)

*B*eing means to be in the *Present*. We cannot yet be in the Future, we are no longer in the Past, but what is the *Present*?

The '*I*' of the Personality, being only a loan, is a temporary '*I*' which man uses in absence of the consciousness of the real '*I*'. With this '*I*' of the Personality, man lives either in the Future or in the Past. The Personality *has no Present*, which only appears to it as an evanescent demarcation line. On reaching this, the Future is transformed mysteriously into the Past. It is for this reason that the existence of the Personality appears to be factitious, unreal. What in our current language we call the *Present* is actually the more or less recent Past, containing our conjectures about the very near Future. A real *Present* seems to be nonexistent for us. This conception is, however, erroneous. In reality, the succession of events in Time, History in all its aspects, is an uninterrupted succession of independent and autonomous particles of the *real Present*. In other words, our representation of the *Present* — as an imaginary line of demarcation where the Future is transformed into the Past — is false. Our classical concept of Past and Future is also false. In fact, everything that exists, exists in Time. To confirm its existence, an object, possessing three dimensions of space and formed of

---

13. Matthew xxv: 13–30.

solid matter, still requires an element of time, a fourth perpendicular. If we do not grant it an instant of time, it cannot exist. *The Present thus necessarily has extension.* For *exterior* man, this extent is very short and moreover individual. But if we reduce this tiny *Present* to the zero we think it is, it becomes purely and simply cessation of existence. It is thus that death actually occurs.

In mathematical terms our existence, as well as that of the whole world in which we live, can be expressed by the following formula:

$$1 = \int_b^d dP$$

where l represents life, where b and d, birth and death, are the limits of the integral, and where dP is the differential of the *Present.*

This formula helps us grasp that—just like any other being—man as we know him is only a series of consecutive sections of an integral being whose existence extends in Time from the moment of birth to that of death. We shall see later that man has another mode of existence, existence in Eternity, with a third mode on the plane of principles, in the heart of the Absolute.

The Tradition teaches us that there—when the promised *Accomplishment* occurs — the pledge of the *general Resurrection* will be redeemed, and the whole Universe and *everything and everyone* that inhabits it, will attain the goal: to pass beyond Imperfection and Asymmetry to the state of Perfection. From the point of view that interests us, this perfection itself is existence in the *real Present*, which for each *Individuality* contains all his Past, and all his Future.

The Accomplishment is the end of *general Evolution*, the interminably slow and dramatic succession of births, suffering and deaths across æons of love and labour. This ensemble of evolution is ruled by a law whose other aspects we have already studied; the *General Law.* Jealously watchful to keep everyone in his place, it leads the ensemble of Creation to the summit by stages so placed that they allow progress in spite of variations in individual rhythm.

Esoteric evolution follows another law and another way. It is, so to speak, *perpendicular to the first.* It follows the *Law of Exception*, which introduces the possibility of more rapid individual regeneration. This is a steep and dangerous path. Courage is needed to begin it, and rapid results can only be obtained at the price of great efforts. In addition, the privilege of forcing the *General Law*, following the *narrow path*[14] and of profiting from the help of a guide—without whom the ascent would not be possible—is given on one express condition: *that he whose individual effort has borne fruit must be ready to do the work again from the start so as to contribute to the general evolution.* This

14. Matthew vii: 14.

rule has a corollary which acts to ensure the continuity in esoteric work by establishing a chain: *nobody can pass to the next degree of evolution without having trained someone else and put them in his place.*

(6)

For living beings the duration of the *Present* is individual. For *exterior* man, this duration is of the order of one breath. In a normal calm state, this will be about three seconds. In psychology, positive science empirically reaches a comparable conclusion by introducing the notion of the *mental Present*. We understand by this term a period of time able to be retained as a whole in a single perception of successive stimuli; its average duration has been estimated at about five to six seconds.[15]

Esoteric science, which is much less concerned with the fixed character of a person than with their possibility of development, says that the individual *Present* can be extended or reduced. The normal respiratory rhythm of *exterior* man in a calm state, 3 to 4 seconds, determines the maximum duration of the present for this kind of man.

As soon as the subject experiences an emotion, the rhythm of his respiration will be accelerated. Unexpected news 'stops the breath'; and respiration can also be considerably accelerated after physical effort. In all these cases, the *Present* undergoes a reduction proportional to the acceleration of the rhythm. Before the person can regain his habitual state on the mental[16] and moral planes, the rhythms of his body, particularly the respiratory rhythm, must return to normal. In contrast, someone who — by the integration of his *Present*—could maintain his physical rhythms in their normal state even under exceptional conditions, would retain a calm detachment that would allow him to take rational decisions. Indeed, the measure to which this mastery exists is the measure of higher being. There is an aphorism which describes this situation in a picturesque way: *in combat, he who hears his horse's hoof-beat will be victorious.*

For someone who yields to *confluence*; who abandons himself to circumstances, the *Present* tends to disappear. If he takes decisions at a time like this, it is probable that he will have many opportunities to regret them later. If *confluence*, combined with accelerated work of one of the lower centres, accelerates respiration and causes a narrowing of the *Present*, all forms of concentration, on the other hand, contribute to its enlargement. The deeper the concentration, the slower the respiration. In the state of contemplation it becomes imperceptible.

---

15. *Vocabulaire de la Psychologie*, published in collaboration with the Association of scientific workers by Henri Piéron, a professor at the College of France, director of the Institute of Psychology of the University of Paris, Presses Universitaires de France, 1951 p. 222.
16. Fr. 'psychique'.

(7)

The *Doctrine of the Present* makes it easier for us to understand the true meaning of man's image as a cross-section of the present moment[17] — as he sees himself, and as he appears to those like him.

Behind all these successive sections, each representing one single instant as each respiration illuminates the *differential of the Present*, we can find an entire *film*. Between the limits drawn by birth and death, this *film* represents the life of each of us, all the beings we have met, and the ensemble of material and moral circumstances which surround us.

This is comparable to what happens when we view the film in a kaleidoscope through its narrow slot. This gives the illusion of movement in Time. The breadth of the slot through which this observation is made is analogous to *the differential of the Present*.

The example of the kaleidoscope allows us to be more precise about this notion of *the duration of the Present*. In reality, the *Present* is not known to endure, and in fact it has no duration. It does not last; all that lasts extends in Time, and so in fact automatically exists in the domain of the Future–Past. The expression: '*duration of the Present*' is a convention. It gives easier access for our intelligence — which takes Time as an absolute category — to the notion of the *Present,* a category which is actually situated *outside Time*. From now on, whenever we use the conventionalized term '*the duration of the Present*', we must take care not to lose this factor from view.

The example of the kaleidoscope, as we were saying, permits us to give real meaning to this conventional expression. It is in fact correct to measure the individual *Present* by means of units of Time; but when we do so we do not measure the *Present* itself, which has no measure, but the *breadth of the slot* through which we observe the film of the kaleidoscope, the *film* of life. Here is another example, chosen to help us better understand this mechanism which rules us.

Let us imagine a being without dimension, a living point endowed with the intelligence of the first dimension. Let us agree that this being lives on a geometrical line, let us say a curve. To him, his whole notion of space is reduced to three representations: what is in front, what is behind, and what is here. In addition, because his mind has no notion of a second dimension, which is necessary to visualize a curve, he believes that the curve on which he lives is a straight line.

The human being, three dimensional in space, is monodimensional in Time. He lives on a straight line in Time, and perceives nothing outside that line. All his notion of Time is reduced, in analogy to the above example, to three representations: ahead — the Future; behind him —

---

17. Fr. 'dans sa coupe de l'instant'.

the Past; and lastly here — the *Present*, which he conceives as without extension.

But if, by appropriate exercises, our living point could acquire a sense of the second dimension, and if he is torn away from the geometrical line on which he lives, believing there is nowhere else — he would realize at that moment, very surprised, that it is possible for him not only to observe the point *here*, but simultaneously to observe two fragments of the line, one in front, and the other behind him.

First case:

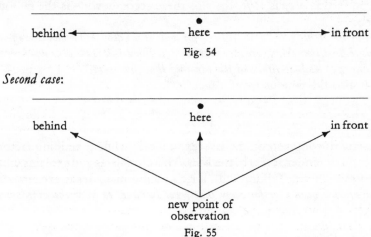

Fig. 54

Second case:

new point of
observation

Fig. 55

The analogy with *exterior* man, who lives on a line of Time, is complete.

We will remember that such a line is curved because of the *Law of Seven*. Monodimensional in Time, the human mind cannot see the deviation of this line in the future. The Future is presented to him not as a curved progression, but as a straight line of Time, a tangent to the present moment. This is one of the principal reasons why man is wrong in his forecasts of the future.

Passing through the stage of man 4, and reaching that of man 5, someone who progresses towards the *Way* begins to acquire the ability to perceive the second dimension of Time. As in the example where the point is torn away from the line, he simultaneously observes the present moment, the Future, and the Past. This means that our concept of Future and Past is a relative concept, belonging to the limited intelligence of *exterior* man, when in reality, objectively, nothing exists except the *Present*, a *film* which — for any given cycle — contains all the Future and all the Past.

We can now understand better this enigmatic and grammatically absurd phrase of Jesus that says '... *before Abraham was, I am*.'[18]

18. John viii: 58.

This being said, we can better understand that *esoteric work on oneself has the essential aim of broadening the individual slot that opens directly on the Present.*

The uninterrupted succession of dP's permits man to live on a line of Time. But the slot belonging to *exterior* man is not sufficient for him to perceive the Future and the Past within the same broad *Present*, and so benefit from this permanent existence. In order to reach this, the slot must be suitably enlarged.

The perception of the '*I*', within a *Present* which embraces Future and Past, is none other than the consciousness of the real '*I*'. The *Present* conceived in this way is *Life*; the slot three seconds wide is the famous *strait gate*.

'*Enter by the strait gate*,' said Jesus: '*for wide is the door and broad is the path that leads to perdition. Many are they that enter it. For strait is the door and narrow is the Path that leads to life, and few are they that find them.*'[19]

This is also the famous *eye of the needle.*[20]

(8)

It is useful to comment on the last text quoted, while examining factors which aid or hinder access to the *Way*. This completes and explains what has been said above. Talking with a rich young man, Jesus exclaimed:

'*Children, how hard is it for them that trust in riches to enter the kingdom of God.*'[21]

Then He added:

'*It is easier for a camel to go through the eye of a needle than for a rich man to enter the kingdom of God.*'[22]

The question is: who is a rich man? Rich, in the esoteric sense, is someone who assigns real value to his Personality; who places his confidence and hopes in it. This is independent of whether he has many belongings or possesses nothing.

To set out on the *Way*, man must necessarily go through an inner collapse of the Personality, what we call *moral bankruptcy*. Then he will know the vain illusion of pride,[23] and the true value of humility. Rich man or beggar, he will have become *poor in spirit*. Now he can easily slip through the *needle's eye*, for it is said:

'*Happy are the poor in spirit, for theirs is the kingdom of heaven.*'[24]

---

19. Matthew vii: 14.
20. Mark x: 25; Luke xviii: 25.
21. Mark x: 24–25; Luke xviii: 24–25.
22. Matthew xix: 23–24; Mark x: 25; Luke xviii: 25.
23. Fr. 'orgeuil'.
24. Matthew v: 3.

CHAPTER XX

(1)

This system of esoteric exercises has been conceived so that people who have already acquired a certain store of theoretical Knowledge can go on to practical work. It is based on the *Doctrine of the Present*. These exercises are divided into three groups, correlated to the structure of the Personality. These three groups of exercises have a single common goal: the acquisition of the *real Present*. They are both physical and psychological. If the psychological exercises are to be fruitful, it is necessary to render the body capable of supporting the required work by a series of physical exercises. Let us not forget that we live *in the body*, and that, properly trained and disciplined, the latter is a marvellous instrument, as well as the only one available to us for achieving the proposed goal. Let us not forget also that esoteric development demands considerable efforts, largely surpassing those we generally make in life. To sustain these efforts, the body must be sound, strong and trained.

The three groups of exercises, practised all along the *Way*, have the following objectives:

— mastery of the body;

— mastery of the Personality;

— establishing contact with higher levels of consciousness.

We can see that these exercises concern the three '*I*'s of man: by training based on a rigid discipline of the '*I*' of the body and the '*I*' of the Personality, we open up for ourselves access to the consciousness of the real '*I*'. This is the theory. The practice has been elaborated since time immemorial: it consists of a ladder of eight groups[1] of exercises.

(2)

The first group relates to *outer cleanliness*: the body must be washed carefully every day; with special attention to the cleanliness of the navel, the feet, and the genital organs. The head must be washed regularly. The nostrils must be cleared to let the air pass through freely.

(3)

The second group aims at *inner cleanliness*: the complete and regular evacuation of the digestive tract must be rigorously observed. Constipation deeply intoxicates the organism. By interrupting at a certain

---

1. Fr. 'groupes-échelons'.

point the working of the digestive system, which normally operates according to the *Law of Seven*, it hinders the transmutation of hydrogens and so deprives the organism of that part of solar energy most precious for esoteric work. Because of this, man loses the possibility of rising above the lower levels of consciousness.

These two groups of exercises have great importance, even though their value is, so to speak, negative. They do not themselves lead towards esoteric evolution, but they are an indispensable condition of this evolution, and must therefore be practised with care.

The maintenance of inner cleanliness is facilitated by daily physical exercise: by walking, gymnastics, and an appropriate dietary regime. Experience will allow us to discover the proper measure for ourselves in this. Here too, we have to guard ourselves against excess. Right measure will be recognized by the sensation of satisfaction it gives us. The activity and regimen we follow must be sound, fortifying, and agreeable. The aim is to restore to the organism its natural balance, generally broken by the artificial conditions in which we live and work. The maintenance of our weight within normal limits also attests to the right choice of our mode of life.

In monastic practice, the conditions of a balanced life are fixed by a *Rule* established centuries ago and practised under the direction of the *Igoumen* (superior). For esoteric work followed in the secular world, these conditions must be studied and applied by the practitioner himself.

(4)

The third group of exercises aims at acquiring *correct posture*. For the practice of psychological exercises, the body must be kept in as perfect a state of equilibrium as possible, so that the attention can be totally concentrated on the object of the exercise. For that, the best posture, called by the Tradition the *posture of the Sage*, must be studied and practised until it can be maintained *in total immobility* for as long as necessary. It is practised seated on a hard chair which does not exceed thirty centimetres in height; legs crossed, knees widespread, hands freely placed on the knees. The position of the arms and hands may be changed, depending on the object of the exercise.

The essential condition is that the head, neck and the vertebral column are kept in a straight vertical line. The shoulders must be held back, and the head high. Dolichocephalic persons must watch to maintain their sinciput horizontally.

All the muscles must be relaxed. This can be done by first contracting them group by group, then suddenly releasing them. The waist must be arched, and if we have followed the instructions just given, the back and head will then naturally take the correct position in a straight line. Bending the back during these exercises must be avoided at all costs. If this becomes a habit, we risk damaging the cerebro-spinal system. In addition, we must pay attention that the vertebral column does not jut out. Lastly, we must watch that all the muscles of the extremities — the hands including the fingers, and the feet including the toes — are completely relaxed.

The eyes must remain motionless. Their position depends upon the purpose of the given exercise, but in general we must look straight ahead, our vision following a line parallel to the ground. To be sure of that, we measure the distance between the eyes and the floor in the sitting position and then fix what the Tradition calls the *sun* on the wall; about four to five metres away and in front of us. This is a black matt circle of three centimetres in diameter, drawn on a white card. Mastery over the eyes is not acquired instantaneously. This is generally the last organ to submit to discipline. That is why the study of the *posture of the Sage* begins with closed eyes. Later on, when we open them, we tolerate their movement on condition that the sight does not leave the limits of the *sun*. Finally, we will achieve immobility of sight.

This is a basic description of the *posture of the Sage*. In practice, we will come up against a multitude of minor difficulties. We must neither worry too much, nor be discouraged. By following the instructions given above, each of us must find his own position of equilibrium. This, as we have said, does not come immediately. When, after repeated trials, the correct posture is finally found and can easily be re-assumed, we will recognize this by the following sign: a sensation of relaxation and of rest which even sleep itself does not give.

The practice of the *posture of the Sage* forms an indispensable condition for the success of the exercises leading to the mastery of physiological processes, and for discipline of the mental[2] life. This is why we must try to find this posture, and perfect it with application and diligence.

The Tradition teaches other postures and other movements: different sorts of genuflections, prostrations and '*stolpostoyanie*'. The latter consists of standing erect like a pole. It was especially used in the primitive church of Egypt. For this type of practice, which demanded considerable mastery of the body and the nerves, even greater than that possessed and exhibited by a professional sailor on the high masts of a sailing ship, they chose highly elevated positions such as the tops of columns.

To practice the psychological method, called the *Royal Way*[3] in the Tradition, the *posture of the Sage*, correctly maintained, is necessary and sufficient for almost all training requirements. Nearly all the psychological

2. Fr. 'psychique'.

3. Tr. In the Indian version of the Tradition this is called Raja Yoga. Readers who are interested in this are referred to Vivekananda's commentaries on Patanjali's Yoga Sutras. This reference by the Author to the Indian Doctrine is intentional, and in another place he has said that the Indian term Agni refers to the Holy Spirit.

exercises, and a great part of the physical exercises, can be done on the basis of this posture.

(5)

The fourth group of exercises concerns *respiration*. If we consider the organism as a machine, respiration represents the flywheel. It regularizes the operation and maintains the rhythm established by the work of the heart. Respiration exerts a direct influence on the metabolism, contributing to the production of the finest energies by the organism, those necessary to establish contact with the higher centres. This influence can be augmented considerably by the control of respiration, particularly by the practice of rhythmic respiration. This possibility is given us by the fact that the movement of the thoracic cage which maintains respiration has dual nervous regulation: the instinctive-automatic system and the voluntary. The possibility of passing from one to the other provides a *bridge*[4] inside our organism between physiological and psychological functions. This bridge is not the only one, but it is very important.

However much they open up seductive perspectives of esoteric evolution, breathing exercises have this risk: badly performed, they can lead to undesirable or even dangerous consequences. They can provoke pulmonary emphysema, for example, or derange the functioning of the heart.

The first precept for the control of breathing is simple. It teaches that, once the lungs have been filled, one must retain the air. We find this instruction in texts of the Orthodox Tradition coming down to us from long ago. However, the duration over which this suspension of the respiratory rhythm is to be maintained is not specified. Since then, a whole series of variations in the practice of this precept have been elaborated. Because of the danger if this is applied without discernment, we must not make use of it except under the personal and constant control of a master.[5]

Since the beginning of the century, we find many books from Hindu, Buddhist or other sources dealing with the question of breath control and rhythm, often commented on by occidental authors. Without going into a critical analysis of the systems and directions given in these books, we must insist on the dangers of practising these breathing exercises when relying on book descriptions only, without the attentive presence of a competent guide.

In Orthodox monastic practice, and especially in the Russian branch of the Tradition, liturgical chant plays an important role by serving as a respiratory exercise. In certain monasteries, for example the Petchera Lavra in Kiev, these chants are carried out in full voice. At the same

---

4. Fr. 'passerelle'.
5. Ed. Many authorities—including P. D. Ouspensky—emphasize the dangers of unsupervised breathing exercises.

time, the choir must concentrate on the theme of the canticle. This mixed exercise, physical, mental[6] and spiritual, uses powerful means and produces remarkable results.

(6)

The fifth group of exercises have as their object *constatation*. With the exercise of constatation we enter fully into the psychological field. By this exercise, we start to face the problem of self study in a practical manner.

To constate means to recognize the state of a thing or phenomenon, to establish a fact *without applying any kind of personal judgement*.

The act of constating therefore implies simple observation of a fact while at the same time being conscious of oneself. Thus — and this is its esoteric meaning — *constatation* demands a doubling of attention; to the object, and to one's own self. This exercise demands all the impartiality of which one is capable. Otherwise, it degenerates into reporting; a unilateral act which, from the esoteric point of view, leads to nothing.

Constatation involves two groups of exercises:

— *Constatation* called *exterior*, where we observe one or several external objects, including ourselves; where we look at ourselves, so to speak, 'from the outside'.

— *Constatation* called *interior*, where we observe one or more traits, facts, or phenomena of our own inner life.

(7)

Constatation includes every mode of the new attitude that forms in a man who starts esoteric work. It is a permanent struggle against the force of mental sleep. We know that one can look without seeing: this is the characteristic of the majority of our visual impressions. We can look and see, in other words, we can *observe*. There is progress there, with attention brought into play; but observing is not enough to obtain esoteric results, since even while we are attentive, the object can still seduce us to the point of making us lose our consciousness of ourselves. It is only when we *observe*, while making a *conscious* effort directed simultaneously towards the exterior and towards the interior, that we reach true *constatation* which itself then produces an esoteric result. Observation of this general rule of doubled attention is demanded throughout the *Way*, all the way to the summit of esoteric evolution. That is the *tresvenic* of the Tradition, to which we have already referred. It is the constant effort to *be watchful*, keeping the idea of the '*I*' present in one's mind, while continuing

6. Fr. 'psychique'.

one's outer activities as before — but better. *Constatation* has for its basis and starting point the general instruction which Jesus taught to his disciples: '*What I say unto you, I say unto all: Watch.*'[7]

But we have already seen that the *exterior* man lives absent from himself. He lives in dreams: dreams at night, and daydreams.

We sleep in life, and sleep deeply. How, in practice, can we get out of this situation? It is difficult, and this is why. A sleeping man retains a sense of the experience of his life in the waking state, with the memory of his name, that symbol of his Personality. When he wakes, these (memories) will allow him to recover his waking consciousness without difficulty. But for the passage from this to the higher level of consciousness, to the consciousness of the real '*I*', these two essential elements are missing: experience of that life, and the knowledge of his name *at that level*. It is by working ceaselessly, 'boring away', by the practice of *constatation*—which comprises and implies a conscious effort of *presence*, to the point where it becomes a true *presence in oneself*—that man can reach the second Birth, the birth of *Individuality*, understood as the indissoluble junction of his developed and born Personality with his real '*I*'. At this time he will obtain his new name, and he will progressively be initiated to that new experience, previously unsuspected, to which the book of Revelation refers:

'*To him that overcometh... to him will I give a white stone and upon the stone, his new name is written, which no one knoweth but he that receiveth it.*'[8]

(8)

External constatation can be *passive*. In this case it relates to objects presented to us on the external film of events, without our exercising any selection between them.

Alternatively it can be *active*, when it is directed at a chosen object. In this active form, *external constatation* can make use of a particular method which, when practised regularly, helps us greatly to know the impression we produce on others. Although not an aim in itself, this exercise is at least a valuable means of discarding a great part of the false representations we have of ourselves. This type of *constatation* can be called *constatation by reflection*, or *taking snapshots* of oneself. These snapshots give the best results when they are taken at meetings,[9] while we are speaking. A sudden effort of *constatation* then permits each of us to *feel ourselves* as we are seen at that moment by those around us. An album of such snapshots allows us to reconstruct in our mind's eye the image we present to others. To know

7. Mark xiii: 37. (Fr. 'veillez'.)
8. Revelation ii: 17.
9. Fr. 'réunions'.

that image even better, a simple exercise with two mirrors is also very useful. We know that our image in a mirror is inverted: the right becomes left, and vice versa. If we look at ourselves by means of two mirrors, our image is corrected. This generally gives us a strange impression. The defects of our faces appear accentuated, because the eye can no longer automatically correct our features, as it did in the case of an inverted image.

The exercise with two mirrors also allows us to see ourselves in profile. We do not know our profile at all. These new visions of ourselves always bring us something.

Orthodox practice knows another form of *tresvenic*, of *active external constatation*, which it commonly uses. It acts in the *prayer of Jesus*, in this form:

'*Lord Jesus Christ, Son of God, have mercy on me, a sinner.*'[10] We can recognize the double objective presented to the attention in this verse: asking for grace, and consciousness of oneself as a sinner. The two elements required for *constatation* are combined here, but only on condition that this prayer is not done mechanically, but by a conscious effort of *presence*. Bishop Theophan says in his commentaries that the force of this prayer does not reside in the words. The words can be modified. The power of the invocation, he says, lies in *constating* our degenerate state before God in His state of perfection. We add that this simultaneous effort of *constatation* creates what we called a difference of potential. This will generate a current of grace. The prayer of Jesus is repeated a great number of times, up to ten or even twenty thousand times a day, both by practising religious, and by laymen.[11]

(9)

The second group of *constatations* are *interior constatations*. This is a vast field of indispensable exercises which, with those already described, will firmly establish us on the *Track* which leads to the *path of Access*, and then to the *Way*.

In these *interior constatations*, we find the same distinction between passive and active exercises as in the case of *outer constatation*.

Interior constatation is to be practised daily in its *passive* form, preferably in the morning, and as far as possible at the same time. The exercise consists of the following: after having remained in the *posture of the Sage* for the time necessary to feel the muscles relax and the rhythm of the body become normal and regular, we must *constate passively* everything that unfolds itself in front of the mental eye. This exercise requires training. It is possible that,

---

10. In the French edition this was translated from the Russian. It is given here as commonly used in English — translated from the original Greek.

11. Ed. Amongst Orthodox monks both the number of repetitions and the speed of repetition varies very much from monastery to monastery.

at the start, we shall see nothing, or very little. By persevering, little by little we will discover a whole *world* rich in life and colours. Later on, this world will become the object of a work whose aim is to bring order to it and, finally, to master it or, in esoteric language, to *overcome* it. But before that, we have to make it emerge totally from the wings of waking consciousness. This is achieved by calm and impartial *passive constatation*. Impartiality is required above all, as man is generally surprised to discover certain emotional and instinctive movements within him, certain ideas which, during the normal state of *waking sleep*, will appear totally foreign to him. The seeker will progressively learn to explore his own moral content. He will constate that only a small part of this content is usually visible on the scene of his waking consciousness, the principal part being shut out somewhere in the wings of his soul. It is with stupefaction, and sometimes with fright, that he will discover coexistences within him that will appear to him impossible and absurd—a poet and a cynic, a hero and a coward. He will perceive that he is essentially an egotist, ready to justify to himself, if necessary by the most fallacious processes of rationalization, any state of soul that he would judge contemptible or criminal in others.

Similar traits—and there are large numbers of them, some more detestable than the others—are dumped behind the scenes of our consciousness, they are instinctively hidden in the 'wings' for two reasons. On the one hand — and this is the general case — man forms a picture of himself far removed from the reality, and then will simply and directly exclude anything that does not correspond to this self-image. Yet these rejected characteristics remain his own. On the other hand, man is afraid of what he really is. As long as he remains inside *exterior* life, he has no need to begin an introspection which will lead him to confront his inner life face to face. In the rare cases where fortuitous circumstances put him momentarily face to face with himself, he turns away his inner eye, immediately returning to the image he has created of himself. This naturally has its source in a systematic lie to himself, but this is not at all surprising, given that *exterior* man is born in lies, lives in lies, and dies in lies. It is only esoteric work which can lead him out of this *wilderness*, this forest full of wild beasts in which he lives. He will then stop being an *exterior* man.

The same exercise of *constatation* yields yet another important result. This is the *recognition of the principal feature of the Personality*.

Each Personality has a principal feature[12] for its axis, and all its qualities and defects gravitate around this. It is not necessary for this trait to be striking; it can be insignificant and even ridiculous. It is remarkable that man recognizes the principal feature in himself only with the greatest

---

12. Tr. For each person, the chief feature will determine the type and number of illusions which form the source of our errors of conception and so of our sins. Because everyone's chief feature is different, they cannot be described for all, so that the guidance of a master is needed to reveal them.

difficulty. Yet it is important to recognize and accept it. We could say, in a pictorial way, that to grasp this is to hold the end of the thread that will allow us to unwind the bobbin. It is by recognizing and studying his principal feature that man will be able to define and recognize his own type, to place himself with no possibility of error in the centre of gravity of his own Personality, in one of the eighteen sectors of his lower centres. Here we pass beyond mere theory to begin our practical work, which starts when we recognize and begin to adjust the functioning of the three centres. This task extends along the whole length of what we have called the *path of Access*.

The diligent practice of *constatation*, particularly in its passive form, as just described, is an instrument of selection. The weak will turn aside from it, abandoning the search for the *Way* to sink further into Illusion. The strong are aware of the terrible reality which their moral contents represent, and they understand — no longer philosophically, as if it concerned somebody else, but with upheaval of soul — that the moment has come to prepare a balance sheet and set it before the Judge. This demands courage.

We have indicated many times already that the *Way* cannot be reached without the seeker accepting his moral bankruptcy and passing beyond this. We are now better placed to understand the reason for and significance of this necessity. From the very beginning of esoteric work, man has every interest in establishing his moral balance sheet: it would be less painful for him to uncover these elements of the balance sheet in stages than to gather them all at once. Whatever the method used, the balance sheet must be arrived at, formulated honestly, and set down. Once having reached the level of man 4; the end of the *path of Access*, to set out upon the *Way*, man can no longer hold a false image of himself. He must *become as a child*, stripped of lies and illusion about himself, rid of all that is artificial which his instruction, education and experience of life have laid down in him. That is the meaning of the words of Jesus: '*Verily I say unto you, except ye turn and become as little children, ye shall not enter into the kingdom of heaven.*'[13]

This exercise of *interior constatation* is the instrument which allows the courageous and persevering seeker to become a *child*. To enter the *Way* of Salvation with a firm tread.

In its active form, *interior constatation* chooses the particular object of our interior life that should be brought to our attention; its typical form is the practice of examining the conscience.

The aim is the same as in active *exterior constatation*.

Either of these exercises can lead to *concentration*. The object of this can either be interior or exterior, since the Kingdom of God is both inside and outside us at the same time. (See Fig. 27).

---

13. Matthew xviii: 3.

(10)

Constatation can take various forms, appropriate to the chosen object and attitude. But doubled attention is always obligatory.

The exercise of *presence* is an effort of *watchfulness*; as we have seen, it is the principal element in this. When done daily, in the form of *passive constatation*, it leads to knowledge of oneself. But because presence must as far as possible become *permanent*—and we emphasize this point because of its importance—the seeker must practise doubled attention as much as he can during all his activities. He will notice in time that this effort of memory, of *presence*, not only does not hinder his activities, but on the contrary it helps greatly in carrying them out.

Presence, among others, takes two forms which must be particularly observed: these are, first, *non-confluence*, and second, *non-considering*.

We have commented on these two attitudes on several occasions. It is, however, necessary to study one particular aspect with greater consideration. *Interior non-considering* must be cultivated in such a way that it becomes total. But we must not confuse this with *exterior non-considering*. Generally, *exterior* man, when in a state of *confluence*, is full of *inner considerings*. On the other hand, he lacks *external consideration*. One must look out for that. *External considering* must be increased as much as possible. *Exterior* life is characterized by mechanicalness on the mental[14] plane as well as on the physical. We know that we must not let our finger slip into the wheels of a working machine: it would be crushed. We might even lose our lives. It is the same on the mental[14] plane: our attention must remain vigilant. Being machines ourselves, we must avoid colliding with the mental[14] mechanisms which surround us.

In broad outline, this is the meaning and purpose of the exercise of *constatation*, and the objectives it allows us to reach. We can now understand why it must be followed all along the *Way*. It serves first as a means to reach these objectives, and then as a means of controlling the results acquired at each stage.

(11)

The sixth group of exercises concerns *concentration*, an active psychological exercise. This consists of withholding the attention from everything which is not the object of moral or physical concentration.

---

14. Fr. 'psychique'.

(12)

The seventh group concerns *contemplation*. This is reached when we are able to keep our concentration on the same object during a specified period of time.

(13)

The last group aims at *ecstasy*. Concentration followed by prolonged contemplation leads man towards *ecstasy*, which is a state of consciousness. As long as this state endures, man finds himself outside the five senses.[15]

(14)

The last three groups of exercises, starting from concentration, cannot be usefully approached until tangible results have been obtained by the prolonged practice of *constatation*. For the time being, we must apply ourselves to that which is accessible to us, and is indispensable if we are to reach the level of man 4. It is only then, as we have tried to show, that the *Way* of esoteric evolution will open to the seeker.

(15)

Let us now recall some of the factors which will help us study a general scheme of the *Way*.

Man lives in his physical body. In this body is his Personality. This is a subtle organism with a provisional 'I'. Behind this organism, the higher organs of the consciousness of the real 'I' and of Consciousness itself are (already) fully formed.

We must draw the attention here to the need for precise terminology. Origen (185–253), in the *Principles*, warned disciples about the intentionally imprecise expressions used in certain texts: it is thus, he said, that the Apostles sometimes spoke of the body when they really meant the soul, and vice versa. But, he would add, sages know how to make the distinction.

A real confusion for *exterior* man comes from the undeveloped state of his Personality. Save for rare exceptions, he knows nothing inside himself other than the Personality. This, by its contrast with his body, presents itself to him as his soul. Nevertheless, due to its hostile attitude towards the real 'I', the Personality is more closely linked to the body than to the true 'I'. This soul-Personality is therefore perishable.

This explains the apparent contradiction in which we attribute immortality to the soul, yet speak as if it is in danger of perishing... and the

---

15. John xi: 33; xiii:21.

213

obligation on our part to care about its salvation. In fact, there is only one means of salvation for the soul-Personality: and that is its intimate junction — through the medium of the higher centres of consciousness — with the true, eternal and imperishable Soul which manifests itself in man under certain conditions.

By this fusion the soul-Personality, which has no light of its own, will shine with the light of the immortal Soul with which, from now on, it will become one. The strength of the real 'I' will then render the personal 'I' — who has thus become identified with it, immortal. This is the meaning of the word Salvation. It is also the meaning of Creation, as analyzed in the previous chapter.

(16)

We know that the junction of the Personality with the higher emotional centre is not realized until the second Birth; this does not happen except after long work on the Personality, with the aim of bringing it to perfection.

From this comes the definition of the *path of Access*: *the path of Access consists of the progressive acquisition of the knowledge[16] and savoir-faire that allow development of the Personality to accomplish the second Birth, its intimate union with the real 'I'. The Individuality born in this way enters the Way in a full sense.*

We will see that the definition above covers only one part of the *Way*—in the broader meaning of the term—known as the *path of Access*. This part is nevertheless the most important for the seeker, for the struggle he has begun against Death ends here in *Victory*.

We can also say that this Victory consists in the absorption of the *magnetic centre* by the higher emotional centre. This happens when the *magnetic centre* absorbs the lower emotional centre, after regulating and balancing the three lower centres of the Personality.

After this Victory, the subsequent part of the *Way*, the *Way* properly speaking, involves work that must be done in totally different conditions, outside any grasp or influence of Death, with all the phenomena which accompany it.

(17)

The *Way* in its ensemble has *seven sections* between *three Thresholds*. According to the Gospel, it leads *from Death to Life*.

The *Way* is conceived according to the *Law of Seven*, and goes from *exterior* life to the *third Threshold*—the limit of the evolution of terrestrial man — in *ten stages*. Man passes through each of these stages by concentrated effort on a creative work conceived to conform to the *Law of Three*.

---

16. Fr. 'savoir'.

Going back to the terminology of primitive Christianity, in these ten stages we can distinguish three states:

— *Catechumens* (tracks)	— those who by discernment of 'B' influences have already created within themselves an embryonic *magnetic centre;*
— *The Faithful* (paths of Access)	— seekers who, having crossed the *first Threshold*, progress towards the *second Threshold;*
— *Christians* (the Way)	— those who, having crossed the *second Threshold*, evolve towards the *third Threshold*.

To follow the *Way* is to put *esotericism* into practice. Let us remind the reader that this notion applies[17] to *catechumens*, to *the faithful*, and to *Christians* — in the meaning the Primitive Church gave to these words — who follow their individual evolution. In the following diagram we distinguish several grades represented by three concentric circles, surrounded by a zone symbolizing the *wilderness*, that is to say, *exterior* life.[18]

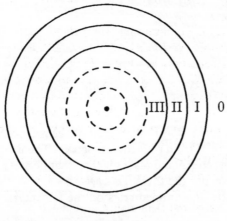

Fig. 56

0 — exterior, the *wilderness*, zone of *exterior* man;
I — *exotericism*, zone of the *catechumens*;
II — *mesotericism*, zone of the *faithful*;
III — *esotericism* proper, zone of the *Christians, interior* men.

---

17. Cf. Chapter VI, p. 50 and Fig. 18.
18. We must not confuse the zones so defined with the hierarchy in the bosom of the Church which comprises — or should comprise — seven grades:

1) Apostles.
2) Prophets.
3) Masters of the Church (also called doctors of the Church).
4) Bishops.
5) Presbyters (priests).
6) Deacons.
7) Faithful.

This last zone is divided in turn into three concentric circles, attributed to men 5 and 6 respectively with man 7 in the middle.

Thus the diagram of the *Way* along its length is as follows:

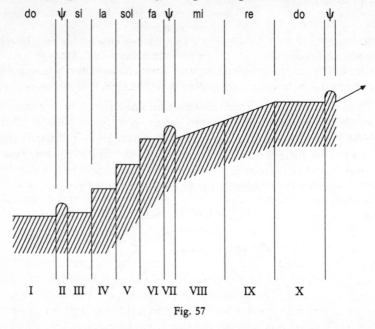

Fig. 57

In this diagram the *Way* is conceived in accordance with a gamut that goes from DO to DO and so forms an octave. The intervals between DO and SI, and between FA and MI, as well as that between DO and SI of the following octave, are the three *Thresholds*.

Let us pass now to commentaries on the ten stages of this diagram.

(18)

First stage

The space to the left of the *first Threshold* represents *exterior* life, characterized by anarchy of the three centres of the Personality. Exact and precise discernment between 'A' and 'B' influences creates the embryo of the *magnetic centre*. Under the influence of the latter, the seeker is drawn towards the *first Threshold*.

Second stage

Having reached this point, man has entered a path. He is placed *face to face with Life*: his own life, with its own soluble and insoluble problems.

This is his first esoteric test. This test consists of a general reassessment of values. The results obtained depend upon the objectivity and courage brought to the task. One must exert a conscious effort upon oneself so as not to 'dodge the issue' or lie to oneself during this reevaluation. One must consider and analyze those about one, face facts and attribute their intrinsic value to them without compromise or pity for oneself or others. One must, naturally, keep the results of this re-evaluation to oneself.

This done, one must draw certain conclusions. Is one losing interest in *exterior* life, which unfolds exclusively under the sway of factors of influence 'A', and to what extent? Is the centre of gravity of the Personality being displaced towards the *magnetic centre*? Is a real emphasis being given to it? (Fig. 20).

At this time, a choice must be made.

It would be better to withdraw before crossing the *first Threshold* than, having cut oneself off from the region of *bourgeois happiness*, to wish to regain it later. The *Way is a one-way street*. After the *Threshold* there is only one option: either to *progress on the Way* or to *fall*. From now on, any return to the original state will be forbidden. If the *magnetic centre* is pure and *sufficiently firm*, a man of influence 'C' (Fig. 20) appears: the *first Threshold* will be crossed under his direction.

Third stage

The *first Threshold* crossed, a link in the chain of esoteric influence will have been forged. Becoming one of the *faithful*, the *catechumen* is *saved in hope*.[19] Yet he will still remain as he was before. All the conscious efforts he has made have allowed him to cross the *Threshold*. This is an enormous step forward. But the sincere desire to get out of *exterior* life, which inspired the crossing, is not in itself enough to free him from all 'A' influences.

On the other side of the *Threshold*, *mesoteric* work will unfold before someone who has reached the note SI. He must be solidly established in this state, and facing forward, as '*Whoever puts his hand to the plough, and looks back, is not fit for the kingdom of God*.'[20] The task for the note SI, is for every

19. Romans viii: 24.
20. Luke ix: 62.

disciple to go back carefully through the *film* of his life, so as to reach a double result:

— To distinguish *objectively*, as far as is possible for him at this phase of his evolution, between permanent, *eternal* elements and *temporary*, karmic ones;

— To stimulate within himself, with the help of this analysis, a strong desire to cross the *second Threshold*.

The strength of this desire, and the firmness of his decision, are the only measures of success. This is why the disciple should attach particular importance to work at the note SI of the *Way*. This is all the more so because this note is short. It is, in fact, only a half tone.

Before the *first Threshold*, man must be aware of his attitude towards *exterior* life in general. This threshold crossed, he must take as objective not this external life, with all its illusions, but instead, the *film of his own life*.

(21)

Fourth, fifth and sixth stages

These correspond to the three notes LA, SOL, and FA of the *Way*. Properly speaking these, with the note SI, form the *path of Access* to the *Way*.

This phase, including the note SI, presents itself as a *Staircase* that man has to climb (cf. Chapter XV, p. 146).

This esoteric staircase has a peculiarity which we must keep in our minds. It is not possible for us to stay on a particular step indefinitely. After a specified delay, sufficient for him to fulfil the task required from him by the note in force, the step will give way.

During evolution through the notes LA, SOL and FA, the *faithful*, climbing the *Staircase* step after step, will have the following tasks to do:

— *note LA* — to make the Personality grow to its fullest possible extent;
— *note SOL* — to develop it;
— *note FA* — to balance the three lower centres by replacing the mechanical ties between them with conscious ties from each centre to the *magnetic centre*, to which the lower centres will then be subordinated.

Climbing the *Staircase* in this way, beginning from the note SI and passing notes LA and SOL, the *faithful* will reach the note FA. By accomplishing the task which has been described for this note, he will become man 4.

The eliminated morality will be replaced inside him by the action of his conscience,[21] the embryonic expression of the consciousness of the real 'I'.

---

21. Fr. 'for intérieur'.

218

The latter's radiance will penetrate, bit by bit, through the *magnetic centre* to the whole Personality of the seeker.

It is to be noted that man 4 remains in several ways an *exterior* man; and he is still *mortal*. But he is ready to cross the *second Threshold*, beyond which, safely sheltered from the 'A' influences and from the *Law of Accident*, the *Way* begins in its true sense.

Once having reached this degree, the disciple becomes a man of influence 'C' (Fig. 20).

One must never lose sight of the fact that everything man does, he does imperfectly. Theoretically, man 4, by the time the note FA is resounding fully, should already be absolute master of himself. The growth and the development of his Personality should have been pushed to their utmost limits. If this were really the case, the absorption of the lower emotional centre by the *magnetic centre* would have occurred in profound joy. But this only happens rarely. This is because man, everywhere and always late, does not fully[22] succeed in accomplishing his task at each step of the *Staircase*. As the time allowed for him to finish his work on each step is limited, he is obliged, from fear of a fall,[23] to pass to the next step while still dragging behind him a part, sometimes a large part, of his karmic debt.

This is allowed, but only on condition that his purification is completed at the note FA.

(22)

Seventh stage

Having reached the *first Threshold*, the *catechumen* has been placed *facing 'life'*. Having reached the *second Threshold*, he is placed *face to face with himself*.

In other words, he will see his Personality in its ensemble and in every detail. In the same way, he will perceive all the results of his *Karma*, as well as all the distortions they have provoked in his *being*, in particular, the distortion that comes from hypocrisy towards oneself, and from the lies we tell ourselves. These are the most difficult elements to constate. Consequently they are the most difficult to neutralize.

This is the second great test.

For the first time in his life, he will see himself objectively, as he is, with no make-up, without the least justification or compromise, and with no *possibility of evasion*.

For the just, this ordeal is full of ineffable joy. To him it will be like the light of dawn.

---

22. Fr. 'intégralement'.
23. Fr. 'effondrement'.

For the unjust—and this is the general case—this vision of oneself seems terrifying.

Perfect equilibrium of the Personality cannot be attained except by complete neutralization of all karmic consequences. Someone who aspires to liberation, although of good faith, cannot appreciate the nature and importance of this. *Born in sin*, he can—and in practice does—consider certain aspects of that *Karma* as being human and thus normal.

Faced with the *second Threshold*, everything that has been learned mechanically loses its force; all the *buffers*, all the *auto-tranquillizers*, must be broken and thrown away. All debts must be paid in the proper coin.

At the same time, the *faithful* has to rid himself of those illusory and imaginary duties which sometimes acquire a hypnotic force, and to which a human being attaches real value.

This confrontation with oneself generally takes a dramatic course because of the karmic debt which each one of us carries. But this is inevitable.

Man must now take stock of all his mental[24] possessions, since until this time the greatest part of these possessions were outside his field of observation, somewhere in the archives of his subconsciousness. He will be surprised, when constating the contents of that subconsciousness, just what he may discover in there; traces of heroic acts, and perhaps of the most ignoble crimes as well.

If he runs away from this monster—in which he must recognize himself—this will be the fall, full of the worst dangers.

His attitude must be one of *attack*. Then, the Personality-monster will give way. At that moment, man will become *master of himself*. It will be the consecration of the position represented by figure 56.

This moment is decisive. From now on, strengthened by the Victory won, the man's task will be to *transfigure his Personality*. He should convey to it an *image of radiant Beauty*. In the language of the Tradition, we can say that at this time the *Betrothed is adorned with her bridal gown*.

This done, the Betrothed of Christ will be ready to meet the Bridegroom.

(23)

With the crossing of the *second Threshold*, the developed and harmonized Personality will be born. This is the second Birth, analogous to physical birth from every point of view. It passes through the same phases. The Doctrine describes detailed parallels between the two, which help the disciple and his master to control the order of this evolution. The book by Nicodemus the Hagiorite called *Unseen Warfare* contains one of the best descriptions of this.

---

24. Fr. 'psychique'.

Having crossed the *second Threshold*, the Personality unites itself with the real '*I*'. Its provisional '*I*', which has not been destroyed but has been developed to its limit, will for evermore be one with the real '*I*': Man 4 then becomes man 5.

This indissoluble union forms the *Individuality*. It is from this moment that man really exists. He *is*, and only at this moment will he be able to say with certainty that he is happy to have been born.

The experiment so often repeated has ended with success.

(24)

The human Personality can have three different states, analogous to the three states of matter.

Before the *first Threshold*, the '*I*' of the Personality is in the solid state. That is to say that 'molecular' forces of attraction in it prevail over centrifugal forces. Psychologically, this state is characterized by egotism: *all for me*. In this *solid* state, man can *understand* nobody. In certain cases, where he is as hard as steel—cases which are relatively rare, it is true—he thinks he is always in the right and attributes his failures to others or to 'accidents'. He is sure of himself.

Then, after reaching the *first Threshold*, the seeker is no longer found in the *solid* state, because he no longer believes in the absolute value of 'A' influences. He will already have had some *doubts* when he perceived the existence of 'B' influences and started to distinguish them from others. Having reached the *first Threshold*, he is no longer *hard*, he is already *malleable*.

By the work between the two *Thresholds*, the mental[25] '*I*' becomes more and more supple, becoming *liquid* at the note FA. In the same way, as a physical liquid is characterized by the faculty of taking the form of a container, so the *liquid* mentality is capable of *understanding* others as itself, in taking their form. In the current language, we describe the state of such a man by the expression 'open minded'.

After crossing the *second Threshold*, man 4, who has now become man 5, acquires a *gaseous* mental[25] state—penetrating everything and permitting him to *understand* all beings and all things.

(25)

Eighth, ninth and tenth stages.

After the *second Threshold*, the true *Way* begins. This consists of three sections, seen as the notes MI, RE and DO.

---

25. Fr. 'psychique'.

Under the aegis of the note MI, the *interior* man enters the higher level of esoteric teaching at the eighth stage. He is now obliged to start teaching others. It is while teaching that he acquires *new faculties corresponding to particular elements of his Individuality*. In the terminology of St Paul, these are the *gifts of the Holy Spirit*.[26]

At this stage man becomes a master, seen from below, but seen from above he has the title of assistant.

The first new basic faculty—common to all *Individualities*, and developed all along the stages MI and RE—is an aptitude for spontaneously distinguishing the true from the false. This aptitude will be the distinguishing sign of the *new man* in the Cycle of the Holy Spirit.

On the next stage, the ninth, placed under the aegis of the note RE, man 5, after having acquired the new faculties that correspond to his *Individuality*, develops them until he gives them their integral expression. He thus acquires *Consciousness*, which manifests in him by the medium of the higher intellectual centre, acting through the higher emotional centre.

This done, he will become man 6.

The tenth stage, last step of the *Way*, is where man 6 becomes man 7. This is characterized by the consecration of the results obtained.

This is the *baptism by Fire and by the Spirit*.[27] Jesus said: '*I came to cast fire upon the earth; and how I wish it were already kindled.*'[28]

This consecration is produced by the sublimation of sex. Thus the circle closes itself. Each manifestation of life starts by a sexual act; at the end of the cycle, the activity of the sexual centre is manifested once more, but on a higher level, that of the higher centres, the level to which—by its nature—this centre belongs.

(26)

Esoteric work has a predominantly negative aspect during the early stages, in the sense that man tries to undo whatever hinders his evolution. Starting from the *second Threshold*, on the contrary, by the eighth and ninth stages, evolution on the *Way* only brings enrichment, with the acquisition of new qualities by work parallel to the actual esoteric work. These stages are out of reach of the *Law of Accident, but a fall still remains possible.*

It is only at the tenth stage, following consecration by Fire and the Spirit, that man 7, the accomplished or perfect man according to the terminology of St Paul, will be guaranteed against all possibility of error and therefore of a fall.

---

26. I Corinthians xiv: 1.

27. Matthew iii: 11; Mark i: 8; Luke iii: 16; Acts i: 5; ii: 2–4.

28. Luke xii: 49. Quoted from the Slavonic text. In the Hindu tradition, the same phenomenon is described as the descent on the Yogi, when he first reaches the desired degree of perfection, of the *dharma megha* or cloud of virtue.

From now on, he possesses in himself '*I*', *Consciousness*, and *Will*.

At that moment, he will have reached the *third Threshold*. This is the limit of possible evolution for terrestrial man of the *Tritocosmos*. Further evolution is certainly possible for him. He can become man 8 and 9. But beyond the *third Threshold* starts the domain of the *Deuterocosmos*.

Because of the slowness of human moral evolution, men 5, 6 and 7 are generally retained to work within human society.

(27)

Weak and pitiful, yet demanding and cruel, *exterior* man always blames other people or circumstances for his lack of success. Everybody and everything are at fault except himself. In such a frenzy of reproaches, we can even go as far as blaming Jesus of Nazareth for not having actually saved humanity...

We can buy food for others; we can cook a dish with this food; we can serve it once it is cooked; we can cut it up; we can even act as if to put the food inside the mouth, as we do for a child or sick person. But at this point, each of us must make the necessary effort to swallow[29] the food for ourselves; this cannot be done by anyone else.

The truth is that the *General Law* keeps man in his place, and if he moves, it will prevent him from advancing or rising. It is the *General Law* also which makes him die. But he must not forget that it is that very law that lets him be born and makes him live. It gives him at least three times the time necessary for developing his Personality completely and finding his real '*I*', with the *second Birth*, and then, after he has crossed the *second Threshold*, for entering the higher section of the *Way*.

The Apostle Paul says: '*When I was a child, I spake as a child, I thought as a child, I reasoned as a child; Now that I am become a man, I have put away childish things.*'[30]

Exterior man is, from the esoteric point of view, only a child; in most cases, a naughty child. He will not become an adult until he has climbed the *Staircase* and crossed the *second Threshold*. At that moment he will *abandon all that was childish*.

Until this happens, the answer of the Oracle to Socrates: '*Know thyself*' remains the primary rule for him who, having crossed the *first Threshold*, has entered the *path of Access*.

He should not forget, while preparing himself to enter it, that this path goes only in one direction; that once upon it he faces the alternatives of brilliant success or a dreadful fall.

---

29. Fr. 'absorber'.
30. I Corinthians xiii: 11.

CHAPTER XXI

(1)

We said in the foreword that esoteric studies help to reveal the meaning of the true evolution of man and of human society. This explains the growing interest these studies arouse in cultivated circles, particularly among those who seek an explanation and remedy for the contradictions of life, whose increasing manifestations and effects weigh ever more heavily on the destiny of man.

Troubles and uncertainties of this kind are normal during a period of transition. Sunrise is always preceded by an increase in night's chill. The coming of Christ followed a century of civil wars, which tore the ancient world apart.

Today man feels acutely the opposition between the tremendous technical progress and the obvious moral deficiency of humanity. In fact, while life on the material plane is moving at an accelerated pace due to the political, social and industrial Revolution which has occurred since 1789, man has made no marked progress on the moral plane. Because of this, he finds himself facing the overwhelming need to begin an *interior Revolution* as soon as possible; a transformation of his being which will permit him to restore the equilibrium between technical and moral levels, now so dangerously compromised.

Today, any being who thinks will feel unhappy; if his *ability* to do is deficient, his overdeveloped sensibility makes his *active will* all the more exacting and refined. This is so much so, that he sees his good intentions wither before they have had the strength to blossom.

There is no reason to hope that the present situation will correct itself automatically. On the contrary, the more technical progress accelerates, the wider grows the gulf in modern man between *wanting* and *the ability to do*. This contradiction can be seen on every plane. For example, fifteen years after the end of the second world war, the world is trapped in a situation which is neither war nor peace. This in itself is an eloquent demonstration of the powerlessness of those in authority. This is true in every field.

To correct the situation, and to resolve the problems that have developed with the march of time, man must now discover new sources of moral energy in the same way that — thanks to the industrial revolution, with steam, electricity and the atom — he has found new sources of physical energy.

The solution of the problem lies, as we have already indicated, in forming a new ruling elite whose latent moral faculties are developed and cultivated. These developed faculties, which will characterize the *new man*, will permit him to surpass the intellectual and the technocrat as the latter surpassed the ecclesiastics and knights of the Middle Ages.

(2)

We have given a general notion of the mental[1] structure of *exterior man*, of his position in the Universe and in relation to the organic life on Earth. Then we have studied the possibilities of progressive psychological development which open to him under certain conditions, to give him access to higher planes of Consciousness.

The *knowledge, understanding* and *savoir-faire* needed to attain this aim have been preserved through the centuries, notably in eastern Orthodoxy. In their ensemble they form the *Way*, whose contents we have analyzed in all its parts. As for the necessary exercises, information has been given so that those who want to enrich their theoretical knowledge and bring it to life will be able to begin practical work. Century after century, while the flame of primitive Christianity burned low, esoteric work — apart from rare exceptions — has remained vigilant. That is to say that on the individual plane, in the world, or in monasteries where several monks worked under the authority of an master-Igoumen, each of them has determined his own aim, and followed it by himself. However, the esoteric meaning of the work done by monks or hermits was a preparatory effort: its objective was to accumulate the necessary energies on the astral plane, and so make it easier for humanity to pass through the great turnings of History.

(3)

It is remarkable that these changes in direction, and the coming of the new era they imply, have been constantly notable for the varied active and eminent roles played by woman. The Gospels testify to this presence. It was to the Samaritan woman near the well of Jacob that Jesus declared *for the first time* that He was the Messiah: *'I that speak to thee am He'*.[2] It was to a woman, Mary Magdalene, that Christ manifested Himself at the resurrection, when He called to her, and she recognized Him.[3]

The principle of woman's intervention is found in all crucial periods of history. We generally place the birth of the Middle Ages at the reign of

1. Fr. 'psychique'.
2. John iv: 7–26.
3. John xx: 11–16.

Justinian the Great. His work was strongly influenced by the powerful personality of his wife, the Empress Theodora. She played a role comparable to that of Aspasia beside Pericles. By supporting him at those times of weakness which the best tempered[4] characters do not escape, she allowed Justinian to give the Christian world an extraordinary impetus, which blossomed during the next few centuries. Let us not forget, too, the fruitful role played by the Ladies in Medieval courts, or the inspiration given to Knights by the 'Dames de la Pensée'.

Periods where the ennobling role of the woman in the life of human society has faded are marked by a triviality of morals and manners, expressed in particular by a taste for realism carried to its utmost limits. The disappearance of the courts, and the political and literary salons where, until the twentieth century, woman played such a key role, deprives international relations of a positive element of understanding, and diplomacy of a suppleness indispensable for settling political problems.

(4)

Today, human relations suffer from a real distortion in the innate role that woman is destined to play at the side of man: instead of being the active force in these relations, the inspiring and fruitful complement to the man, the woman tends to follow a parallel path, which no longer permits her to exercise her own creative vocation. The cycle of the Holy Spirit will not perpetuate this imbalance. The picture of the blossoming era of the Holy Spirit — given by the Apostle Peter — gives a precise indication. He describes it as *'new heavens and a new earth where truth will dwell.'*[5]

Quoted before, this text needs further comment from another point of view. In the cycle of the Father and that of the Son man, identifying himself with the 'I' of an undeveloped Personality, becomes isolated from his real 'I', and lives outside the bosom of the Lord. In other words, he remains in his fallen state, which is a result of the original sin. During these two cycles, he takes Illusion for Reality. For thousands of years, this identification with the 'I' of the Personality has divided the previously indivisible consciousness of polar beings; of the man and woman who once formed a *single Being*, endowed with the unique consciousness of the real *Self*; the *Being* described in the myth of the *Androgyne*.

The incomplete 'I' of the Personality, unfinished and powerless, wanders in life with no faith and no true affection. It goes from error to error, from weakness to weakness, and from lie to lie. A prisoner — perhaps voluntarily, but nevertheless a prisoner — man does not do what he wants to do

---

4. Fr. 'mieux trempé'.
5. II Peter iii: 13.

in life, but does what he hates,[6] blindly obeying a diabolical mechanical-ness which, under its three aspects: *fear*, *hunger* and *sexuality*,[7] rules his life. This purely factitious existence has nothing real except the possibility of evolution — which remains latent, and forms the objective of esoteric studies and work. Apart from this seed, everything in *exterior* life is based on lies. Yet nothing based on lies will ever be able to resist the life-giving breath of the new heavens and the new earth announced for the coming era. Before all else, the lies which dominate relations between man and woman — the least culpable form of which is Illusion — will disappear.

If the fall is a direct consequence of identifying with the 'I' of Personality, and the solitude of polar beings separated by the fall is the source of weakness in humans who have in this way become mortal, the return to Unity appears to be an inexhaustible source of new energies. These energies are necessary to man, and to restore the dangerously disturbed equilibrium of today's public and private life, he must seek them out.

However, this return to the perfect unity of polar beings is not given freely. It is the exclusive privilege of those who have crossed, or are ready to cross, the *second Threshold* of the *Way*. It is through realization of the totally indivisible unity of their real 'I', by two polar *Individualities* arrived at the *second Birth*, that the original sin can and must be redeemed. This is the solution for private and for public life. This is also *the peace of the Lord*.[8]

What is the real 'I', Soul of our soul and core of our *Individuality*, if not a divine spark, a particle of Christ's body? It is in this way that we have to understand the meaning of the text of St Paul, quoted in the introduction to this book: '*In the Lord, neither is the woman without the man, nor the man without the woman*'[9] and also: '*for as the woman has been taken from the man, so also does man exist by the woman, and all comes from God.*'[10]

(5)

This is the solution to the problem, posed at the beginning of this chapter, of the need to find a new source of moral energy. We have reached this solution by means of the positive method of esoteric study. It can also be reached by means of the negative method described in chapter XVII, p. 173.

Exterior man, as his Personality is under-developed, has a field of search and action limited by the faculties of the three lower centres.

---

6. Romans vii: 15.
7. Cf. ch. VIII, pp. 68–69.
8. John xiv: 27.
9. I Corinthians xi: 11.
10. *Ibid.*, 12.

The motor centre, which already acts in the spermatozoa, is strongly developed in man. This development can be pushed farther still, well above the level considered as normal. We can, for example, raise the instinctive life from its ordinary level to that of waking consciousness, and thus establish control over certain physiological processes. Well conducted, this intervention in the instinctive life can improve health and prolong life. But this is where its effects stop. Developing the abilities of the motor centre gives man a healthy and vigorous body, but does not give him any new source of moral energy. In our civilization we do not preoccupy ourselves with perfecting the motor centre. We live in an imperfect body, sickly and ageing while its growth is hardly completed. Man does not even try to fight these inconveniences by natural procedures. He accepts them passively, as if they were inevitable.

Contemporary man concentrates his efforts on the development and education of his intellectual centre. Everything is organized methodically to perfect this centre sector by sector. Primary education, which aims to furnish man with an *instrument for work*, specially exercises the motor sector of the intellectual centre. Secondary education, which seeks to give the student a basis of *general culture*, works mainly on the emotional sector of the intellectual centre, which then works together with the motor sector of the same centre. Higher education is intended to initiate the student to *specialized culture* by developing the intellectual sector of the intellectual centre. As a result of this development, man becomes what we call an intellectual. However, the resources of the intellectual centre which allow man to make miracles in the domain of pure or applied positive science are limited to this. The works of both Kant and Virchow have shown us that the field of action of the human intellect is, so to say, encircled by an impenetrable wall.[11]

We are left to examine the position of the emotional centre briefly. In our civilization, it is curious to note how much the growth and development of this centre are left purely to chance. The emotional life, if deprived of methodical training, is the source of unforeseen events that are rarely agreeable for man, and even more rarely happy. Its consequences are generally heavy to bear. In *exterior* man, because of the absence in our civilization of an obligatory emotional training to equal our intellectual training, the underdeveloped and uncared for emotional centre falls under the influence of the other centres: motor, intellectual and finally sexual. We do not exaggerate when we say that the emotional centre occupies the place of a poor relation in the mental[12] life of man. Yet it is only by the appropriate development of this centre that man can open up for himself the new source of moral energy, for which his need is so very pressing.

---

11. Ed. The discovery or recognition of this 'wall' appears itself to be the subject of intellectual training in certain versions of the Tradition.

To return to this source, the chief practical objectives are mastery of the sexual centre, and the training of the emotional centre.

(6)

Before we go on to deeper examination of the problem of evolution and its conditions, we shall examine an important recommendation, which must be followed from the beginning of the work until the second Birth. It is one of the *Golden rules* of the Tradition: *man must link together the work of the intellectual and emotional centres*. This is how it is done:

If the question to be studied and solved is of an intellectual nature, then, after the intellectual centre has elucidated it, before reaching a conclusion or final decision, and before taking action, man must consult his emotional centre. Conversely, he must not act impulsively or exclusively under the influence of the emotional centre: before acting, he must consult his intellectual centre.

In general, man must cultivate in himself the ability to grasp any phenomenon and any problem — in the inner or outer worlds — by simultaneously using the two centres, emotional and intellectual.

(7)

The natural growth of the Personality stops long before it is complete. It has an individual limit which depends upon a whole ensemble of factors including: civilization, race, caste, family and social surroundings, education and instruction.

Without continuous conscious effort, the development of the Personality beyond this limit can never occur. All that man brings with him at birth are his predispositions, in other words, *talents*. With the growth of the Personality, these predispositions reveal themselves, and that is all. To take their development further, conscious efforts must be made. The rule is exact: *whoever does not develop his talents loses them*.[13]

We generally seek to develop these talents through education. As long as our studies or researches continue, the Personality continues to grow, although often in a not very harmonious way. But when studies and researches end, and we start to exploit the knowledge we have acquired in this routine manner, the development of the Personality ceases.

The most important and most difficult stage of the *Way* to pass is the *Staircase*, also called the *path of Access*, which leads to the level of man 4.[14] Anyone who seeks to climb this must make this effort the *principal aim of his*

---

13. Matthew xxv: 14-30; Mark,iv: 25; Luke xix: 26.
14. Cf. ch. XV, pp. 146–7; ch. XX, pp. 217–9 and fig. 57.

life. From now on, esoteric work must become the axis of his existence, round which the inner and outer circumstances of his life revolve.

This categorical demand must not frighten us. At the same time, we must realize that the tests[15] begin from the first step of the *Staircase*.

To cross the *first Threshold*, man must undergo the first test successfully *without looking back*:[16] he must be ablaze with the *ardent desire* to overcome the entanglement[17] of life in the *wilderness*, so that he can throw himself into the unknown in a search for a new, reasonable, and real life.

This desire for transformation, if it has enough vigour and intensity, will fill the interval between the notes DO and SI, which is the *first Threshold*, and the seeker will then stand with a firm footing on the first step of the *Staircase*.

The four notes which form the *Staircase* are linked by a deep interdependence, since their resonance draws its strength from the initial impulse of *Desire*. This means that if this initial Desire does not unite all man's existence in obedience, if it does not dominate his whole being, it is better for him to stop in time and not cross the *Threshold*. We repeat: the *Way* is a path of no return. This is the real reason for this test of *Desire*. This *Desire* must have the strength of thirst, says the Tradition.

Next, having reached the first step, man must undergo the test of *Faith*. To *Believe* is not enough; one must *have faith*. The test takes the form of a need for man to surmount his fear of 'abandonment' to Faith. Jesus reassured His sheep on this subject: '*Be not therefore anxious saying, What shall we eat? or What shall we drink? or Wherewithal shall we be clothed? For after all these things do the Gentiles seek; your heavenly Father knoweth that ye have need of all these things. But seek ye first the Kingdom of God and His truth; and all these things shall be added unto you.*'[18]

On the second step, a test of *Strength* awaits those who have committed themselves on the *Staircase*. '*The Kingdom of Heaven*' said Jesus, '*is taken by force, and it is those who do violence to themselves who will hold it.*'[19]

On the third step, the test is of *Discernment* and *Skill*. To understand what this is about, one must meditate on the meaning of the parable of the *unjust Steward*,[20] a parable which seems difficult to understand. It is a test. He who can see this in terms of the precept: '*you cannot serve God and Mammon*',[21] will be better prepared to withstand this test.

---

15. Ed. The Greek word used for these tests, 'peirasmos', is translated in the Lord's prayer and elsewhere as 'temptations'.

16. Luke ix: 62.

17. Fr. 'houppée'.

18. Matthew vi: 31–34.

19. Matthew xi: 12; Luke xvi: 16. Slavonic text: 'and those who do violence to themselves will grasp it.'

20. Luke xvi: 1-13.

21. Matthew vi: 24; Luke xvi: 13.

On the fourth step, one must confront the test of *Love*, of true life-giving love, a consuming fire quite different from what now smoulders under the ashes. What that true love is, we have already indicated when we quoted St Paul.[22] One should learn this text by heart. It is a blazing sword whose flames burn up all alloy mixtures; all that man takes for love — within him or towards him — when it is not quite that. If we keep these words before our minds, we will immediately be able to judge every movement of the heart, and will know whether or not it contains traces of true *Love*.

Having passed this test, man has nothing within him but *pure Love*, which contains the elements of transfigured Desire; of Faith, Strength, and Discernment.[23]

We can see that the test at the fourth step is decisive. Until then man can drag along the defects of his past, and usually does so: lying, weakness, self-pity, inner compromise. Generally, he has the time, the opportunity and the possibility to rid himself of them before committing himself to the fourth step; but because of the weight of this past he wastes time, and lets many of the opportunities which present themselves escape him. On the fourth step, the balance sheet must be drawn up and accounts settled. Man, poor and naked, is accepted at the *second Threshold*, but only on condition that he is consistent and pure. The essential is that he be consistent, meaning that he contains within himself true Love. Everything false within him will be burnt by the flames of this blazing sword...

It is to be noted that all these tests happen together, and on all the steps of the *Staircase*. But they are distributed unequally according to the particularities of our Personalities, all of them being driven by the force of *Desire*. On each step, a shift in emphasis puts the ensemble in resonance with the note with which it corresponds: SI first then LA, SOL and FA.

To study in greater depth the elements of personal progress on the *Staircase*, elements which constitute the *film* of life, it is not superfluous to review the doctrine of *Karma*.

The karmic law, derived from the *principle of Equilibrium*, is defined by St Paul in the Tradition: '*Be not deceived; God is not mocked: for whatsoever a man soweth, that shall he also reap.*'[24] We should also remember the words by which Jesus warned us against *Karma* and indicated the attitude to be taken to neutralize it. '*Agree with thine adversary quickly,*' He says, '*while thou art with him in the way; lest haply he delivers thee to the Judge, and the Judge deliver thee to the officer,*[25] *and thou be cast into prison. Verily I say unto thee, thou shalt by no means come out thence, till thou hast paid the last farthing.*'[26]

---

22. I Corinthians xiii: 4–8; Cf. chap. XVII, pp. 166–7.
23. Romans xiii,10.
24. Galatians vi: 7.
25. '*Torturer*', in the Slavonic text.
26. Matthew v: 25–26; Luke xii: 58–59.

In *exterior* life, man lives on credit in more than one way, even if he does not force the hand of others. Without being aware of it, he draws behind him the moral burden of his unpaid debts, and of his transgressions against the *principle of Equilibrium*. All these unpaid debts, and all their karmic consequences, must be fully paid before the *second Threshold*.

The action of *Karma* is mechanical; in each separate case it acts automatically so as to restore the equilibrium broken by the *free movements* of man. In consequence, *Karma* acts by compensation not globally, but independently on each sector of the activities of man.

(8)

In stepping onto the *Staircase*, to approach and then cross the *second Threshold*, man adopts a new attitude towards himself: from this point on, *he takes his fate in his own hands*.

This task is both heavy and delicate. Man, in fact, does not live in a void, but in everyday life, surrounded by his peers.[27] To take his fate in his own hands presupposes and demands from man a sensible and conscientious attitude, one which excludes all impulsive and simplistic decisions concerning those around him.

The problems met will generally appear insoluble. They must be solved, yet no solution will be positive — in the esoteric sense — unless every person of those around him is taken into account[28] according to the importance of the role they play. In this respect, we must act in accordance with the instruction given by Jesus and quoted above.

To follow these principles is not easy, but it is possible, on condition that man stops lying to himself, and that he no longer retains any trace of hypocrisy or cheating in his heart.

(9)

The life of man is a *film*. It is certainly difficult for our Cartesian minds to grasp this concept. Our three-dimensional minds are badly adapted to ideas and facts which touch on the domain of the eternal.

Incomprehensible as it may seem, our life is truly a *film* produced in accordance with a *script*. This *film* goes on continuously, without stopping, in such a way that, at the time of his death, man is born again. What seems absurd is that he is born in the same place, at the same date where he was born before, and of the same parents. So the *film* goes on again.

---

27. Fr. 'semblables'.
28. Cf. ch. XI, p. 100.

(10)

Each human being, then, is born with his own particular *film*. This represents the field of action in which man is called to apply his conscious efforts. The repetition of the *film* is not reincarnation, although these two notions are often confused. For the reasons we have already mentioned, *exterior* man, who lives in the system of the Future-Past, cannot embrace in a single moment the ensemble of his *film*, nor even the part that contains his immediate future. To do so, he would need to enlarge the slot of his *Present*. It thus happens to him that, faced with certain events, he will feel that he has already seen or lived those events. Some see in such phenomena the proof of so called reincarnation. In reality, phenomena of this sort are the result of a casual and temporary surge of fine energies in the organism: the slot of the individual *Present* then enlarges for a few instants, and some significant facts of the immediate future slip into the waking consciousness. In this way, the impression is created of a return of another time.

In a certain way this is true, although the impression of having lived before is only caused by *mechanical* unfolding of the *film*. By reincarnation, we must understand a phenomenon of a very different order. Although the theoretical *film* revolves integrally on the plane of *possibilities*, meaning in eternity, the *film* of the *exterior* man clings to the plane of realization, that is, of *Time*, but only to the extent strictly necessary to satisfy the ends of the *Ray of Creation*. True reincarnation, on the other hand, occurs entirely in time, and belongs integrally to the domain of the *Real*, well understood as part of the broader frame of Manifestation. We have insisted on the fact that the human Personality is not a reality in the proper sense of the word, but a possibility. It plays a role in the *film* to which it is attached, from which it will not disappear until the moment of the second Birth. At that moment, it will cease to be a Personality. Because of its indestructible union with the real 'I', it will be transfigured, and so it will become an *Individuality*.

As long as man lives in the *wilderness*, self-satisfied and immersed in lies and illusions, the *film* will unfold with mechanical inflexibility, and the Personality will remain entirely unchanged. These circumstances start to change the moment man crosses the *first Threshold*. This passage can be compared to the conception of the future *Individuality*. The *Staircase* symbolizes the period of gestation, and the crossing of the *second Threshold* represents the second Birth, the birth of *Individuality*. During his later development, corresponding to the notes MI and RE of the *Way*, the *Individuality* becomes progressively integrated with the higher cosmoses. By acquiring the gifts of the Holy Spirit appropriate to his nature, he progressively participates in real, objective existence, which finally characterizes his *being*. This is Salvation; liberation from the bonds of the *film*.

It is only at this point of evolution that true individual reincarnation becomes possible. This is not mechanical; it is done consciously, generally to accomplish a mission.

An example of reincarnation is given by the Gospels. When Jesus was talking with Peter, James and John when they descended from the mountain after the Transfiguration, the disciples asked Him this question: '*Why do the scribes say that Elijah must come first.*'[29] He answered and said: '*it is true that Elijah must come to make everything ready: but I say unto you that Elijah has come already, and they knew him not, but did unto him whatsoever they would. Even so shall the Son of man also suffer of them. Then understood the disciples that He spake unto them of John the Baptist.*'[30]

Elsewhere, talking of John the Baptist, Jesus was categorical. '*If ye are willing to understand it, this is Elijah that is to come,*' and He added: '*He that hath ears let him hear.*'[31]

It is important to grasp clearly the difference which exists between the *film*, a mixture of possibilities, and reincarnation in time, which belongs to the domain of the Real, and to understand the meaning of this difference. At the time of the second Birth, that is to say, by crossing the *second Threshold*, man escapes his bondage to the *film*, and enters the domain of redemption. He is then admitted into the Sacred Brotherhood of *living Beings*, called in the Tradition: *The Great esoteric Brotherhood*. The Apostle Paul tells us: '*and we know that to them that love God, all things work together for good, to them that are called according to His purpose. For whom He foreknew, He also foreordained to be similar to the image of His Son, that he may be the first-born among many brethren.*'[32]

The *Great esoteric Brotherhood* is an unshakeable force: those who are part of it are no longer subject to illness or sorrow. Death loses its hold over them. On their own scale, following the example of the Lord, they too have *overcome the world*.[33]

(11)

In theory, the *film* in which man is born and in which he lives can go on until the end of the world, on condition that he is happy, satisfied with himself, attributing his virtues to himself, and blaming others for his

---

29. Malachi iv: 5.
30. Matthew xvii: 10–13: Mark ix: 13.
31. Matthew xi: 14.
32. Romans viii: 28–29.
33. John xvi: 33.

mistakes and misfortunes. Properly speaking, this kind of existence cannot be considered as human; it could be described as *anthropoid*. This term is justified in the sense that *exterior* man, immersed in self-satisfaction, represents the crowning achievement of millions of years of evolution of the species from its animal ancestors, yet, from the point of view of esoteric evolution, he is a possibility which has not yet been realized.

If we envisage the problem of esoteric evolution from the point of view of the *film* and the different parts man can play in it, it is clear that this kind of evolution is impossible as long as the *film* can always be considered as turning in the same circle. People who perform in such a *film* are those we have called *anthropoids*, puppets, the *dead* who, in the words of Jesus, 'believe themselves to be alive'.[34] Esoteric evolution starts when man, by his conscious efforts, proves capable of breaking the circle and transforming it into an ascending spiral (see Fig. 58 overleaf)

The spiral represents an intermediate state between the position where the human Personality is found to be trapped in the *film*, which revolves mechanically in a way hardly separated from the eternal plane, and that of the perfect, free *Individuality*, who is able, if need arises, to reincarnate consciously in Time.

This is an intermediate state in this sense, that the *film* definitely departs from the plane of the eternal, from the plane of possibilities. The curve of life, which for *exterior* man does not in practice differ from a circle, transforms itself into a spiral and does not end—as it did previously—almost at its point of departure: the distance between these two points now marks a definite progression in Time. The *film* in the form of a spiral belongs to men who climb the *Staircase:* we have seen that complete disengagement of the *film* is produced at the moment of crossing the *second Threshold*. If man is able to do that successfully during a single life, so breaking the circle for the very first time, he does not return to it. Such a case is very rare: it is the lot of the *just*. Generally, this liberation requires several lives; several revolutions of the spiral.

As a general rule, each revolution occurs in Time, and consequently can appear to be a reincarnation. In reality, it is nothing but a return to *exterior* life. A pseudo-reincarnation like this is neither conscious nor personal: it is the actors in the *film* who return, and they do not remember any previous experiences.

However, a change is possible as soon as the conscious efforts of man increase the effect of the Time factor by enlarging perception of the *Present*.

In a film which unfolds in a spiral in this way, the contents of the play change; they change in two ways: first in each life, that is, during each revolution, and also from spiral to spiral. The composition of the cast, the circumstances, and the scenery all change. Two elements however remain

---

34. Matthew viii: 22: Revelation iii: 1.

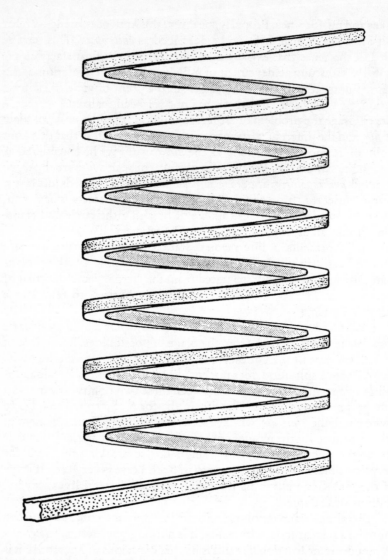

Fig. 58

permanent: first, the general *aim*, to reach and cross the *second Threshold;* then the absolute *condition* for crossing this *Threshold*, that all the karmic debts which have been accumulated in the present life, as well as during previous spirals, must be neutralized and liquidated. *Before the second Threshold*, says the Tradition, *every drama must be played out to its denouement.*

The work is hard and difficult because man constantly makes mistakes. The attentive reader has understood that following the spiral, or climbing the *Staircase*, is reserved for men who have already absorbed a certain quantity of 'B' influences, and who thus possess a more or less developed *magnetic centre*. We must emphasize that this state in no way guarantees that they will make no further errors. It is true that from the time man first mounts the *Staircase* he is watched, especially if he makes sincere and considerable efforts. The *Great esoteric Brotherhood* offers him a helping hand. Certain meetings, a play of favourable circumstances, are the forms taken by this help. This assistance does not, however, free him of the need to work on himself and to go on making conscious efforts. In addition, it must be said that often the proffered help is not used, because man does not listen to the advice given, or because he does not grasp the meaning of the favourable circumstances and the possibilities of progress which open before him. Still more than half a creature of the domain of Illusion, he continues to take frequent impulsive decisions, and often turns against his own avowed aims. In most cases, although he may be able to disentangle certain situations at the level of each spiral, he will also introduce new complications into the *film*, especially in his relations with those around him. It must therefore be understood that as long as man has not attained and crossed the *second Threshold*, he will have to start all over again. He will restart every spiral in the *wilderness*, he will once again have to discern the 'B' influences, cross the *first Threshold*, and climb the *Staircase* step by step. It is true that no conscious effort is ever lost; but the experience acquired in one spiral only appears in the next in the form of innate personal aptitudes, or vague recollections of people in the cast.

One of the great obstacles to evolution is that man does not generally think of his esoteric evolution except in old age, when he has already accumulated a considerable amount of error and new complications in his life. He often introduces into the play new characters, quite foreign to the underlying meaning of his life, or to the reason for which his team is created. He sometimes takes on commitments which tie him narrowly, when he most urgently needs all his liberty of action to catch up with time wasted in enterprises or causes which have nothing to do with esoteric evolution.

The day will come when he will become aware of his situation. Woe to him if, frightened, he tries to brutally break the ties which he has knotted. Instead of attaining the liberty he seeks, he will then fall into much harder and more senseless new slavery, added to the old. We have given an idea,[35] in chapter XVI, of the attitude man should adopt towards those around him. We are now going to attempt to suggest measures that can be taken to find a denouement or unravelling.

We should know that, at the end of a spiral, a comparison is made between the *film* as it was conceived at the time of birth and what it

---

35. Fr. 'aperçu'.

has become at the time of death. The balance sheet between these two states is drawn up, as in accountancy, by listing assets and liabilities, followed by a *profit and loss* account. This will show the result of the elapsed life objectively. This balance sheet furnishes the basic elements for composing the *film* at the start of the following spiral. If we could avoid all errors and complications in this new experience, produced as a result of *free movements*, esoteric evolution would then occur in a harmonious rising curve. Generally, this is not the case. As we have just said, man most often comes to this idea of evolution after he has already complicated the *film* to which he belongs. But true evolution cannot occur except *on the basis of the original film*—after all artificially added elements have been eliminated. The latter is conditional on a return to the purity of the centres, especially the emotional centre which—at least at the start—is the sole receptacle of 'B' influences, and seat of the *magnetic centre*. The heart must therefore be pure, and if not already pure it must be purified. This is the *sine qua non* condition of success. All the information contained in Chapter XVII, which was concerned with 'lying' in all its aspects, was given essentially to emphasize the absolute need for purifying the heart, and for beginning to re-educate the emotional centre in a positive direction.

This necessity explains the meaning of the words of Jesus: '*Except ye turn, and become as little children, ye shall in no wise enter into the kingdom of heaven.*'[36]

This verse specifically refers to the emotional life. However, since the times of the Early Church, there has been a tendency to interpret and understand this instruction by our Lord as a restriction on the development of the intellectual life. This is a mistake. Intelligence must be developed and stimulated, and the admonition: *become as little children*, only points to a need for purity of the centres, not to a need to keep them in a primitive state. St Paul the Apostle gives a precise commentary on this which leaves no room for ambiguity: '*Brothers*', said he, '*be not children in that which concerns judgement,*[37] *be children in what concerns malice, but as to judgement, be fully grown men.*'[38] Supporting this admonition, the Apostle also drew the attention of his contemporaries to the fact that at that time, man was already very retarded on the way of evolution. He said, in fact : '*for when by reason of the time ye ought to be teachers, ye have need again that someone teach you the first principles of the oracles of God: and have come to need milk, and not solid food. For every one that partaketh of milk is without experience of the word of truth.*'[39]

---

36. Matthew xviii: 3.
37. In the Slavonic text: 'with respect to your intelligence'.
38. I Corinthians xiv: 20.
39. Hebrews v: 12–13.

Since the time of St Paul it is doubtful whether man has caught up from being behind. If today we want to obtain real results from the point of view of esoteric evolution, we must make haste to abandon the diet of *milk* and take the risk of adopting *solid food*.

This is exactly what we are trying to aid by presenting this Doctrine to the reader in systematic form, instead of in parables: this is *solid food*. It is now necessary for us to give instruction in the same form on a possible *short cut* in esoteric work which can rapidly take us to the *second Threshold*. We have already indicated that this possibility is offered to polar beings, to those couples described by the ancient Tradition in the myth of the *Androgyne*. We will now reconsider this question more precisely from both theoretical and practical points of view.

(12)

On the basis of the preceding analysis, the essential data for the *film* of any ordinary person can be described as follows: as the hero of the romance of his own life, the subject must necessarily be the star of the *film*. But he can also play a minor role in the *film* of people who play a secondary role in his own *film*. In this way, each *film* gets enmeshed with other *films*, where the same people are found in totally different situations. One must also distinguish between two categories of actors. The first are really part of the cast. A definite role is assigned to them: they are organically tied to the *film*. The second group only appear by accident in the *film*, drawn into the action by the *free movements* of the hero. This complexity is further increased because some of the actors who have genuine parts in the *film* play their roles badly, while others play roles which are not their own. Situations like this are widespread. Let us examine this phenomenon in more detail.

The human Personality, as we know, is an organism with multiple parts or facets: 987 to be exact. In the ideal case, only realized by polar beings, and the only effective one from the esoteric point of view, the 987 facets of man and woman are strictly polar. These are the predestined husband and wife whose union will create a true couple. However, the cast contains other people, who play roles organically tied to that of the hero, and who are necessary to bring the *film* in its ensemble to its natural end. These are friend-souls, brother-souls, sister-souls, collaborating-souls and servant-souls etc. The Personalities of each of them have a certain number of facets identical to those of the hero, for actors of the same sex, while for the actors of the opposite sex they are polar. In the case of brothers and sisters, the number of identical or polar facets can be as many as half or even more. The lack of discernment and of sincerity towards ourselves, the innate desire to find a perfect resonance to the vibration of our soul, and the impatience that follows, all multiplied by the action of the *General Law*, induce us too often to contract unions which can only result in absurd situations. Instead of resisting the mirage; instead of waiting and seeking, we slip into imperfect unions, which are a source of suffering both for the partners and their children. In addition, these unions alter the meaning of the *film* in its ensemble, and so corrupt the personal lives of all the actors in the drama. Lastly, the esoteric results foreseen in the initial composition of the *film* are gravely compromised.

Our lives very often resemble a well conceived theatre play in which the roles are upset by a person searching for an absurdity; each of us is this mischievous or comic being.

It is as a result of *considering* on the matrimonial plane, or through lack of *consideration* on the purely sexual plane, that most of our errors are committed, including those which demand the heaviest payment. Even beings of good faith are not exempt from error. To confuse a *brother* or *sister* for husband or wife compounds a very complicated situation, especially from the esoteric point of view. The situation is all the more confused when children are born from such unions.

Life then takes on the character of a perpetual compromise with oneself. The moral and physical health of 'accidentally united couples' suffers: with changes in the intellectual centre due to cheating and lying; heart disease if the emotional centre is sensitive and still aspires to the truth; also diseases of obscure origin, of which cancer is one that attacks the body in its most fragile parts. In every case, the condition necessarily leads to permanent loss of fine energies which, in its turn, brings on accelerated aging and leads to premature death.

Difficult as are these situations that arise out of our errors, they must not prevent anyone who throws himself into esoteric work from finding the courage in himself to look them in the face, and to search for a satisfactory outcome. If the *Devil*—the *General Law*—tries to lead us into new errors to obstruct our esoteric evolution, the supporting hand of the Lord, gentle yet firm, is always stretched out to help us. Yet our minds, too rational and too realistic, often stop us from sensing this help.

We have already indicated the form of a just and objective solution to the problems that face us when a situation has been entangled by our errors: the *Gordian knots* must not be cut, they must be untied in such a way that the participants, both tied by the same *knot*, feel only relief at the disappearance of a situation which was simply a source of suffering for both.

If the situation is truly resolved, to the benefit of *all* those originally concerned, the original meaning of the *film* and its normal development can be found.

(13)

The ensemble of people organically linked in one *film* forms a *team*. In the initial conception of the *film*, this *team* must attain a predetermined aim as a result of the way the participants play their roles in the *play-of-life*. This aim is different from the aims we follow in a life ruled by 'A' influences, which are instruments of the *General Law* in its development of the *Ray of Creation*. The objective for such a *team* always has an esoteric meaning: in fact, although the Personalities which compose it may be very different, they will share a deep need: a desire to end lies and illusions once and for all, to escape the domination of the 'A' influences and, in one form or another, to reach that objective existence in which man finds his real 'I', and identifies himself with it.

Here, we must describe the principal law which underlies the formation of these *teams*. On the human plane, the greatest reward goes to him who commands. In esotericism, on the contrary, it goes to him who knows how best to serve. The confusion between these two important master-ideas — of *commanding*, and of *serving* — sometimes appears dramatic. We can even see this in the disciples of Jesus. The question of knowing who was greatest amongst them tormented them. The Gospel mentions this more than once.[40]

(14)

To better understand the significance of how the *team* is made up, and the kind of mission entrusted to it, it must be remembered that the spiral of the *film* unwinds itself in an intermediate position, between rotation without issue in the plane of eternity, and progress in time through conscious reincarnation.

The more evolved the *team*, the more important the task entrusted to it. History provides examples of the work of *teams* in all fields: legislative, military, political and religious. The role of women in *teams* is particularly marked in crucial periods of the history of peoples.

We shall consider two significant examples of profane *teams*.

Although legend has intervened and distorted our picture of the life of Alexander the Great, historical data allows us to discern the meaning of his mission. His *team*, much of which his father had already gathered, was going to create a new world, the *Hellenistic world*, an immense audience which, three centuries later, was destined to receive the Word of the Gospel and so become the cradle of Christian civilization. It is through looking at this essential aspect of his work that some primitive Churches,

---

40. Matthew xx: 20–28; xxiii: 11; Mark ix: 34; x: 43–45; Luke ix: 46; xxii: 24.

and later the Qur'ān itself, considered Alexander as a Messenger and a Saint.

The history of the *team* of Peter the Great is even better known to us. It seems that, when still very young, the Tzar was conscious of the role he would have to play. Klioutchevsky, one of the best historians of the emperor, arrived at a conclusion which, when written by a man gifted with a critical mind and scientific integrity, seems absurd: he said that to explain his work it must be admitted that Peter came to the world with an already established plan of reform. It is clear that to understand the historical importance of his reign, the rational considerations valid for other cases—especially that of Alexander—will prove insufficient. Voltaire used to say that Peter was the greatest legislator since Mohammed. But this is appreciation, not explanation. Peter wanted to eliminate the consequences of two and a half centuries of the Mongol yoke. By letting Russia, the last survivor and last heir of the ancient Orient, be born anew, the emperor was going to stimulate the awakening of all the Orient, and show it the path to a new Renaissance. This is the way his mission should be understood.

The contribution of woman to his work was considerable. He leaned on her for the reform of social life. He made her come out of the nursery, where she whiled away her days cut off from masculine society. He made her participate in his famous *assemblies*, and in the life of the Court. Catherine's role at Peter's side was a most important one, as S. M. Soloviev has quite clearly shown. The friend of his heart, as the emperor used to call her, formed part of himself, so to speak, sharing his joys and the worst dangers.

At the end of a relatively short life—he died at the age of fifty two—Peter was slowly abandoned by everybody. This is the fate reserved for heroes and prophets. Nevertheless, his courage, strength of soul, and lucidity never abandoned him: he dictated his last decision a few hours before his death.

We find here an example of *team-work* aiming at a clearly defined objective. We certainly do not know, and will never know, the intimate details of relations between the characters in *Peter's film*. We know that their work together sometimes met with difficulties and failures. But these latter stimulated Peter's energy. By his unshakeable faith, he himself stimulated the faith of his *team* and the courage of all the people. If the *team* of Peter the Great showed some signs of weakness at the end of his life, we must not forget that the *principle of Imperfection* reigns in the world. However, this weakness did not appear until the work had been achieved in broad outline.

The Bible contains certain descriptions of *team-work* for both profane and religious objectives. We know very little about the composition of Noah's *team*. The Scriptures only say that the Ark received two of each species. As for the work of Moses, which was both military and legislative, data about this *team* are more precise, and information concerning King David is still more precise. If the role of woman seems obscure in the case of Moses, it is all the more visible in that of David.

On all levels, particularly that of religion, an example of incomparable grandeur is given to us by the *team* of the Apostles, directed by our Lord Jesus Christ. His task was to bring about the rebirth of the whole world into the Cycle of the Son, and to plant the seed of another Cycle, the last; that of the Holy Spirit. We know — and it was without doubt revealed intentionally — that even in this *team* everything did not occur without difficulties, without errors, and without lack of faith. Acting in this world, the team's members were themselves subject to the influence of the *principle of Imperfection*. Jesus alone, together with His Mother, were perfect, without the slightest blemish, without any backsliding or hesitation. The Apostles showed weakness more than once. Their task was nevertheless achieved and today, after twenty centuries, we bear witness to that: for the words of Jesus were obeyed by the Apostles. The Good News was to be preached to the whole of creation,[41] and this has been accomplished: *the Gospels have, in fact, been spread all over the world.* With this spread, the principles of Christian civilization are recognized everywhere, now more and more even by the non-Christian world. The essential condition for moving on to the last Cycle, the era of the Holy Spirit, is thus realized.

The constated imperfections in the work of all *teams* such as those of Alexander and Peter, and even more in the *team* of the Apostles, are a great comfort for us. They show us that we must not be discouraged by our own weaknesses, as long as the *essential* has been done. Our failures and falls must be analyzed, and must serve as lessons. Courageously, we may then resume the game, having nothing in our minds but a single important idea: to understand our role better, and to play it to the end with its original meaning restored.

(15)

The *film*, freed from karmic elements introduced by our *free movements* during our present life, will still contain the *Karma* of previous experiences. In other words, since nothing in the Universe is lost, we are born with a *script* already burdened with the consequences of our previous *free movements*. Karmic elements, and the traces of accomplished conscious efforts, are both found in latent state in our subconsciousness. There they exert a certain influence on our life in the form of our predispositions; our inclinations and dislikes.

---

41. Mark xvi: 15.

As we have just indicated, it is only at the summit of the *Staircase*, at the note FA of the *Way*, that man will see all the contents[42] of his *being* truly and in every detail. Nevertheless, once the *first Threshold* is crossed, esoteric work will begin to reveal the true meaning of the *film*. Man must proceed with an impartial analysis of its contents: the role that each of the actors plays in it — and the value of this role — must be passed through a sieve. Gradually, as this stripping work progresses, the positive or negative character of different roles emerges more and more clearly. After this, inappropriate elements tend to disappear from the scene. At the end of this analysis, the *film* will contain only a reduced number of actors. But all of them are organically bound together, and with the hero, by the contents of the play, as it was conceived from the beginning of these experiences ... which are pursued by the real 'I' through centuries or even millennia. The play must then be played out to its resolution or denouement.

The basic task of man, once he has crossed the *first Threshold*, is to shelter himself from the karmic influences which are the effects of errors committed in his *free movements*, either in the present life or in the past. To facilitate their task, these workers used to go to some monastery or create a hermitage for themselves, a 'desert', in the language of the Orthodox Tradition. The pupil was thus sheltered from a large part of the 'A' influences, and this enabled him to concentrate his efforts more effectively on introspective work. In our times this formula is old-fashioned. Monasteries and hermitages are no longer available to everyone, as they were at one time. Today one must work in the esoteric plane while remaining in the secular world. This is particularly true because the rhythm of everyday life is different. Our times require energetic and rapid methods.

(16)

Our last question is to discover if there is a sort of esoteric *shortcut*, allowing the *Staircase* between the two *Thresholds* to be climbed more quickly, while we remain and work in the contemporary world.

This means exists: we have referred to it more than once: it is *to work as a couple*. We must believe that in the new era which approaches, this method will be favoured more and more, will be protected, and will eventually become obligatory. However, for this esoteric work to be completed successfully by two people, it is essential that the two beings — man and woman — *are integrally polar*.

The method of working here is the reverse of that described above where, by successive elimination based on long and minute analysis of

---

42. Fr. 'contenu intégral'.

his *film*, and after new errors and new failures, man must *end* by finding his legitimate spouse, a fully integral polar being with whom to unite himself.

In this case, man must instead *begin* by a conscious search for his polar being. If found, they can *work together* on the *film* which — in its origin — is common to them both.

A man alone is incomplete. But just where he is weak, his polar being is strong. Together, they form an integral being: their union leads to the fusion of their Personalities and a faster crystallization of their complete subtle bodies, united into a common second Birth. This is the redemption of the original sin.

The system of *films* is conceived in such a way that polar beings will *necessarily* meet in life, in certain cases more than once. Only the confused ties contracted in this life by each of them, as a result of their *free movements*, combined with the karmic consequences of one or more previous experiences, can divert the man or woman from the *only* being with whom they could form a *Microcosmos*.

If there were no karmic debt, everything would go wonderfully: two young people would meet in the most favourable family and social atmosphere, and their union would represent a true fairy-tale. But this is not reality. Obeying the *principle of Imperfection*, and moved by the action of the *General Law*, the two predestined beings will commit errors. Deeply buried in lies, they do not generally know how to appreciate the gift they are given. Often, they do not even recognize each other.

If this is the case, then an agonizing question is put: is there one or more means to detect our polar being, and if so, what are these means? To meet that person, to do so without recognition, to let our polar being pass by, is the worst mistake we could possibly make: because we would remain in our factitious life, without light. Must not *everything* be sacrificed in favour of a union which is the only chance of our life: the promise of return to paradise lost?

Nevertheless, we should beware of the last trap, one we can fall into just at the moment when ineffable happiness seems to smile upon us. We have just said: all must be *sacrificed;* we have not said: all must be *broken*. If, having recognized one another, the two polar beings triumph over this last ordeal or test, often the most painful, the new life will open in front of them, as they are then called to be *One* on earth and in heaven.

But let us now return to the question of knowing how not to pass by after having met our true *alter ego*, the pledge of happiness and salvation?

There is a whole series of subjective and objective clues which assist us in recognizing our polar being. The polarization is manifested on all planes simultaneously: sexual, physical, mental[43] and spiritual.

Two elements must be taken into consideration.

---

43. Fr. 'psychique'.

The first is objective. It is a consequence of the *principle of Imperfection*, manifesting, here as elsewhere, as one of the great principles which condition and rule life. If it is correct to say that the predestined man and woman are *absolutely* polar beings, this polarity is not simple because, to a certain measure, both are physically, mentally and spiritually *hermaphroditic* beings. That measure, that proportion, is at the same time *sufficient and necessary*. It is necessary to permit every being coming into this world to carry *within himself* the image of the polar being; this image is expressed, in each case, by means of the organ of the opposite sex which exists in every being in a state of non-development. It is, so to say, a part of the flesh and blood of his polar being that each one of us carries within himself. This proportion is sufficient, that is, it is the absolute minimum that will not jeopardize the complete polarity, since the proportion of hermaphroditism in both polar beings is strictly equivalent.

The second element, which is subjective, is the distortion of our Personality due to conscious or unconscious deviations to which the initial *film* was subject in our life, or more exactly, during the course of our existence. Distortions of this kind make it more difficult to recognize the polar being, and can make us less willing to exert ourselves to unite with that being.

(17)

L et us now examine the initial phenomenon of Creation, and the polarization of the sexes in its application to man. We know the complete diagram of the human being:

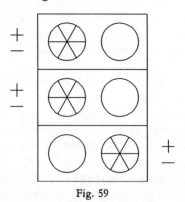

Fig. 59

This diagram does not show the polarization of the indivisible centres. With the higher and sexual centres polarized, the diagram for a man would look as follows:

246

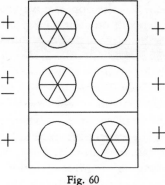

Fig. 60

The diagram for a woman is naturally polarized in relation to that of man. Placed one beside the other, these figures give the following configuration:

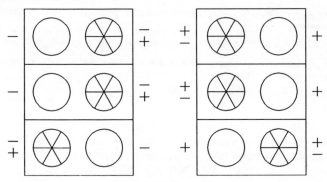

Fig. 61

In its ensemble, the last diagram represents the complete being. As such, this being integrally reflects the manifested Absolute in the created Universe — in all its aspects.

We can clearly see now that it is the *Androgyne* who constitutes a true *Microcosmos*, not the isolated man or woman. On an infinitesimal scale,[44] this encompasses all the elements which the *Macrocosmos* contains in infinitely great proportions. We must note regarding this subject that, according to the Bible, the creation of man *in the image and likeness of God* was in the form of the *Androgyne*: this description in fact refers to the time *before* the fall of Adam, meaning, before the disintegration of the joint astral body of the two polar beings.[45]

---

44. Fr. 'échelle'.
45. Genesis i: 27; Fall, *ibid.*, iii: 7.

For man as for woman, but the opposite way round, salvation in the bosom of the Absolute depends on their reintegration in the *Microcosmos*, as St Paul indicates explicitly in the text already quoted: *'neither is the woman without the man, nor the man without the woman in the Lord.'*[46] Man and woman are in fact incomplete beings who — taken apart — cannot reflect in His fullness the image of God *who is all in all.*[47]

It is an axiom that every man and every woman has a polar being: this explains the wonderful numeric equilibrium between the sexes. Nevertheless, not all humans feel the imperative need to be united to their polar being. Beings who live *enclosed*[48] in their Personality without thinking deeply[49] — and they constitute the great majority of humanity — enthusiastically involve themselves in a life ruled by 'A' influences, and do not really feel the need for such a union. For them, the polar being is on the same plane as everyone else. The Personality does not perceive anything exceptional in him, and if by some chance an extraordinary impression is experienced, it is instead felt as something abnormal and embarrassing. Particularly difficult situations are born from such misapprehensions.[50] In this context we can speak of couples formed under the influence of the *Law of Accident*, in which the partners have opposite aspirations: one aspires towards the 'A' influences and the other searches for the *Way*. At the base of such unions we often find, beside a double error of judgement, the influence of karmic debt, remote or recent; for example, an 'arranged' marriage, or passion without love. The most intelligent attitude to take on such occasions is to unite the efforts of the couple to unravel the situation to their mutual benefit. Left to itself, the situation will only get worse. Very special care must be taken of children of such a union, as they suffer. Everything must be done to remedy this. As a general rule, we must not lose sight of the fact that, even if it is permitted to the human being to offer himself in sacrifice, he has no right to accept the sacrifice of others.

We can say, however, that accelerated evolution of the hero of the *film* brings him nearer to his polar being. At the same time, it automatically removes from the *film* those Personalities who have entered it fortuitously.

(18)

After the formation of the *magnetic centre* within him man starts to feel the desire, then the need, to be united to his polar being. This desire

---

46. I Corinthians xi: 11. Cf. p. 227.
47. I Corinthians xv: 28.
48. Fr. *'ancrés'*.
49. Fr. 'intensément'.
50. Fr. 'méconnaissance'.

and need will increase in proportion to the growth of the latter. This is why, as we have just said, the concept of the *Androgyne* has purely mythical or theoretical value for ordinary man. We can now realize that for man, a living aspiration to be re-integrated in the *Microcosmos* — the most direct way to the re-integration in the Absolute — is the fruit of a high moral culture. As we have mentioned several times, esoteric evolution is conditioned at the start by a bankruptcy, a moral breakdown. To make progress after this, man must know exactly where he stands, meaning that he must *see himself*. St Isaac the Syrian said that he who has been able to see himself as he is is better than he who has been able to see the angels.[51]

What we call bankruptcy, the Tradition calls 'death'. It is death while still in a living body. One must first die, then be resurrected. Jesus says: '*except a grain of wheat fall into the earth and die, it abideth by itself alone; but if it die, it beareth much fruit*'[52] and he adds the comment: that '*he that loveth his soul loseth it* (the Personality) *and he that hateth his soul* (again the Personality) *in this world shall keep it unto life eternal.*'[53]

(19)

By progressively taking his fate into his own hands, man at the same time takes responsibility for *all* the partners in his *film*.

It has already been said that he must restore the original meaning of his *film*, then push the development of the latter in such a way that the 'play' be properly played out to its intended denouement. The hero, while working on himself, must apply himself to *create new circumstances around him*, which will enhance the unfolding of the action towards its originally intended conclusion. His exterior efforts must above all be directed towards the creation of these *circumstances*, not towards seeking direct influence over people: this kind of influence often seems opportune, but in the great majority of cases it is an error. Instead of unravelling the situation, the influence creates karmic debts which complicate things all the more. One must be very prudent and circumspect. Yet new circumstances must be created in a way that effectively helps those interested to act in the direction desired. Once again, man should seek to serve, not to impose himself. Patience, perseverance and faith are qualities of great practical value in this work.

---

51. *Philokalia*, sermons of St Isaac the Syrian.
52. John xii: 24; Matthew x: 39; Mark viii: 35; Luke ix: 24.
53. *Ibid.*

For man to recognize his polar being, he must be fully attentive on all planes accessible to his consciousness. In fact, as a result of the distortion of the *film*, the meeting always occurs in circumstances and in a manner least expected, generally at a moment and in a form which resemble nothing he could have ever imagined.

The rule enforced is precise: *to recognize his polar being, man must know himself.* This is obviously logical: to recognize his *alter ego*, man must first recognize his own *ego*.

We are thus confronted once again with the problem of the search for the *Way*.

It is true that the 'I' of the body, like the 'I' of the Personality, aspires to find the perfect response from another being. Nevertheless, it is only by identifying himself more and more with his real 'I' that man *magnetizes*[54] the union with his polar being.

It is with a heart full of faith, sharpening within himself his highest faculties of intuition and attention, his sense of critical analysis taken to the highest point of alertness, that man will go in search of the being without whom he is not real. As it was for the troubadour long ago, it is in *courtly love* that he can hope to find and recognize 'la Dame de ses Pensées'.

The difficulty we find in discovering our polar beings lies in the fact that we are deformed, and constantly distort our *film* by *free movements*. These are the first two points that need to be corrected: we must rectify our own distortion and renounce our impulsive movements. This explains the prescription not to act under the influence of only one centre. It is the necessity to correct for our distortions, which, logically, imposes on us the need, both in *reception* and *transmission*, for conscious effort to make our emotional and intellectual centres work together to face the problems which confront us.

The complexity of a human being can be compared in principle to that of an orchestra, and that of his life to a symphony where each instrument follows its part in a harmonious ensemble. In working on himself, he must act as the orchestra leader acts during the rehearsals of a new musical performance.

All this is preparatory work. But when polar beings meet, by what immediately perceptible signs can humans who are still imperfect, still

---

54. Fr. 'aimante'.

deformed by karmic debts, be certain in all objectivity that they are not making a mistake?

Here are some indispensable criteria that can have objective value in mutual recognition. From the first meeting, in the presence of the polar being, both the 'I' of the Personality and the 'I' of the body vibrate in a manner which resembles nothing felt before. The reason for this is that these I's find themselves then in the presence of their *first love* which continues through the centuries. Without clearly being conscious of it, the polar beings know each other; and this knowledge, as ancient as they are themselves, is expressed by the voice of their subconsciousness. This creates an atmosphere of absolute confidence and sincerity from the moment they meet.

There is a touchstone here: *polar beings do not lie to each other*. They do not need to lie, for inwardly both are one single being, from the depths of which the real 'I' issues his call and gives his assent. After this, that absolute, spontaneous sincerity constitutes the basis of their relations, and this in turn will give these two beings the otherwise inconceivable feeling of *freedom in unity*, which ends the impression of servitude and isolation under which we ordinarily live.

Soon afterwards, vague reminiscences of past *experiences* will start to come to the surface in their waking consciousness.

The reader will now understand the deepest reason why lying to oneself is forbidden: he who lies to himself will also lie to his *alter ego*. That will be the end of the miracle. The wonderful side of the meeting will disappear behind a curtain of trivial lies, which will rapidly take the aspect of an impassable wall. Behind this wall, relations with the polar being will no longer be distinguished from those that a man can have with other women: wives, mistresses and adventures. Once more, the experience will be spoiled.

This is how and why *exterior* man passes by his polar being without recognizing her. This is why practical work on the esoteric *Way* starts and necessarily continues with a struggle against lying to oneself. Success in this field is indispensable. To reach this aim, no price whatsoever is too high to pay.

(22)

If they are open to the truth, and if their meeting makes chords — silent until now — vibrate in harmony within them both, the way is then marked out, for polar beings, by their conscious efforts to re-create the *Microcosmos* which had formerly been dissociated and broken. They will traverse the *Staircase* like an arrow and will suddenly find themselves in front of the *second Threshold*.

The *catechumen* crosses the *first Threshold* under the impetus of a *negative* feeling: the horror of life in the *wilderness*, and the ardent desire to escape from it. To reach the *second Threshold*, the two polar beings who present themselves in front of it must be holders of a *positive* password, which will be required from them at that precise moment.

The *Way* opens to those who know what they want; know what they aspire to, on the *Way* and outside the *Way*, in an *exterior* life which after this can never again be detached from esoteric work. Happy are those who can be useful in it. The Door which leads to Life will open before them, and they will read on the pediment of the wall the sacramental inscription:

'The labourer is worthy of his hire.'[55]

---

55. Luke x: 7.

POSTSCRIPT

Since earliest antiquity, man has striven to solve the problem of *absolute Knowledge*. A classical initiation formula says: *try to grasp that which, once learned, you will know all*. They used to teach novices this: that to understand all, it is necessary to know very little — but before we can grasp this trifle, a great deal must be learned. In the minds of the ancients this order of ideas, the notion of Gnosis, represented not just simple knowledge, but living[1] Knowledge, superior to both Reason and Faith.

In the words of St Paul, used as an epigraph to this work, *Gnosis* — the one Gnosis — appeared as *mysterious and hidden Wisdom*. Its purpose, in revealing different aspects of this wisdom is to allow us to perceive the hermetic meaning of the title.

As for the subtitle, this should not only be applied to the abstract idea of Gnosis, as just described, but to its manifestation in the world, particularly during that critical period which preceded and followed the Advent of Christ.

During the Cycle of the Father, the divine Gnosis had been revealed in the form of mysteries — the *mysteries of the Promise* — which later found their justification in Jesus as the *mystery of Realization*.

With the Advent of Christ, the strict rule of silence previously imposed upon the initiated came to an end. A flood of gnostic ideas was then released. Spontaneously there appeared at the same time in many parts of the ancient world teachings, theories and systems based on both the Tradition of the *mysteries of the Promise*, and on the *mystery of Jesus* which was shaking the ancient order of initiation.

In the mixture and interpenetration of ideas which resulted, we can soon distinguish two diverging currents, both starting from the same basic postulate. That is, both began from an objective statement of the imperfection of the world of phenomena.

Certain *gnostics* tried to explain this imperfection as a fall of light into matter, a catastrophe supposedly beyond the intervention of a God who was Perfect and unmanifested, or by means of an error, or even by a malevolent intention of the Creator.

At the basis of these errors we always find a confusion between planes[2]. Reason attributes to the divine an attitude, a weakness, and even more often, purely human motives. We recognize here, amongst other things, the mark of Hellenic thought, which tended to humanize the divinities. The Good News announced by Jesus reversed this ancient conception,

---

1. Or vivifying.
2. Fr. 'plans'.

calling for the divinization of the human in man by a second Birth; the gateway to the Kingdom of God.

These struggles between ideas ended in victory for Orthodoxy. The heretical tendencies that then manifested themselves were fought and overcome, one after the other, by the work of the Apostles and that of the doctors of the œcumenical Church, who have made the doctrine of Christ, the doctrine of Love, shine brightly in its Truth because of their dedication and perseverance.

Because of this it was possible — notably in the oriental Orthodoxy — to preserve the esoteric Tradition mysteriously hidden in its original purity, just as it had been transmitted by the Apostles and their disciples.

Geneva, November 1958–June 1959.

END OF THE FIRST VOLUME

BIBLIOGRAPHY
Prepared with the collaboration of
Dr. Albert-Jean LUCAS

A bibliography on the ensemble of subjects treated in Gnosis could be considerably larger than this. The sole aim of the publications listed below is to allow the reader, if he so wishes, to study in greater depth various elements which form the context of the present work. Such study will make it easier to understand the theses that are presented in it.

Legend: St-P — published by the Monastery of Saint Panteleimon on Mount Athos. For Russian titles, the modern orthography has been used.

ENGLISH LANGUAGE[1]
and languages other than French
I.
The BIBLE: OLD and NEW TESTAMENT

THE BIBLE or HOLY SCRIPTURE BOOKS OF THE OLD AND NEW TESTAMENT. Slavonic text. (БИБЛИЯ сиречь КНИГИ СВЯЩЕННОГО ПИСАНИЯ ВЕТХОГО И НОВОГО ЗАВЕТА (Славянский текст)). Text edited, corrected and published by order of Empress Elisabeth I. Moscow, State Press, 1762.

NOVUM TESTAMENTUM *graece et latine. Textum graecum recensuit, latinum ex Vulgata. Tertia editio critica recognita.* By Frédéric Brandscheid. Fribourg. Vol. I — 1901; Vol. II — 1907.

GOSPEL OF JOHN. Chap. I–XIV — Bodmer Papyrus, II. Bibl. bodmeriana, 5. Published by Prof. Victor Martin. Geneva, 1956.

II
Concordances, Dictionaries, Encyclopædias

THE NEW CATHOLIC DICTIONARY. A complete work of reference of every subject in the life, belief, tradition, rites, symbolism, devotions, history... of the Church... comp. and ed. under the direction of Conde B. Pallen (and) John J. Wynne... under the auspices of the editors of the Catholic Encyclopædia. New York, The Universal Knowledge Foundation, 1929.

THE CATHOLIC ENCYCLOPÆDIA. An international work of reference on the constitution, doctrine, discipline and history of the Catholic Church. Ed. by Charles Herbermann and others. London, Caxton Pub. Co., 1907–1912. 15 vols.
Supplementary volume containing revisions of the articles on canon law according to the code of canon law of Pius X. prom. by Pope Benedict XV. By Andrew A. Macerlean. New York, The Encyclopædia Press, 1918.

---

1. Ed. To aid the English reader, the original order of this bibliography has been changed. Titles in the French language have been placed in a separate section. Some of the titles shown in the English language section of this bibliography have been added for this English edition. These are marked §.

ENCICLOPEDIA CATTOLICA. Direttore Mons. Pio Paschini, Rettore magnifico del Pontificio atenco lateranense. Citta del Vaticano, Ente per l'Enciclopedia cattolica e per il libro cattolico, 1948.

THE JEWISH ENCYCLOPÆDIA. A descriptive record of the history, religion, literature and customs of the Jewish people from the earliest times to the present day, prepared under the direction... of Cyrus Adler... (and others), Isidore Singer Ph. D. projector and managing editor, assisted by American and foreign boards of consulting editors. New York and London, Funk and Wagnalls Co., 1901–1916. 12 vols.

THE UNIVERSAL JEWISH ENCYCLOPÆDIA. An authoritative and popular presentation of Jews and Judaism since the earliest times. Ed. by Isaac Landman. New York, Universal Jewish Encyclopædia Co. Inc., 1948. 10 vols. Supplement. A reading guide and index. Comp. by Simon Cohen. New York, Universal Jewish Encyclopædia Co. Inc., 1948.

ENCYCLOPÆDIA OF RELIGION AND ETHICS. Ed. by James Hastings... with the assistance of John A. Selbie... and other scholars. Edinburgh, T. and T. Clark. New York, C. Scribner's Sons, 1908–1926. 13 vols.

III
APOCRYPHA

THE APOCRYPHAL NEW TESTAMENT. Translated by M. R. James. Oxford, At the Clarendon Press, 1955.

THE GOSPEL ACCORDING TO THOMAS. Coptic text established and translated by A. Guillaumont, H.-C. Puech, G. Quispel, W. Till and † Yassah 'Abd Al Masiḥ. Collins, London, 1959; E. J. Brill, Leiden, 1959. §

THE APOCALYPSE OF BARUCH. By R. H. Charles. London, Macmillan, 1918.

THE APOCALYPSE OF EZRA (II Ezra III–XIV). Translated and annotated by G. H. Box. London, Soc. for promoting Christian knowledge, 1917.

ADAM and EVE (*The book of...*) also called: the *Conflict of Adam and Eve with Satan*. A book of the early Eastern Church by the Rev. S. C. Malan. London, Williams and Norgate, 1882.

THE ASCENSION OF ISAIAH. Transl. from the Ethiopic version which together with the New Greek Testament, the Latin versions and the Latin translation of the Slavonic is here published in full by R. H. Charles. London, A. Black, 1900.

THE PSALMS OF SOLOMON. Edited by Henry Barclay Swete. Cambridge, The Univ. Press, 1899.

THE TESTAMENT OF ABRAHAM. By W. E. Barnes. Cambridge, The Univ. Press, 1892.

THE TESTAMENT OF SOLOMON. Edited by Chester Charlton McCown. Leipzig, J. C. Hinrichs, 1922.

IV
VARIOUS

AFANASIEV, A.N. (АФАНАСЬЕВ, А. Н.). *Nature as seen in Slav poetry.* (Поэтические воззрения Славян на природу). Moscow, K. Soldatenkov, 1865–1869. 3 vols.

ALEXANDRIAN CHRISTIANITY. Selected translations of Clement and Origen with introductions and notes by John Ernest Leonard Oulton ... and Henry Chadwick. [Consisting of the Stromateis, books 3 and 7, by Clement of Alexandria, and the treatises entitled 'On Prayer,' 'Exhortation to Martyrdom' and 'Dialogue with Heraclides by Origen.] London, SCM Press, 1954. §

THE ATHOS PATERIKON or THE LIVES OF SAINTS WHO REACHED GLORIFICATION ON HOLY MOUNT ATHOS. (АФОНСКИЙ ПАТЕРИК или ЖИЗНЕОПИСАНИЕ СВЯТЫХ НА СВЯТОЙ ГОРЕ АФОНСКОЙ ПРОСИЯВШИХ). Description of more than a hundred ascetics of ancient times and the Middle Ages. Moscow, St-P, 1897. In 2 parts. 7th ed.

THE BEAUTY OF THE EASTER SERVICES (КРАСОТА ПАСХАЛЬНОГО БОГОСЛУЖЕНИЯ). Homily during vespers on Easter Sunday. Moscow, St-P, 1912.

BOEHME. Jacob. *The Way to Christ discovered ... To which are added some other pieces ... also a Treatise on the Four Complexions.* The translations are those published in 1648, with alterations and with the marginal explanations incorporated in the text. Bath, S. Hazard; Bristol, T. Mills, 1775. §

BORISKOVSKY, P. I. *The most distant past of humanity* (Борисковский, П. И., Древнейшее прошлое человечества). Moscow, The Academy of Sciences, 1957.

BROWN, Allan R. *Paul the Sower.* A study of the purpose and meaning of the Epistle to the Romans. Introduction by Herbert Parrish D.D. New York, Fleming H. Revell Co., 1932.

BURCKHARDT, Titus. *Sacred art in East and West — its principles and methods.* Translated by Lord Northbourne. Bedfont, Perennial Books, 1976. §

BURROWS Miller. *The Dead Sea Scrolls.* With translations by the author. London, Secker & Warburg, 1956. §

THE CEREMONY OF RENOUNCEMENT OF SATAN AND UNION WITH CHRIST. Which forms part of the reception into the Catechumenate. (ОБРЯД ОТРЕЧЕНИЯ ОТ САТАНЫ И СОЧЕТАНИЯ ХРИСТУ — в чине оглашения). Moscow, St-P, 1907.

COLLECTED LETTERS OF BISHOP THEOPHAN THE RECLUSE. (СОБРАНИЕ ПИСЕМ СВЯТИТЕЛЯ ФЕОФАНА). Moscow, St-P, 1898–1901. 8 fasc.

CONTEMPORARY ASCETICS OF HOLY MOUNT ATHOS (АФОНСКИЕ СОВРЕМЕННЫЕ ПОДВИЖНИКИ). Ascetic monks: Nicodemus, Païssy, Gabriel, Neophyte and Antheme facing the glory of God. Moscow, St-P, 1904. 10th ed.

DAY Langston and WARR, George de la. *New Worlds Beyond the Atom.* London, V. Stuart, 1956.

DAY OF RESURRECTION! (ВОСКРЕСЕНИЯ ДЕНЬ!). According to several sources, especially Bishop Theophan the Recluse. Moscow, St-P, 1904. 2nd ed.

DEMETRIUS (Archbishop of Tauric Chersonese). *Flowers of the garden.* (ЦВЕТЫ ИЗ САДА Димитрия, Архиепископа Херсонского). Moscow, St-P, 1889–1890. 7 fasc.

DIONYSIUS THE AREOPAGITE. *The Celestial and Ecclesiastical Hierarchy.* Transl. by Rev. John Parker. London, Skeffington & Son, 1894. §

DOSTOEVSKY, F. *Complete works.* St Petersburg, Panteleff Press, 1906. 9 vols. (ДОСТОЕВСКИЙ, Ф. М., Полное собрание сочинений).

EPIPHANIUS. *Epiphanii contra Haereses.* Basileae, 1562.

EUSEBIUS OF CÆSAREA. *An Ecclesiastical History to the year 324 of the Christian era..* Translated by C. F. Cruse. London, 1838. §

EVANGELICAL HISTORY OF THE SON OF GOD – INCARNATED FOR OUR SALVATION (ЕВАНГЕЛЬСКАЯ ИСТОРИЯ О БОГЕ-СЫНЕ ВОПЛОТИВШЕМСЯ НАШЕГО РАДИ СПАСЕНИЯ). Gospel history exposed in consecutive order by the words of the Holy Evangelists, by Bishop Theophan the Recluse, with a preface to the reader by him. Moscow, St-P, 1895. 2nd ed.

FEDOROV, Nicolai Fed. *Philosophy of the common cause.* (ФЕДОРОВ, Николай Фед., Философия Общего Дела). Articles, thoughts and letters. Ed. under the supervision of V. A. Kozhevnikov and N. A. Peterson. Moscow, Verny, 1906–1913. 2 vols.

FREUD, Sigmund. *The basic writings of...* Psychopathology of everyday life. The interpretation of dreams. The contribution to the theory of sex. Wit and its relation to the unconscious. Totem and taboo. The history of the psychoanalytic movement. Translated and edited, with an introduction by Dr. A. A. Brill. Index. New York, The Modern Library, Cop. 1938.

HARNACK, Adolphe von. *History of Dogma.* Transl. from German by Niel Buchanan. London, Williams and Norgate, 1897–1899. 2nd ed. 7 vols.

JOSEPHUS FLAVIUS *Complete Works.* Transl. by William Whiston etc. London, Pickering & Inglis, 1963. §

JUNG C. G. *Modern man in search of a soul.* Transl. by W. S. Dell and Cary F. Baynes. London, Ark Paperbacks, 1984. §

JUNG C. G. *Symbols of Transformation.* Translated by R. F. C. Hull. London, Routledge and Kegan Paul, 1956. §

JUNG C. G. *Psychological types.* London, Routledge and Kegan Paul, 1971. §

LEGENDS CONCERNING HOLY MOUNT ATHOS. (СКАЗАНИЯ О СВ. ГОРЕ АФОНСКОЙ). Explanation of the word 'holy' as well as the other attribute: 'The domain of the Mother of God'. Extract from a XVth century manuscript from the de la Laure Library of the Holy Trinity–St Sergius monastery, attributed to Stephen the ascetic of Mount Athos. Moscow, St-P, 1897. 5th ed.

LEGENDS CONCERNING THE LIFE OF THE HOLY VIRGIN ON EARTH. (СКАЗАНИЯ О ЗЕМНОЙ ЖИЗНИ ПРЕСВЯТОЙ БОГОРОДНЦЫ). Moscow, St-P, 1904. 8th ed.

THE LIFE OF SAINT ATHANASIUS OF ATHOS. (ЖИТИЕ ПРЕПОДОБНО-ГО АФАНАСИЯ АФОНСКОГО). Founder of the monastic life of Mount Athos. Moscow, St-P, 1908. 8th ed.

THE LIFE AND MIRACLES OF SAINT SERGIUS OF RADONEZH. (ЖИТИЕ И ЧУДЕСА ПРЕПОДОБНОГО СЕРГИЯ РАДОНЕЖСКОГО). Moscow, St-P, 1897.

THE LIFE AND SUFFERING OF SAINT THOMAS THE APOSTLE. (ЖИТИЕ И СТРАДАНИЯ СВ. АПОСТОЛА ФОМЫ). Moscow, St-P, 1902. 10th ed.

MENOLOGY. (ЧЕТЬИ МИНЕИ В ПОУЧЕНИЯХ НА КАЖДЫЙ ДЕНЬ ГОДА). Lives of the saints with homilies for each day of the year. In 4 vols. collected by Archpriest Victor Guriev.
— Vol.   I — September, October, November,
— Vol.   II — December, January, February,
— Vol. III — March, April, May,
— Vol. IV — June, July, August.
Moscow, St-P, 1896.

MOUNT ATHOS. (СВЯТАЯ ГОРА АФОН). *Gate of Heavens*. Domain of the Most Holy Virgin on earth — Holy Mount Athos. (Врата Небесная — Удел Пресвятыя Богородицы на земле — Святая Гора Афон). Paris, 1958.

MOUNT ATHOS. (СВЯТАЯ ГОРА АФОН). *History of the Saint Andreas Monastery*. (История Андреевского Скита). Moscow, St-P, no date.

NICODEMUS THE HAGIORITE. *The Cross — protector of the whole Universe*. (НИКОДИМ СВЯТОГОРЕЦ. Крест — Хранитель всея Вселенной). Exegesis on the canon of the vivifying exaltation of the Holy Cross of Our Lord (14th September). Transl. from Greek by Prof. I. N. Korsunsky. Moscow, St-P, 1899.

NICODEMUS THE HAGIORITE. *Unseen Warfare*. (НИКОДИМ СВЯТОГОРЕЦ. Невидимая Брань). Transl. from Greek by Bishop Theophan the Recluse. Moscow, St-P, 1904. 4th ed.

NICOLL, Maurice. *The New Man*. New York, Hermitage House, 1951.

ORAGE, A. R. *The Active Mind*. New York, Hermitage House, 1954.

ORIGEN. *Contre Celsum*. Translated [from the Latin] with an introduction and notes by Henry Chadwick. Cambridge, Cambridge University Press, 1980. §

ORIGEN. *The Song of Songs*. Commentary and homilies. Translated and annotated by R. P. Lawson [or rather, Sister Penelope]. Westminster, Newman Press, 1957. §

ORIGEN. *Origen on First Principles*. Being Koetschau's text of De Principiis translated into English, together with an introduction and notes, by G. W. Butterworth. Madras, printed London, S.P.C.K., 1936. §

ORIGEN'S TREATISE ON PRAYER. Translation and notes with an account of the practice and doctrine of prayer from New Testament times to Origen by Eric George Jay. London, S.P.C.K., 1954.

ORIGEN. *An exhortation to martyrdom; [and] Prayer; [and] First principles, book IV; [and] Prologue to the commentary on 'The song of songs'; [and] Homily XXVII on 'Numbers'.* Translation [from the Latin] and introduction by Rowan A. Greer, preface by Hans Urs von Balthasar. London, S.P.C.K., 1979. §

OUSPENSKY, P. D. (УСПЕНСКИЙ, П. Д.). *The Inner Circle.* (Внутренний Круг). St Petersburg, 1913.

OUSPENSKY, P. D. *Fragments of an unknown teaching.* London, Routledge & Kegan Paul, 1950. §

OUSPENSKY, P. D. *The Psychology of man's possible evolution.* New York, Knopf, 1945.

OUSPENSKY, P. D. *The Fourth Way. A record of talks and answers to questions based on the teaching of G. I. Gurdjieff.* New York, Knopf, 1959.

PHILOKALIA, Vol. I. (ДОБРОТОЛЮБИЕ, том 1-й). Transl. directed, and introduction by Bishop Theophan the Recluse. This volume includes the works of Anthony the Great; Macarius the Great; Abba Isaiah the Hermit; Mark the Ascetic and Abba Evagrius. Moscow, St-P, 1905. 4th ed.

PHILOKALIA, Vol. II. (ДОБРОТОЛЮБИЕ, том 2-й). Transl. directed by Bishop Theophan the Recluse. This volume includes the works of: John Cassian the Roman; Hesychius of Jerusalem; Nilus of Sinai; Ephraim of Syria; John Climacus; Barsanuphius and John; Abba Dorotheus and Isaac the Syrian. Moscow, St-P, 1895. 2nd ed.

PHILOKALIA, Vol. III. (ДОБРОТОЛЮБИЕ, том 3-й). Transl. directed by Bishop Theophan the Recluse. This volume includes the works of: Diadoch; John of Carpathos; Abba Zossima; Maximus the Confessor; Thalassius; Theodore; Philotheus of Sinai; Elias the Priest, then the report concerning Abba Philemon. Moscow, St-P, 1900. 2nd ed.

PHILOKALIA, Vol. IV. (ДОБРОТОЛЮБИЕ, том 4-й). Transl. directed, and introduction by Bishop Theophan the Recluse. This volume includes extracts from all known teaching, whether printed or in manuscript form, of the venerable father, messenger of God, Theodore the Studite. Moscow, St-P, 1901. 2nd ed.

PHILOKALIA, Vol. V. (ДОБРОТОЛЮБИЕ, том 5-й). Transl. by Bishop Theophan the Recluse. This volume includes the works of: St Simeon the New Theologian; Simeon the Devout; most venerated Nicetas Stethatos; Theoleptus, Metropolitan of Philadelphia; Gregory of Sinai; Nicephorus the Solitary; Gregory Palamas; Patriarch Callistus and his fellow ascetic Ignatius of Xanthopoulos; Callistus Telecudes; Simeon, Archbishop of Thessalonica, and others. Moscow, St-P, 1900. 2nd ed.

PHILOKALIA, Index. (ДОБРОТОЛЮБИЕ, Указатель). Moscow, St-P, 1900.

PHILOKALIA (*Early Fathers from the*...) together with some writings of St Abba Dorotheus, St Isaac of Syria and St Gregory Palamas. Selected and translated from the Russian text 'Dobrotolubiye' by E. Kadloubovsky and G. E. H. Palmer. London, Faber and Faber Ltd., 1954.

PHILOKALIA (*Writings from the... on prayer of the heart*). Translated from the Russian text 'Dobrotolubiye' by E. Kadloubovsky and G. E. H. Palmer. London, Faber and Faber Ltd., 1957. 3rd. rev. ed.

PHILOTHEUS, monk. (ЛОФЕЙ, Старец). *Epistle to Vasily III.* (Послание Государю Царю и Вел. Князю Василию 3-у). In *Pravoslavny Sobessednik* (Православный Собеседник). Orthodox Review no. 1, St Petersburg, 1863.

PISTIS SOPHIA. Opus gnosticum. Valentino Adiudicatum e condice Manuscripto coptico londinensi. Descriptit et latine vertit M. G. Schwartze. Editit J. H. Petermann. Berolini, in Fred Duemmleri Libraria, 1851.

PISTIS SOPHIA. Leipzig, Carl Schmidt, 1925.

PISTIS SOPHIA. Englished, with an introduction and annotated bibliography by G. R. S. Mead ... New and completely revised edition. London, J. M. Watkins, 1921. §

PLATO. *The portable Plato.* 'Protagoras', 'Symposium', 'Phaedo', and 'The Republic', complete, translated from the Greek by Benjamin Jowett. Harmondsworth, Penguin, 1977. §

PLOTINUS. *The Enneads.* Translated by Stephen MacKenna. Third edition revised by B. S. Page. With ... an introduction by Professor Paul Henry. London, Faber & Faber, 1962. §

THE PRAYER TO THE MOST SWEET LORD JESUS—AT THE MOMENT OF SEPARATION OF THE SOUL FROM THE BODY. (МОЛЕНИЕ СЛАДЧАЙШЕМУ ГОСПОДУ ИИСУСУ, ПРИ ИСХОДЕ ДУШИ ИЗ ТЕЛА). Moscow, St-P, 1912. 12th ed.

REASON AND COURAGE. (*Of worldly vanity and freedom from care*). (О РАЗУМЕ И МУЖЕСТВЕ, О житейской суете и беспечалии). Moscow, St-P, 1903. 3rd ed. (From the Mount Athos Tradition).

REITZENSTEIN Richard. *Poïmandres.* Studien zur griechisch-aegyptischen und fruehchristlichen Literatur. Leipzig, 1904.

REITZENSTEIN Richard. *Die hellenistischen Mysterien Religionen, ihre Grundgedanken und Wirkungen.* Leipzig and Berlin, Teubner, 1927. 3 Aufl.

RULES OF ANCIENT TIMES FOR PRACTISING ASCETICS. (ДРЕВНИЕ ИНОЧЕСКИЕ УСТАВЫ). Of Pachomius the Great, Basil the Great, John Cassian the Blessed, Benedict the Blessed, collected by Bishop Theophan the Recluse. Moscow, St-P, 1892.

SAINT ANDREAS Archbishop of Cæsarea. (СВ. Архиепископ Кесарийский). *Exegeses on the Apocalypse.* (Толкование на Апокалипсис). Moscow, St-P, 1897. 4th ed.

SAINT ISAAC THE SYRIAN. (СВ. ИСААК СИРИЯНИН). *Works.* Moscow, St-P, no date.

SAINT JOHN OF THE LADDER. (СВ. ИОАНН ЛЕСТВИЧНИК). *Ladder of Heaven* (Climacus). (Лествица Небесная). Moscow, St-P, no date.

SAINT JOHN CLIMACUS. *Ladder of Divine Ascent.* Transl. by Colm Lubbheid and Norman Russell, introduction by Kallistos Ware. London S.P.C.K., 1982. §

SCHOLEM, Gershom G. *Major Trends in Jewish Mysticism.* New York, Schocken, 1954. 3rd rev. ed.

SCHOLEM, Gershom G. *Zohar — The Book of Splendor.* Selection by Gershom Scholem. New York, Schocken, 1949.

SIGNS OF THE COMING OF THE ANTICHRIST. (ЗНАМЕНИЯ ПРИШЕСТВИЯ АНТИХРИСТА). According to the holy writings with commentaries by the Holy Fathers and Doctors of the Church: John Chrysostom, Andreas of Cæsarea, John of Damascus, Ephraim of Syria, Theodorites and others. Moscow, St-P, 1902.

SNEGIREV, I. M. (СНЕГИРЕВ, И. М.). *Russian popular festivals and superstitious ceremonies.* (Русские простонародные праздники и суеверные обряды). Moscow, University Press, 1837–1839. 2 vols.

SRESNEVSKY, I. I. (СРЕЗНЕВСКИЙ, И. И.). *Adoration of the sun by the ancient Slavs.* (Об обожании Солнца у древних Славян). In the Journal of the Ministry of Public Education II, St Petersburg, 1848.

THE 'STARTZY' PAISSY VELICHKOVSKY AND MACARIUS OF THE OPTINA MONASTERY and their ascetic and literary activity. (СТАРЦЫ О. ПАИСИЙ ВЕЛИЧКОВСКИЙ И О. МАКАРИЙ ОПТИНСКИЙ и их литературно-аскетическая деятельность). Moscow, St-P, 1908.

TEILHARD DE CHARDIN *Works:*
— The phenomenon of Man,
— The appearance of man,
— Vision of the Past,
— Milieu Divin,
— The future of Man.
London, Collins, 1960–66. §

THEOPHAN THE RECLUSE. (ФЕОФАН ЗАТВОРНИК). *How should one live?* (Как жить?). Reasoned advice from Bishop Theophan the Recluse. Moscow, St-P, 1909. 3rd ed.

THEOPHAN THE RECLUSE. (ФЕОФАН ЗАТВОРНИК). *Commentaries on the epistles of St Paul.* (Толкование посланий Св. Апостола Павла). Romans, I Corinthians, II Corinthians, Galatians, Ephesians, Colossians and Philemon; Philippians and Thessalonians, I and II; Titus and Timothy I and II. Moscow, St-P, 1890–1895. 8 fasc.

THEOPHAN THE RECLUSE. (ФЕОФАН ЗАТВОРНИК). *St Paul's epistle to the Hebrews.* (О посланий Св. Апостола Павла к Евреям). Introduction and the beginning of the work found after the Bishop's death. Moscow, St-P, 1896.

THEOPHAN THE RECLUSE. (ФЕОФАН ЗАТВОРНИК). *Letters on Christian life.* (Письма о христианской жизни). Moscow, St-P, 1908. 4th ed.

THEOPHAN THE RECLUSE. (ФЕОФАН ЗАТВОРНИК). *Letters on the spiritual life.* (Письма о духовной жизни). Moscow, St-P., 1892. 2nd ed.

THEOPHAN THE RECLUSE. (ФЕОФАН ЗАТВОРНИК). *Psalm XXXIII.* (Псалом Тридцать третий). Commentaries. Moscow, St-P, 1900.

THEOPHAN THE RECLUSE. (ФЕОФАН ЗАТВОРНИК). *Psalm CXVIII.* (Псалом Сто-Осмнадцатый). Commentaries. Moscow, St-P, 1891. 2nd ed.

THEOPHAN THE RECLUSE. (ФЕОФАН ЗАТВОРНИК). Three sermons: *to the outraged, the outrageous and the afflicted.* (Три слова обидимым, обидящим и скорбящим). Moscow, St-P, 1903. 4th ed.

THOMAS A-KEMPIS. (ФОМА КЕМПИЙСКИЙ). *The Imitation of Christ.* (Подражание Христу). Moscow, St-P, no date.

THOMAS A-KEMPIS. *The Imitation of Christ*. London, Blackie and Son, no date. §

THREE FORMS OF ATTENTION AND PRAYER. (О ТРЕХ ОБРАЗАХ ВНИ-
МАНИЯ И МОЛИТВЫ). Extract from the sermons of Simeon the New
Theologian. Moscow, St-P, 1901.

TROITSKY, S. V. (ТРОИЦКИЙ, С. В.). *On the names of God and onomatologists.*
(Об Именах Божиих и Имябожниках). St Petersburg, Saint Synod Press,
1914.

TURGENEV, Ivan S. *Poems in prose*. London, Moscow Progress, 1982. §

UNSEEN WARFARE. Being the *Spiritual combat* and *Path to Paradise* of Lorenzo
Scupoli as edited by Nicodemus of the Holy Mountain and revised by
Theophan the Recluse. Translated into English from Theophan's Russian
text by E. Kadloubovsky and G. E. H. Palmer with an introduction by
H. A. Hodges, M.A., D.Phil., Professor of philosophy at the University of
Reading. London, Faber and Faber Ltd., 1952.

VELICHKOVSKY, Paissy. Blessed staretz, ascetic and archimandrite. (ВЕЛИЧ-
КОВСКИЙ, Паисий). *Of inner prayer in the spirit.* (Об умной или внутренней
молитве). Moscow, St-P, 1902. 3rd ed.

THE WAY OF A PILGRIM. Trans. from the Russian by R. M. French. London,
S.P.C.K., 1942. §

WEINFURTER, Karel. *Man's highest Purpose.* The lost word regained. Translated by
Prof. Arnold Capleton and Charles Unger. London, Rider and Co., Paternoster House, Paternoster Row, no date.

THE ZOHAR. Translated by Harry Sperling and Maurice Simon. Introduction by
Dr. J. Abelson. London and Bournemouth, Soncino Press, 1949.

FRENCH LANGUAGE
I.
The BIBLE: OLD AND NEW TESTAMENT

LA PREMIERE PARTIE DU NOUVEAU TESTAMENT, en françays, nouvelle-
ment reveu et corrigé, traduction par Le Fèvre. Lyon, Nicolas Petit, 1540.

LA BIBLE. *Qui est toute la Sainte-Ecriture du Vieil et Nouveau Testament.* La Rochelle,
de l'Imprimerie de H. Hauttin par Corneille Hertmann, 1616.

LA SAINTE BIBLE, contenant:
— le texte sacré de la Vulgate,
— la traduction française du R. P. de Carrières,
— la Concordance des Livres saints,
— les commentaires de Ménochus,
— des préfaces et des notes historiques et théologiques.
Par Mgr. Drioux, 12ᵉ éd. Paris, Berche et Tralin, 1900. 8 vol.

LA SAINTE BIBLE. Traduite en français sous la direction de l'Ecole biblique de
Jérusalem. Paris, Ed. du Cerf, 1956.

LE SAINT EVANGILE DE N. S. JESUS-CHRIST ET LES ACTES DES
APOTRES. Marseille, Ed. de Saint-Jérôme, 1931.

LE NOUVEAU TESTAMENT ET LES PSAUMES. Traduction par Louis Segond. Nouvelle édition. Paris, 1932.

EVANGILE DE JEAN. Chap. I–XIV — Papyrus Bodmer, II. Bibl. bodmeriana, 5. Publié par le Prof. Victor Martin. Genève, 1956.

II
Concordances, Dictionaries, Encyclopædias

CONCORDANCE DES SAINTES ECRITURES. Précédée des analyses chronologiques de l'Ancien et Nouveau Testament. Paris, L. D. Delay, 1844.

CONCORDANCE DES SAINTES ECRITURES. D'après les versions Segond et synodale. Société biblique auxiliaire du Canton de Vaud. Genève-Paris, Lausanne, Maison de la Bible, 1954.

DICTIONNAIRE DES ANTIQUITES GRECQUES ET ROMAINES. Fondé par Ch. Daremberg et Edm. Soglio. Paris, Hachette, 1877–1912. 5 tomes en 9 vol.

DICTIONNAIRE DE LA BIBLE. Publié par F. Vigoureux, prêtre de Saint-Sulpice, avec le concours d'un grand nombre de collaborateurs. A.–Z. Paris, Letouzey et Ané, 1895–1912. 5 vol.

DICTIONNAIRE DE THEOLOGIE CATHOLIQUE. Fondé par A. Vacant. Paris, Letouzey et Ané, 1903–1950. 15 tomes en 17 vol.

VOCABULAIRE TECHNIQUE ET CRITIQUE DE LA PHILOSOPHIE. Par André Lalande, Membre de l'Institut. Paris, Presses Universitaires de France, 1956. 7e éd.

VOCABULAIRE DE LA PSYCHOLOGIE. Publié avec la collaboration de l'Association des travailleurs scientifiques. Par Henri Piéron, Prof. au Collège de France, Dir. de l'Institut de psychologie de l'Université de Paris. Paris, Presses Universitaires de France, 1951.

III
APOCRYPHA

APOCRYPHES. (*Dictionnaire des*). Collection de tous les livres apocryphes relatifs à l'Ancien ou au Nouveau Testament. Paris, Migné, 1856. 2 vol.

APOCRYPHES DE L'ANCIEN TESTAMENT. Documents pour l'étude de la Bible publiés sous la direction de François Martin. Paris, Letouzey et Ané, 1906.

LES APOCRYPHES ETHIOPIENS. Trad. française de René Basset. Paris, Librairie de l'Art indépendant, 1893–1895. 10 vol.

QUATRIEME LIVRE DES MACHABEES. Introduction et notes par André Dupont-Sommer. Paris, H. Champion, 1939. (Bibl. de l'Ecole des Hautes études scient., histor. et philol.).

LES EVANGILES APOCRYPHES. D'après l'édition de J. C. Thilo, par Gustave Brunet. Suivis d'une notice sur les principaux livres apocryphes de l'Ancien Testament. Paris, Franck, 1848.

LES APOCRYPHES DU NOUVEAU TESTAMENT. Publiés sous la direction de J. Bousquet et B. Amman: documents pour servir à l'étude des origines chrétiennes. Paris, 1910–1922. 3 vol.

EVANGILES APOCRYPHES. Par Ch. Michel. Paris, Picard, 1924.

LA BIBLE APOCRYPHE — EVANGILES APOCRYPHES. Par F. Amiot. Paris, Librairie Arthème Fayard, coll. *Textes pour l'histoire sacrée*, choisis et présentés par Daniel Rops, 1952.

DOCTRINE DES XII APOTRES (Didachè). Texte grec, trad. française. Introduction et index. par H. Hemmer, G. Oger et A. Lorent. Paris, Auguste Picard, coll. *Les Pères apostoliques*, 1926. 2ᵉ éd.

PROTEVANGILE DE JACQUES. Et ses remaniements latins. *Pseudo Matthieu. Nativité de Marie.* Introduction. Textes, traduction et commentaires par Elime Amman. Paris, Letouzey et Ané, 1910.

L'EVANGILE DE PIERRE. Par Léon Vaganay. Paris, J. Gabalda, 1930.

L'EVANGILE SELON THOMAS, ou *les Paroles secrètes de Jésus.* (Tome II des *Livres secrets des Gnostiques d'Egypte*). Par Jean Doresse. Paris, Plon, 1959.

L'EVANGILE SELON THOMAS. Texte copte établi et traduit par A. Guillaumont, H.-C. Puech, G. Quispel, W. Till et † Yassah 'Abd Al Masiḥ. Paris, Presses Universitaires de France, 1959.

EVANGELIUM VERITATIS. Codex Jung, édité par Michel Malinine, Henri-Charles Puech, Gilles Quispel. Zürich, Rascher Verlag, 1956.

UN LOGION DE JESUS SUR BANDELETTE FUNERAIRE. Par Henri-Charles Puech. Paris, Bulletin de la Sté. Ernest Renan, n° 3, 1954.

UNE COLLECTION DE PAROLES DE JESUS RECEMMENT RE-TROUVEES. Paris, Comptes-rendus de l'Académie des inscriptions, 1958.

DORESSE, Jean. *Introduction aux écrits gnostiques coptes découverts à Khénoboskion.* (Tome I des *Livres secrets des Gnostiques d'Egypte*). Paris, Plon, 1958.

ACTES DE PAUL et ses lettres apocryphes. Introd., textes, trad. et commentaires par Léon Vouaux. Paris, Letouzey et Ané, 1913.

ACTES DE PIERRE. Introd., textes, trad. et commentaires par Léon Vouaux. Paris, Letouzey et Ané, 1922.

FRAGMENTS RETROUVES DE L'APOCALYPSE D'ALLOGENE. Par Henri-Charles Puech. Dans Mélanges, s.l., Franz Cumont, 1936.

L'APOCALYPSE ARABE DE DANIEL. Paris, Leroux, 1904.

EPITRE DE BARNABE. Texte grec, trad. française, introduction et index par H. Hemmer, G. Oger et A. Lorent. Paris, Auguste Picard, coll. *Les Pères apostoliques*, 1926. 2ᵉ éd.

LES ODES DE SALOMON. Une œuvre chrétienne des environs de l'an 100–120. Trad. de J. Labourt et P. Battifol. Paris, J. Gabalda, 1911.

IV
VARIOUS

AHIKAR LE SYRIEN. (*Histoire et sagesse d'*). Trad. François Nau. Paris, Letouzey et Ané, 1906.

ALLENDY, Dr. R. *Le symbolisme des nombres: Essai d'Arithmosophie.* Paris, Chacornac, 1948.

AUDET, Jean-Paul. *La Didachè — Instructions des Apôtres.* Paris, J. Gabalda, 1958.

BLANC DE SAINT-BONNET, Antoine. *De l'unité spirituelle ou de la société et de son but au-delà du temps.* Paris, Langlois et Leclerc, 1845. 3 vol.

BOEHME, Jacob. *Le chemin pour aller à Christ.* Du vieux Seidenbourg, nommé communément Theo-Philosophe Teutonique. Trad. de l'Allemand. Berlin, Impr. Gottard Schleichtiger, 1722.
Comprend neuf petits traités réduits en huit:
— De la vraie repentance,
— De la sainte prière,
— De la vraie équanamité, dit l'abandon,
— De la régénération,
— Dialogue de la vie supersensuelle,
— De la contemplation divine,
— Entretien d'une âme illuminée avec une autre âme qui n'est pas illuminée,
— Des quatre complexions.

BOUCHER, Jules (J. B.). *La symbolique maçonnique* ou l'Art Royal remis en lumière et restitué selon les règles de la symbolique ésotérique et traditionnelle. Paris, Dervy, coll. *Histoire et Tradition,* 1953.

BREHIER, E. *Les idées philosophiques et religieuses de Philon d'Alexandrie.* Paris, Vrin, 1950.

BURCKHARDT, Titus. *Principes et méthodes de l'Art sacré.* Lyon, Derain, coll. *Les trois lotus,* publiée sous la direction de H. et J. Herbert, 1958.

BURROWS, Miller. *Les manuscrits de la Mer Morte.* Traduit de l'américain par M. Glotz et M. T. Franck. Paris, Robert Lafont, 1957. 2 vol.

CLEMENT D'ALEXANDRIE. *Extraits de Théodote.* Texte grec, introd., trad. et notes par François M. Sagnard. Paris, Ed. du Cerf (série non-chrétienne), 1948. (Thèse de lettres).

CLEMENT D'ALEXANDRIE. *Les Stromates.* Introd. de Claude Mondésert, trad. et notes de Marcel Carter. Paris, Ed. du Cerf, coll. *Sources chrétiennes,* 1951–1954. 2 vol.

DELCOURT, Marie. *Hermaphrodite.* Mythes et rites de la Bisexualité dans l'Antiquité classique. Paris, Presses Universitaires de France, 1958.

DENYS L'AREOPAGITE. *La hiérarchie céleste.* Introduction par René Roques. Etude et texte critique par Günter Heil. Trad. et notes par Maurice de Gandillac. Paris, Ed. du Cerf, coll. *Sources chrétiennes,* 1958.

DIADOQUE DE PHOTICE. *Cent chapitres sur la perfection spirituelle.* Paris, Ed. du Cerf, coll. *Sources chrétiennes,* 1943.

DORESSE, Jean. *Un rituel magique gnostique.* Paris, Ed. H. Roudil, Revue de la Tour Saint-Jacques, n°⁸ 11–12, juillet–décembre 1957.

DORESSE, Jean. *L'Empire du Prêtre Jean.* Paris, Plon, 1957.

DRAGUET, R. *Les pères du désert.* Paris, Plon, 1942.

ECKHART (Maître). *Œuvres de Maître Eckhart. Sermons-Traités.* Trad. de Paul Petit. Paris, Gallimard, 1942.

EUSEBE DE CESAREE. *Histoire ecclésiastique.* Texte grec, traduction et annotations par Gustave Badry, correspondant de l'Institut. T. I — Livres I–IV; T. II — Livres V–VII. Paris, Ed. du Cerf, coll. *Sources chrétiennes,* 1952–1955. 2 vol.

FABRE D'OLIVET, Antoine. *La vraie maçonnerie et la céleste culture.* Texte inédit avec introd. et notes critiques par Léon Cellier. Paris, Presses Universitaires de France, 1952.

FABRE D'OLIVET, Antoine. *Pythagore. Les vers dorés. Discours.* Traduit par F. d'O. Paris, 1813.

FESTUGIERE, A. J. *La révélation d'Hermès Trismégiste.* Paris, J. Gabalda, 1949–1954. 4 vol.

GUENON, René. *Aperçu sur l'ésotérisme chrétien.* Paris, Ed. Traditionnelles, 1954.

GUENON, René. *Les états multiples de l'Etre.* Paris, Ed. Vega, coll. *L'Anneau d'Or,* 1947.

HERMES TRISMEGISTE (CORPUS HERMETICUM). Texte établi par A. D. Nock et traduit par A. J. Festugière. Paris, Ed. Les Belles-Lettres, 1945. 4 vol.

HIPPOLYTE DE ROME. *Philosophoumena* ou *Réfutation de toutes les hérésies.* Première trad. française avec introd. et notes par A. Siouville. Paris, Rieder, 1928. 2 vol.

HISTOIRE GENERALE DES RELIGIONS. Publiée sous la direction de M. Gorce et R. Mortier.
— I. Introduction générale, les primitifs, l'Ancien Orient, les Indo-Européens.
— II. La Grèce, Rome.
— III. Les Indo-Iraniens, le judaïsme, les origines chrétiennes, les christianismes orientaux.
Paris, Quillet, 1944–48. 2 vol.

HUTIN, Serge. *Les gnostiques.* Paris, Presses Univ. de France, coll. *Que sais-je?,* n° 808, 1959.

HUTIN, Serge. *Les sociétés secrètes.* Paris, Presses Univ. de France, coll. *Que sais-je?,* n° 515, 1952.

JASPERS, Karl. *Origine et sens de l'histoire.* Trad. de l'allemand par Hélène Naef, avec la collaboration de Wolfgang Achterberg. Paris, Plon, 1954.

JOSEPHE FLAVIUS. *Œuvres complètes.* Trad. en français sous la direction de
Théodore Reinach:
— *Antiquités judaïques* (I –   V)
— Dito   (VI –   X)
— Dito   (XI –   XV)
— Dito   (XVI –XXII)
— *Guerre des Juifs*   (I –   III)
— Dito   (IV – VII)
— Fasc. I — *De l'ancienneté du peuple juif,* trad. par Léon Blum. Publié par la
Société des études juives. Paris, E. Leroux, 1900–1904. 5 vol + 1 fasc.

JUNG, C.G. *L'homme à la découverte de son âme.* Trad. et préface de R. Cahen-
Salabelle. Genève, Ed. du Mont-Blanc, coll. *Action et Pensée,* 1946.

JUNG, C.G. *Métamorphoses de l'âme et ses symboles.* Trad. et préface de Y. Le Lay.
Genève, Goerg et Co., 1953.

JUNG, C.G. *Types psychologiques.* Trad. et préface de Y. Le Lay. Publication en
français sous la direction du Dr. R. Cahen. Genève, Goerg et Co., 1958.

KERENYI, Charles. *La religion antique.* Trad. de Y. Le Lay. Genève, Goerg et Co.,
coll. *Analyse et synthèse,* sous la direction du Dr. R. Cahen-Salabelle, 1957.

LANZA DEL VASTO. *Commentaire de l'Evangile.* Préface de l'abbé A. Vaton. Paris,
Denoël, 1951.

LOISELEUR, J. *La doctrine secrète des Templiers.* Orléans, 1872.

MATTER. *Histoire critique du gnosticisme.* Son influence sur les sectes religieuses et
philosophiques des six premiers siècles de l'ère chrétienne. Paris, Leuvrault,
1928. 3 tomes en 2 vol.

MOURAVIEFF, André. *Questions religieuses d'Orient et d'Occident.* St.-Pétersbourg,
1858–1859.

MOURAVIEFF, Boris. *L'histoire a-t-elle un sens?* Revue suisse d'Histoire, t. IV,
fasc. 4, Zürich, 1954.

MOURAVIEFF, Boris. *Liberté. Egalité. Fraternité.* Revue Synthèses, n° 129, Bruxelles, 1957.

MOURAVIEFF, Boris. *Le problème de l'autorité super-étatique.* Neuchâtel-Paris, La
Baconnière, 1950.

MOURAVIEFF, Boris. *Ouspensky, Gurdjieff et les Fragments d'un enseignement inconnu.*
Revue Synthèses, n° 138, Bruxelles, 1957.

MOURAVIEFF, Boris. *Des croyances slaves pré-chrétiennes.* Revue Synthèses, n° 161,
Bruxelles, 1959.

NELLI, René. *Ecritures cathares.* Comprenant:
— La Cène secrète,
— Le Livre des deux Principes,
— Le Rituel latin et le Rituel Occitan.
Textes précathares et cathares présentés, traduits et commentés avec une
introduction sur les origines et l'esprit du catharisme, par René Nelli. Paris,
Denoël, coll. *La Tour Saint-Jacques,* 1959.

ORIGENE. *Commentaires inédits des Psaumes.* Etude sur les textes d'Origène contenus dans le manuscrit Vindobonensis 8, par René Cadiou. Paris, Protat Frères, coll. d'études anciennes publiées sous le patronage de l'Association Guillaume Budé, 1936.

ORIGENE. *Extraits des Livres I et II du Contre Celse.* (Papyrus n° 88.747 du Musée du Caire). Ed. et introduction, notes de Jean Scherer. Le Caire, Imprimerie de l'Institut français d'Archéologie orientale, 1956.

ORIGENE. *Homélies sur le Cantique des Cantiques.* Introd., trad. et notes de Dom O. Rousseau. Paris, Ed. du Cerf, coll. *Sources chrétiennes,* 1954.

ORIGENE. *Homélies sur l'Exode.* Trad. de P. Fortier. Introd. et notes de Henri de Lubac. Paris, Ed. du Cerf, coll. *Sources chrétiennes,* 1947.

ORIGENE. *Homélies sur la Genèse.* Trad. et notes de Louis Doutreleau, introd. de Henri de Lubac. Paris, Ed. du Cerf, coll. *Sources chrétiennes,* 1944.

ORIGENE. *Homélies sur les Nombres.* Introduction et traduction de André Méhat. Paris, Ed. du Cerf, coll. *Sources chrétiennes,* 1951.

ORIGENE. *De principiis.* Tome V du *Corpus* comprenant les œuvres d'ensemble d'Origène. Berlin, Koetschau, s. d.

ORIGENE. *Entretien avec Héraclide et les Evêques ses collègues sur le Père, le Fils et l'âme.* Texte grec. préf., introduction et trad. par Jean Scherer. Le Caire, Institut français d'Archéologie orientale, 1949.

OUSPENSKY, Pierre. *Fragments d'un enseignement inconnu.* Trad. de l'anglais par Philippe Lavastine. Paris, Stock, 1950.

PAULY, Jean de. *Sepher Ha-Zohar. Le livre de la Splendeur.* Doctrine ésotérique des Israélites. Paris, Emile Lafuma-Giraud, 1909–1911. 6 vol.

PETREMENT, Simone. *Le dualisme chez Platon, les Gnostiques et les Manichéens.* Paris, Presses Univ. de France, 1947.

PETITE PHILOCALIE DE LA PRIERE DU CŒUR. Traduite et présentée par Jean Gouillard. Paris, Cahiers du Sud, coll. *Documents spirituels,* 1953.

PLATON. *Œuvres complètes.* Traduction nouvelle et notes par Léon Robin avec la collaboraction de M. J. Moreau. Paris, NRF, Bibliothèque de la Pléiade, Librairie Gallimard, 1950.

PLOTIN. *Ennéades.* Texte établi et traduit par Emile Bréhier. Paris, Ed. Les Belles-Lettres, 1954. 7 vol.

POLIVKA, Jirt. *Les nombres 9 et 3 x 9 dans les contes slaves de l'est.* Dans la Revue des Etudes slaves, t. VII, fasc. 3 et 4, p. 217–223, Paris, 1927.

PUECH, Henri-Charles. *La gnose et le temps.* Dans *Eranos Jahrbuch,* t. XX, p. 57–113, Zürich, Rascher Verlag, 1952.

PUECH, Henri-Charles. *Le manichéisme, son fondateur, sa doctrine.* Paris, Musée Guimet, *Bibliothèque de diffusion,* t. LVI, 1949.

PUECH, Henri-Charles. *Où en est le problème du gnosticisme?* Dans Revue de l'Université de Bruxelles, t. XXXIX, p. 137–158 et 295–314, Bruxelles, 1934–1935.

RECIT D'UN PELERIN RUSSE. Trad. du Russe par Jean Gauvin (Laloi). Neuchâtel, La Baconnière, 1948.

SAINT IRENEE, Evêque de Lyon. *Contre les Hérésies*. Mise en lumière et réfutation de la prétendue 'Connaissance'. Texte latin, fragments grecs. Introduction, traduction et notes de F. Sagnard. Edition critique. Paris, Ed. du Cerf, coll. *Sources chrétiennes*, 1952.

SAINT MAXIME LE CONFESSEUR. *Centuries sur la charité*. Introduction et trad. de Joseph Pegon, S. J. Paris, Ed. du Cerf, coll. *Sources chrétiennes*, 1943.

SCHUON, Frithjof. *L'œil du cœur*. Paris, Gallimard, coll. *Tradition*, 1950.

SCHUON, Frithjof. *Sentiers de gnose*. Paris, La Colombe, 1957.

SCHWALLER DE LUBICZ, R. A. *Le temple de l'homme*. Paris, Ed. Caractères, 1957.

SEROUYA, Henri. *La Kabbale*. Ses origines, sa psychologie mystique, sa métaphysique. Paris, Grasset, 1947.

TEILHARD DE CHARDIN. *Œuvres:*
— Le phénomène humain,
— L'apparition de l'homme,
— La vision du passé,
— Le milieu divin,
— L'avenir de l'homme.
Paris, Ed. du Seuil, 1957–1959.

TOURGUENEFF, Ivan S. *Poèmes en prose*. Première traduction intégrale publiée dans l'ordre du manuscrit original autographe, avec des notes par Charles Salomon. Gap, Impr. Louis Jean, 1931.

VALENTIN. *Homélies*. Citées par Clément d'Alexandrie dans les *Stromates* IV, 13, p. 89. Paris, Ed. du Cerf, coll. *Sources chrétiennes*, 1951–1954.

VULLIAUD, Paul. *La Kabbale juive*. Histoire et doctrine. Paris, Impr. spéc. de libr. Emile Nourry, 1923. 2 vol.

VULLIAUD, Paul. *Siphra de Tzeniutha II*. F° 176b 179a. Comprend deux versions. Paris, Emile Nourry, coll. *Textes fondamentaux de la Kabbale*, n° 1, 1930.

Appendix

SIN AS 'ERROR OF CONCEPTION'

A key to the therapeutic value of self-knowledge.

A pupil of the author has asked us to draw the reader's attention to the related ideas of sin and repentance in the form they take in this book. The text (Chapter 14, p. 133) says: 'Errors of conception are the actual source of sins.' This difficult idea is more easily understood through example than in theory. So important is this whole idea that we can only draw the reader's attention to it strongly and comment on a few key expressions:

To repent is to pave the way for Jesus Christ. This was the task of the Precursor, John the Baptist. It is by repenting that we compensate for our sins so that we may gradually become Just. This idea of Justice is a third concept that makes this meaning of sin and repentance clearer. The Just do not err. Repentance is thus the first essential condition towards becoming objective and of stepping forward on the Way towards the purity of self-consciousness and the second Birth. But what is the true meaning of this repentance?

Mythology as case history:

Here we will find it necessary to discuss colourful examples from life's rich experience. The ancients sometimes approached similar questions in a similar—but slightly different—way. Instead of discussing these matters in the abstract, they used the rich stories from their mythology as the only way they could grasp things which the dry intellect cannot conceive.

First living example — Errors of conception:

Let us suppose that a man has been angered by his wife as he rose from sleep. He avoided any further quarrel, but cut himself badly while shaving, and this infuriates him. As a last straw, he finds a flat tyre on his car. Finding nobody to call, he changes the tyre, soiling his hands before going to his office — and is still boiling with repressed anger and contained violence when he arrives there. Once in his office, he calls his secretary, and is compelled to wait two minutes before she arrives. When she finally enters, it is quite apparent that she was drinking her coffee. Asked for a special file, she answers that it has not yet been completed: that important papers have been given to a co-director. This is enough for him to burst into a fit of uncontrollably violent rage. Later, arguing the matter with himself, he asks whether he can say objectively that the secretary showed contempt for the work, and that this made him lose his temper.

Comment:

The real question should be: what contempt? Why does he not make allowance for the cumulative effects of earlier events and the simmering anger these had led to. Would he then have seen contempt? Would he have burst into fury had he been in a happy mood? If he had hoped to make a pass at his secretary, would he not have forgiven her worse than this? Yet let us suppose, as often happens, that he persists in believing he has a clear and objective view of the situation.

In this we can see what is meant by 'an error of conception' of the world and of oneself. He should have made allowance for his anger against his wife, and for his guilt—rapidly killed in himself—when he almost lost his temper in front of her. He should have remembered his cowardice... his ridiculous anger at the razor when he cut himself; and how he understandably threw it on the floor, as it was not his awkwardness that was the cause. Also, how does he have the nerve to curse Fate, and accuse it of almost giving him a heart attack while changing the tyre of his car? What can he honestly say about Fate or about God, when all his religious and moral convictions are restricted to superstitious consultation of the astrological predictions in the daily newspapers, to attending a few funerals, to talking with contempt about both religious people and atheists — and sometimes to lying at night, terrified by the idea of death, of annihilation.

Yet this is a man who believes in being modern, rational, cool, even unbeatable. There are many more impulsively distorted errors of this kind in his conception of himself, of his actions, and of his world... he is literally blinded by these lies, he does not exist; he is neither the unfounded ideas he holds, nor the morals he lacks; nor the instincts of the cruel beast within him, which he fears... and whose existence he denies. Nor is he his latent motives, formed in adolescence, which he now drags behind him like a ball and chain. His fears, his secret shame, his exaggerated ambitions, his old hatred of his mother or brothers plotting against him... all these blind him not once but a hundred times. He is a living, moving heap of sin, that is, of crusted, hardened and tenacious errors of conception.

Behind these errors of conception, we can find an arrogant pride: 'I am always right', greedy ambitions, and the impulses of sex. They are hidden in the past, tacitly forgotten dark forces and animal rapacity. Once, many years ago, when he was just a pure-hearted boy, these dark forces of raving and boasting were the underlying supports of the contradictory and elaborate considerations by which he justified in his own eyes, all the wrong he did... with them he silenced — he killed — the criticisms that came from his heart's inner sense of morality. Eventually his heart died. For man and for woman, this is the form that is taken by the Fall.

Second example: Repentance as an act of consciousness:

A child whose mother has forbidden him to eat a cake starts building up more and more considerations to justify him eating that cake... instead of simply feeling guilty and combatting his rapacious appetite. This avid hunger that is heightened by interdiction is the Serpent of Genesis. It leads to complex self-justifications, formed from a whirling flow of dualistic evaluations which divide the world into compartmented regions of good and evil. For example, he may say to himself: 'my mother is afraid I shall fall sick, but I won't. True,' he might continue, 'when my sister ate the cake behind my mother's back, she got diarrhœa — but she had eaten too much, I won't. My mother told me that this is the only remaining cake, kept for my older brother, but I know she hides a lot from us, so why not eat'.

Comment:

There can be other interwoven justifications for our greed. They become elaborated into a vast system of dualities built on incorrect evaluation of good and bad circumstances. This is what is called 'eating the fruit of the tree of the knowledge of good and evil,' the tree of the agnostic intellect; this is the part of the mind which so easily finds 50% for and 50% against and by this indecision releases our greed and our rapacity.

From this compounding of misconceptions comes mental darkness. Set against this, repentance is an act of Consciousness, and consciousness is Light. To be conscious of something is to put that thing inside the light of awareness. 'And what comes to light' says St Paul very profoundly, 'vanishes and is absorbed in the light.' This is the theory and practice of the forgiveness of these errors of conception that we call sin.

What is it that prevents the case described above from becoming conscious and aware of the accumulated errors of conception which utterly blind him to the light? Sins, blindness, light and consciousness are the terms that come naturally when we discuss the subject we are facing now. Simply, before everything else, what prevents this man seeing himself is the fact that he will have to abandon all the proud illusions he had about himself: he is not always right as he believed. It would be better to say he has never been right. Since childhood he has replaced his child's purity by his dualistic thought, branching and bifurcating thoughts endlessly so as to hide his simple animal avidity and his mischievous cunning, to get a cake: he was not the child of innocence that he believes he was, and which he describes to his friends and children. He was — to use expressive terms — a twisted, cowardly hypocrite, a contemptible, ridiculous and pitiable little gnome. Why use such terms? It is because, if he faces facts, this is just how he must think of himself, emotionally, painfully. He has sullied his own purity by so many lies, by boasting, by elaborating empty excuses for himself and imposing them on others. He has enjoyed the fear he created in the faces of others even while aware of his own cowardice. He has so often given himself what he did not deserve that, to lose all that justified his life will mean pain, pain and more pain, when he no longer has an ounce of moral strength. He lacks moral strength because by this constant compromise he has gradually given away all his moral strength by refusing to face up to his animal image, his guilt and his lies.

Does not such a man, hopelessly drowned in these erroneous conceptions, in this helpless weakness, in his deadly fear of the light of awareness and consciousness — does he not deserve everything St Paul said to the Romans: 'Being filled with all unrighteousness, wickedness, fornication, covetousness, maliciousness; full of envy, murder, strife, deceit, malignity; whisperers, backbiters, hateful to God, insolent, haughty, boastful, inventors of evil things, disobedient to parents, without understanding, covenant-breakers, without natural affection, unmerciful etc...(Romans i: 29–32).

Between him and the light of repentance, between him and the act of conscious awareness that will purify him in the Light of Consciousness, stands his extreme weakness, his extreme fear of pain, his fear of losing this inflated view of his own emptiness.

If we can understand this, we can clearly grasp that there are no unforgivable sins. It is enough to want to repent. The refusal to make this act of consciousness, painful as it may be, is the refusal to be forgiven.